# DEMYSTIFYING THE MYSTERY OF CAPITAL: LAND TENURE AND POVERTY IN AFRICA AND THE CARIBBEAN

Edited by
**Robert Home**
Reader in Land Management
Anglia Polytechnic University
and
**Hilary Lim**
Principal Lecturer
University of East London

Cavendish
Publishing
Limited

London • Sydney • Portland, Oregon

First published in Great Britain 2004 by
The GlassHouse Press, The Glass House,
Wharton Street, London WC1X 9PX, United Kingdom
Telephone: + 44 (0)20 7278 8000   Facsimile: + 44 (0)20 7278 8080
Email: info@cavendishpublishing.com
Website: www.cavendishpublishing.com

Published in the United States by Cavendish Publishing
c/o International Specialized Book Services,
5824 NE Hassalo Street, Portland,
Oregon 97213-3644, USA

Published in Australia by The GlassHouse Press,
45 Beach Street, Coogee, NSW 2034, Australia
Telephone: + 61 (2)9664 0909   Facsimile: +61 (2)9664 5420
Email: info@cavendishpublishing.com.au
Website: www.cavendishpublishing.com.au

British Library Cataloguing in Publication Data
Demystifying the mystery of capital: land tenure in Africa and the Caribbean
1 Land tenure – law and legislation – Africa
2 Land tenure – law and legislation – Caribbean area
I Home, Robert K  II Lim, Hilary
346.6'0432

Library of Congress Cataloguing in Publication Data
Data available

ISBN 1-90438-513-3

1 3 5 7 9 10 8 6 4 2

Printed and bound in Great Britain

# Foreword

This book presents the main findings of a research project commissioned by what was the Infrastructure and Urban Development Group of the Department for International Development, as part of their Knowledge and Research (KAR) Programme. The KAR Programme was concerned with the generation, dissemination, adoption and impact evaluation of knowledge that can help eliminate poverty, in six sectors: energy, geosciences, ICT (information communication and technology), transport, urbanisation and water. It supported not only the work of DFID, but of other agencies, national governments and NGOs in moving towards international development goals.

This book addresses important housing and urban development issues: how to improve access to secure land tenure for the poor in peri-urban areas, and whether State-guaranteed land title in its various forms will contribute towards poverty reduction. The urbanisation process needs to be managed, and DFID policy seeks to help the poor (men, women and children) to participate in, and benefit from, dynamic urban development, emphasising equity, sustainability and social justice within a rights-based framework. Tenure security is a fundamental requirement for the progressive integration of the urban poor into the city, with infrastructure upgrading linked to improved protection against forced eviction.

Through the research project covered by this book, DFID links to the collective international effort in poverty reduction, through such evolving initiatives as the Habitat Campaign for Secure Tenure, the World Bank's land policy, and pro-poor shelter strategies. DFID has supported discussion of the project's work at specialist international meetings such as IRGLUS (International Research Group on Law and Urban Space, Porto Alegre, Brazil, July 2002), the symposium on land redistribution in Southern Africa (Pretoria, South Africa, November 2002), the workshop on land policy, administration and management for the English-Speaking Caribbean (Port-of-Spain, Trinidad, March 2003) and the Nigerian Centre for Urban Development and Housing (Minna, Nigeria, February 2004).

Recognising the need to strengthen capacity within developing countries to acquire, use and generate knowledge, this KAR project involved a team of six senior researchers, three of whom were from universities in each of the three case-study countries (the University of Botswana, Copperbelt University and University of the West Indies). They were supported by excellent local interviewers, and the backing to the project from the Botswana Government Department of Surveys and Mapping deserves particular mention. The six senior researchers have each contributed a chapter to this book, and provide a multi-disciplinary perspective through their academic and professional expertise in land surveying, law, planning and social anthropology. To achieve the women and gender perspectives increasingly acknowledged as key to successful shelter policy, the core team comprised an equal balance of men and women, while the local interviewers were predominantly women.

This research has also focused on giving the poor a greater say, improving their take-up of research results, and recognising the diversity within the over-arching term 'the poor'. The researchers have actively sought 'a voice for the poor' in their field research, organising meetings which involve them as well as officials and policy-makers. Indeed, the words from those interviewed are incorporated in the case studies of all three countries, and the project has sought to strengthen the capacity of local authorities and community-based organisations 'on the ground'.

This research has already been publicised through such outlets as the DFID-supported *Urbanisation* and *Insights* newsletters, reaching a wide readership in the international development and urban poverty sector, and already generating much useful communication and feedback. It is hoped that this book, as the main output of the project, will reach even more readers, and it will be distributed particularly within the three case study countries with DFID financial support. Through such sharing of new knowledge, the authors hope to make their contribution towards the ambitious aim of world poverty reduction.

*Michael Parkes*
*Senior Adviser in Architecture and Urban Development, DFID (London)*

# Acknowledgments

The authors particularly wish to thank the informants, who were interviewed in the three countries, and the following for their contributions.

In Botswana: interviewers Rosinah and Onalenna Gabathuse, and Phetogo Bafisi, Roger Blake, Godfrey Habana (and other staff of the Department of Surveying and Mapping), Joel Kutlapye, Segemotso Maroba, and former Surveying and Mapping students of the University of East London.

In Trinidad: interviewer Salisha Ali-Bellamy, and Sam Anderson, Asad Mohammed, Ack Baksh, Samuel Campbell, Ainsley Charles, Carol Cuffy-Dowlat, Musa Ndengu, Erica Prentice-Pierre, Robin Rajack, Lennox Sankersingh, Keith Scott, Raid Al-Tahir and the Digital Map Production Facility of the Lands and Surveys Division, Port of Spain.

In Zambia: Nalumino Akakandelwa, Jacob Babarinde, Priscilla Kangwa, John Lungu, Manya Mooya, Maliti Musole, Emmanuel Mutale and Manfred Welter.

Others: Cara Annett, Pat Berwick, Allan Brimicombe, Beverley Brown, Richard Bullard, Rahi Choudhury, Bob Dixon-Gough, Fiona Fairweather, Richard Farr, Jonathan Jackson, Sheila Johnson, Jon Lloyd, Michelle McCanna, Alec McEwen, Michael Mattingly, Linda Murking, Michael Mutter, Michael Parkes, Geoffrey Payne, Christina Smith, Graham Tipple, Jim Tuohy, Paul van der Molen, Elaine Verspeak, John White.

# List of contributors

**Clarissa Fourie,** MA, PhD, is a social anthropologist who formerly worked in a South African university land surveying department. She now heads the Land Tenure Unit at Habitat (UNCHS), Nairobi. Her doctoral thesis was on tribal land tenure in informal settlements in South Africa.

**Charisse Griffith-Charles,** MPhil, TTLS, is a lecturer in Cadastral Surveying in the Department of Surveying and Land Information at the University of the West Indies, St Augustine, and a licensed cadastral surveyor in Trinidad and Tobago. She is currently pursuing a PhD, in Geomatics at the University of Florida, Gainesville. The focus of her research is land titling and cadastral programmes, and the sustainability of the systems that they establish.

**Robert Home,** MA, DipTP, PhD, MRTPI, is a land use planner working in the Law Department of Anglia Polytechnic University, who has published on town planning in British colonial history and contemporary less developed countries. His doctoral research was on the influence of colonial policy upon Nigerian urbanisation.

**John Kangwa** is a land surveyor and lectures in the Department of Urban and Regional Planning at the Copperbelt University. He has undertaken research in social impact assessment around mining projects, urban management and land delivery.

**Hilary Lim,** BA, MA, PhD, is a property lawyer and teaches in the School of Law, University of East London (UK). Her research interests are in the field of critical rights theory and postcolonialism. She has published in the field of children's rights and is currently editing (with Anne Bottomley) a collection on women and property (to be published by Glasshouse Press).

**Chadzimula Molebatsi,** BA, MA, PhD, lectures in the Department of Environmental Sciences, University of Botswana, Gaborone, Botswana. His PhD at the University of Newcastle-upon-Tyne was on urban planning in Botswana, and he has published on environmental planning.

# Contents

# List of acronyms and abbreviations

| | |
|---|---|
| AIDS | Acquired Immune Deficiency Syndrome |
| ALSP | Accelerated Land Servicing Programme (Botswana) |
| APU | Anglia Polytechnic University (UK) |
| BDP | Botswana Democratic Party |
| BHC | Botswana Housing Corporation |
| BSA | British South Africa Company |
| CASLE | Commonwealth Association of Surveyors and Land Economists |
| CBO | Community Based Organisation |
| CBU | Copperbelt University (Zambia) |
| CEDAW | Convention for the Elimination of Discrimination Against Women (UN) |
| CO | Colonial Office (UK) |
| COC | Certificate of Comfort (Trinidad) |
| COR | Certificate of Rights (Botswana) |
| CSO | Central Statistical Office (Zambia) |
| CUP | Cambridge University Press |
| DC | District Commissioner |
| DDC | District Development Committee (Botswana) |
| DFID | Department for International Development (UK) |
| DPU | Development Planning Unit (University College London) |
| DSM | Department of Surveys and Mapping (Botswana) |
| DTRP | Department of Town and Regional Planning (Botswana) |
| FAO | Food and Agriculture Organisation |
| FIG | International Federation of Surveyors |
| FPSG | Fixed Period State Grant (Botswana) |
| GIS | Geographic Information Systems |
| GPS | Global Positioning Satellite |
| Ha | Hectares |
| GRZ | Government of the Republic of Zambia |
| HIV | Human Immunodeficiency Virus |
| HMSO | Her Majesty's Stationery Office |
| IIED | International Institute for Economic Development |
| IRGLUS | International Research Group on Land and Urban Space |
| ITDG | Intermediate Technology Development Group |
| K | Kwacha (Zambian currency: approx K7,000 = £1 sterling) |
| KAR | Knowledge and Research |
| KCC | Kitwe City Council (Zambia) |
| LSA | Land Settlement Agency (Trinidad) |
| LTC | Land Tenure Centre (University of Wisconsin) |
| LUPAP | Land Use and Policy Administration Project (Trinidad) |
| m | metre |
| MMD | Movement for Multi-Party Democracy (Zambia) |
| MOLA | Meeting on Land Administration |
| MP | Member of Parliament |
| NGO | Non-Governmental Organisation |
| NHA | National Housing Authority (Trinidad) |
| NHP | National Housing Policy (Zambia) |

NRI       Natural Resources Institute (UK)
OUP       Oxford University Press
P         Pula (Botswana currency: approx P8 = £1 sterling)
PNM       People's National Movement (Trinidad)
PRO       Public Record Office
RDC       Residents Development Committee (Zambia)
ROB       Republic of Botswana
SADC      Southern African Development Community
SAP       Structural Adjustment Programme
SARPN     South African Regional Poverty Network
SDI       Spatial data infrastructure
SHHA      Self-Help Housing Agency (Botswana)
sq m      square metre
TLB       Tribal Land Board (Botswana)
TT        Trinidad and Tobago
TT$       Trinidad and Tobago dollars (approx TT$12 = £1 sterling)
UEL       University of East London (UK)
UK        United Kingdom
UNAIDS    United Nations AIDS organisation
UNC       United National Congress (Trinidad)
UNCHS     United Nations Commission for Human Settlements (Habitat)
UNDP      United Nations Development Programme
UNECE     United Nations Economic Commission for Europe
UNICEF    United Nations Children's Fund
UNIP      United National Independence Party (Zambia)
UP        University Press
USAID     United States Assistance for International Development
UWI       University of West Indies
WASA      Water and Sewage Agency (Trinidad)
WHO       World Health Organisation
WLSA      Women and Law in Southern Africa
WPLA      Working Party on Land Administration (UNECE)
ZCCM      Zambia Consolidated Copper Mines

# Chapter 1
## Introduction:
## Demystifying 'The Mystery of Capital'
### Robert Home and Hilary Lim

The millions of people in the world who lack access to land where they can find secure shelter present a great global challenge to law, governance and civil society. About half of the world's population (three billion people) now live in urban areas, and nearly a billion are estimated to be living in informal, illegal settlements, mostly in the urban and peri-urban areas of less developed countries (DFID 2001). The UNCHS (Habitat) Global Campaign for Secure Tenure, launched in 1999, has been encouraging the progressive regularisation of unauthorised and informal settlements through changes in legal frameworks, policies and standards (Fernandes and Varley 1998; Durand-Lasserve and Royston 2002; Payne 2002).

The vast scale of housing and land tenure problems has moved both governments and donor agencies from direct provision of mass housing to a neo-liberal, facilitative and enabling role for the State. In turn, this has given rise to a greater acceptance of all kinds of self-help in housing, a policy shift traceable to the writings of John Turner in the 1970s (Turner 1976; Burgess 1982). These changes have been reflected in a change in terminology, shifting from 'squatter' or 'slum' areas to 'informal', 'extralegal' or 'unauthorised' settlements. If such areas are indeed 'here to stay' (to deploy the title of Hindson and McCarthy 1994), then governments need to find ways to regularise their land tenure arrangements.

The large donor agencies have long been committed to a framework of secure, transparent and enforceable property rights as a critical precondition for investment, economic growth and poverty alleviation, and continue to shape the agenda (Deininger and Binswanger 1999; Manji 2003). The linkages between land titling and development remained, however, a largely closed discourse within the communities of development policy-makers, until a more flamboyant, 'magic bullet', view of property rights appeared in Hernando de Soto's best-selling book, *The Mystery of Capital: Why Capitalism Triumphs in the West and Fails Everywhere Else* (de Soto 2000). De Soto claims that the registration of property rights offers the key to ending Third World poverty and creating happy capitalists everywhere. His seemingly simple recipe, which 'neither condemns nor criticizes' (Lea 2002), has proven attractive to donor agencies and influential Western opinion-makers (Clinton 2001; USAID 2002).

The de Soto argument addresses poverty in both developing and former Eastern bloc countries by claiming that property only becomes useful capital when it is recognised by a formal legal system. Without such a system, the property held by the world's poor is merely so much 'dead capital'. They regard property as a thing – their homes or businesses mere material objects, devoid of titles and addresses; places to use and live in – but of no value in itself. Reinforcing his message with his typically vivid imagery, de Soto depicts the poor as locked in the 'grubby basement of the pre-capitalist world' (de Soto 2000: 55). The formalisation of property can raise them from the basement into the upper floors, where property is not a thing but a series of dynamic, interlocking relationships expressed in law (Lea 2002: 63–64).

For de Soto, there are six 'property effects' which make Western capitalism successful: fixing the economic potential of assets; integrating dispersed information into one system; making people accountable; making assets fungible (ie, capable of being divided, combined or mobilised to suit any transaction); networking people; and protecting transactions through the rule of law (de Soto 2000: Chapter 3). His 'mystery of capital' is the representation through documentary title of material property, liberating its economic and transactional potential to generate capital. He ambitiously compares the release of 'dead' property capital with nuclear fission: 'similar to the process that Einstein taught us whereby a single brick can be made to release a huge amount of energy in the form of an atomic explosion' (de Soto 2000: 37).

The de Soto thesis has its critics. Academics have found his methodology and supporting research suspect, and have disputed his basic argument (Bourbeau 2001; Gilbert 2002; Fernandes 2002). He evades some difficult issues, such as the cost of cadastral reform, the future of communal land tenure systems and the colonial sanctioning of pre-emption (Lea 2002: 63–65). He does not much question the role of capitalism and land title in perpetuating colonial power structures and inequalities, and indeed in creating greater inequalities, as the poor are pushed out by larger, wealthier and possibly foreign investors attracted by the latent capital in land. He seems to conclude that the benefits outweigh the possible costs for poor people, who can chose how to use their new-found capital (Asp 2003: 9–10), but does not address other difficult aspects of land and property systems, such as the farm-size efficiency debate or the continued strength of large-scale hereditary land-holding. Nevertheless, the power and simplicity of his arguments have commanded attention, and are stimulating much current research.

## Land Tenure Regularisation in Practice

If integrated property systems are the key to capitalist economic development, then cadastral and land registration systems need to be strengthened, democratised and expanded. Rai has commented upon the reshaping of property in the colonial engagement: 'modern capitalist relations required a "rational" systematisation of property relations; the inclusion of colonised States into the world economy necessitated recognisable property relations that could not be achieved without disturbing the "alien/uncivil" social relations' (Rai 2002: 23). Where pre-colonial land tenure structures were acknowledged at all, they were reconfigured and reconstructed by the colonial administration into its perception of customary tenure, which it deemed to be holding back economic progress. Thus a formal legal pluralism was instituted, with the overlay of 'received' law from the colonial power. Postcolonial nation-States, especially if they claim democratic credentials and have to face conditions of a legal pluralism fashioned in colonialism, offering conflicting sources of legitimacy and often unpredictable or contradictory outcomes (McAuslan 2000).

The 'jewel in the crown' for British colonial land managers was the Torrens system of State-guaranteed property registration. The power of the idea of Torrens in the Western common law consciousness is evident from the recent claim, in the opening pages of an English land law text, that, 'Land was made to be registered ... The attractions ... are irresistibly obvious' (Sparkes 2003: 1–2). Developed (significantly) by a businessman for business purposes, the Torrens system embedded in the nation-State the concept, derived from John Locke, of possessive individualism and private property rights, free of feudal or communal overriding interests, which was receptive to and facilitative of the Western property categories of leasehold and freehold.

Adapting Torrens-style land registration to conditions of legal pluralism, however, is neither simple nor cheap. Land registration procedures are time-consuming and demanding. Specialists are needed to undertake field surveys, check cadastral plans, prepare legal documentation, keep and update records, transfer property, compensate for errors and enforce the law. With the complex associated procedures, often involving large land areas and populations, it is not surprising that cadastral coverage and land information systems in developing countries are weak. Numerous costly initiatives during the last decade to modernise land information in those countries have produced disappointing results and been questioned by both the potential beneficiaries and the cadastral specialists. Many postcolonial governments have come to recognise the limitations of State-directed land management. Recent innovatory approaches, in which the post-*apartheid* Southern African region (combining as it does 'modern' technological and educational expertise with the problems of less developed countries) has been a pioneer, have attempted to combine effective records with local community control, bringing land registration to the people on the ground (Christensen and Hojgaard 1997; Durand-Lasserve and Royston 2002). As de Soto puts it:

> It is up to the government to find out what these extralegal arrangements are and then find ways to integrate them into the formal property system. But they will not be able to do that by hiring lawyers in high-rise offices in Delhi, Jakarta or Moscow to draft new laws. They will have to go out into the streets and roads and listen to the barking dogs (de Soto 2000: 189).

Such a participatory approach (listening to the people, rather than to the dogs, and to community-based organisations and urban social movements) requires a rethinking of professional roles, stakeholder relationships, dispute resolution methods and record-keeping systems. Unfortunately, if centralised land titling has proved expensive for less developed countries, the participatory approach, which has to take account of multiple claims to property rights, is unlikely to be less so and will require legal and regulatory reform. The ideas of de Soto depend upon an educated cadre of professional surveyors, adjudicators and other civil servants for their delivery (de Waal 2003).

Land titling refers to formal conferment of the right to use or own a landed property, normally expressed in legally recognised and accepted documentation. Owners can use the documents to access financial resources (through mortgages or hypothecation), enjoy security of tenure and undertake improvements to their property. In Trinidad, the Certificate of Comfort has since 1988 conferred on the holder a personal right that he will not be ejected from his house plot, unless it is necessary for him or her to relocate, in which case an alternative plot is identified and made available. The certificate was intended as a simple document with a measure of security of tenure pending more detailed legal processes. In Botswana, a Certificate of Right bestows a similar security on State land and a customary grant on tribal land. All such intermediate titles, often negotiated under traditional formalities and/or extralegally, have to be upgraded, legalised and formalised within a State-guaranteed land registration system.

## Seeking the 'Voice of the Poor'

Research for the World Development Report has drawn upon the exchanges and shared views of a range of poor people in diverse countries, so as to inform and contribute 'lived experiences' into the shaping of aid policy – 'the voice of the poor' (Narayan and Petesch 2002). As Dean argues, 'in the 1990s participatory poverty assessments have re-established themselves as a qualitative investigative technique by which to define the task of poverty alleviation – as it were, from "the bottom up"' (Dean 2001: 59). De Soto's call for the voices of the poor (or their barking dogs) to be heard resonates with this attention to everyday experience and popular discourse. The forces of globalisation and modernisation, and the crisis of the failing nation-State are reflected in individual experiences of everyday life. Recent research has attempted to relate the bureaucratic process of development back to the everyday lives of those in informal settlements, perceiving that social science has become detached from lived realities. Community-based participatory processes in poverty assessment and reduction draw upon the experiences of the poor themselves, seeing social policy as filtered through networks of relationships, and shared assumptions and meanings, which vary greatly between societies. Formal systems are played out in interaction with dynamic, shifting, informal cultures and structures, but also through the lives and strategies of individuals. One of de Soto's striking images is to liken the poor to a lake, and the makers of property systems to the engineers whose skills can transform that placid lake's potential energy into hydro-electricity, but this image is one which devalues and erases the diversity of the poor.

Various academic research tools have been developed in an effort to 'prise open' the different dimensions of lived totality, interweaving human and socio-political development: biographic method, oral history and postcolonial theory (Gubrium and Holstein 2003). Participative techniques can make manifest what might have been hidden by the deployment of more conventional tools of social science. Oral historians have adopted life-history methods as tools of emancipation and empowerment, particularly helpful in reaching those sections of society, in the past or present, whose experience could not be directly tapped through documentary or formal survey sources. Oral history can reveal what is important to ordinary people: 'how nearly everyone planned, plotted and schemed to do as well as they could for themselves, their children, and for their communities' (Barnes and Win 1992: 9). For it is 'through such discourses that people disclose the different ways in which they negotiate the everyday realities of living in an unequal society' (Dean 2001: 61). Another technique, the biographical interpretative method, seeks to differentiate the objective life story (identifying family history and key life events) from the 'told story', that is, how the individual presents his or her own story and its underlying themes and turning points (Chamberlayne and others 2001; Wengraf 2001).

These techniques have their limitations. It is worth remembering that:

> Life is not a (Western) drama of four or five acts. Sometimes it just drifts along; it may go on year after year without development, without climax, without definite beginnings or endings ... In life, we usually don't know when an event is occurring; we think it is starting when it is already ending; and we don't see its in/significance (Trinh T Minh-ha 1989: 143).

One of the 'weapons of the weak' (Dean 2001: 60) is resistance and mundane acts of sabotage against those they regard as oppressors (including researchers). This may involve turning the language of the powerful back on itself, or picking up the inflections in the researcher's words or behaviour and responding accordingly. Scott (1990: 4–5) deploys the term 'hidden transcript' to denote a discourse in popular vernacular that takes place 'off-stage', beyond the observation of the powerful audience, composed of speech, gestures and practices which may dovetail with what is revealed in the public but may also be contradictory or add subtle nuances. The hidden transcript is 'the privileged site of non-hegemonic, contrapuntal, dissident, subversive discourse' (Scott 1990: 25).

De Soto's focusing of attention upon the voices of the poor is linked to postcolonial theory, which seeks to fill the gaps and silences in narratives where a dominant culture and language speaks for submerged voices. The 'Subaltern Studies' historians (Guha 1987; Spivak 1994; Otto 1999), for instance, were concerned to provide a platform for those whose position was so marginal that their subjectivity and agency was obscured from view in most historical accounts. Spivak envisages the notion of the subaltern as 'a space cut off from the lines of mobility in a colonised country', which always has 'something of a not-speakingness' within it (Spivak in Landry and Maclean 1996: 288–89). Making space for excluded voices may be based upon an untenable assumption that 'we possess a discourse which can engage with the excluded', but even so it has the potential to disrupt the power of Western legal discourse and present alternatives (Lim 2001).

## Constructing the Research

To investigate de Soto's arguments, the UK government's Department for International Development commissioned the research which is presented in this book within its policy theme concerned with increasing access by low-income households to adequate, safe shelter. The research contractor was first the School of Surveying, University of East London, and subsequently the Law School of Anglia Polytechnic University, and was undertaken between 2001 and 2004. The aim was to explore the role of local land titling in poverty alleviation in peri-urban settlements under different land tenure regimes, comparing the experience of African and Caribbean countries within the Commonwealth. The outputs included case studies, good practice guidelines and a strengthening of in-country capacity through workshops. The main research aim was to test de Soto's thesis of a linkage between land titling and poverty alleviation improvements through exploring the life experiences and attitudes of residents in informal peri-urban settlements.

The senior researchers comprised academics and professionals, one in each of the three case-study countries, together with three other subject specialists. It was felt important that those who undertook the field research for the three case studies shared a language and urban experience and possessed a similar cultural understanding to those from whom they sought information. The intention was to bring together the two professional and academic disciplines which have been most closely involved in land titling programmes: lawyers and land surveyors. Both have been attacked by de Soto: the lawyers for their resistance to change, and the surveyors (or 'technicians') for preparing mere inventories, which say little about how property rights are organised (de Soto 2000: 209–17). The contribution of other disciplines, particularly planning and social anthropology, has been incorporated into the research project with the intention of improving understanding of the social context within which law and surveying operates (Larsson and Elander 2001). Given the importance of gender dimensions in the study, it was helpful that three of the six senior researchers, and all of the in-country junior interviewers, were women.

Much of the research associated with land titling and the de Soto thesis has been undertaken in Asia and Latin America, and in large countries with complex bureaucratic and policy machinery, which have tended to dominate the discourse. By selecting small countries, it was felt that the policy and procedures were less of an obstacle to direct access to the experience of the poor, and the peri-urban areas chosen for study were more manageable research locations. The three countries for study were selected partly pragmatically (where suitable in-country researchers were available), and were all former British colonies (or protectorates) now within the Commonwealth. They illustrate a mixture of tenure forms, co-existing within a pluralistic, postcolonial legal system mostly deriving from British legal culture. The table below presents basic statistical indicators for the three countries, using the UK as a comparator.

## Country data profiles

| Indicator | Botswana | Trinidad | Zambia | United Kingdom |
|---|---|---|---|---|
| Surface area (thousand sq km) | 581.7 | 5.13 | 752.6 | 242.9 |
| Population total (million) | 1.7 | 1.3 | 10.3 | 58.8 |
| Population density (per sq km) | 0.002 | 255 | 14 | 242 |
| Annual population growth (%) | 1.0 | 0.7 | 1.7 | 0.1 |
| Life expectancy (years) | 38.5 | 72.5 | 37.5 | 77.4 |
| Infant mortality rate (per 1,000 live births) | 80.0 | 17.0 | 112.0 | 6.0 |
| Prevalence of HIV (female; % ages 15–24) | 37.5 | 3.2 | 21.0 | 0.1 |
| Illiteracy (female; % age 15 and above) | 19.4 | 2.2 | 27.3 | — |
| GNI per capita; Atlas method (current US$) | 3,100.0 | 5,960 | 320.0 | 25,120.0 |
| GDP growth (annual %) | 6.3 | 5.0 | 4.9 | 2.2 |

Source: *World Bank Country Statistics* 2001

The land areas and population densities varied widely, although all three of the chosen countries have high population and economic growth rates by comparison with the UK. Botswana is predominantly semi-arid with very low population densities but a rapidly urbanising population. Trinidad is a medium-sized Caribbean island with rapid growth rates and life expectancies and infant mortality rates that are (of the three countries) closest to the UK. Zambia has low population densities but established urban traditions concentrated in the capital (Lusaka) and the Copperbelt.

Measures of poverty vary widely, but an accepted statistical measure is average gross national income per capita, which for all three countries was less than a quarter that of the UK. Zambia is at present classified as one of the poorest nations in the world, reflected in a high infant mortality rate, and income per capita of less than a dollar a day; its strong mining-based economy at independence has been devastated by falling copper prices and structural adjustment, resulting in a negative growth rate and a sharp increase in poverty in the 1990s.

The economic and social impact of AIDS has been particularly strong in Africa, Botswana and Zambia being no exception. One accepted statistical indicator is the percentage of young women estimated to be living with HIV/AIDS. The situation in the Caribbean is less acute, but some 420,000 adults are believed to be living with HIV/AIDS in the region (UNAIDS 2002: 198), with young women particularly affected. The relationship between poverty and HIV/AIDS has profound implications for families, land tenure and land reform, especially inheritance practices and laws, a theme that has been effectively ignored by de Soto.

Access by the poor to land for shelter reflects land-ownership patterns and classifications. Botswana has private freehold (6%), State land (23%) and tribal or communal land (71%). Zambia no longer recognises private freehold, but classifies land as either State (6% of land area) or customary (the rest and a category which includes forest reserves, national parks and game management areas). Trinidad, on the other hand, has no customary or tribal land, but divides its ownership more or less equally between private (47%) and public (53%), the latter including forest. The three countries were chosen partly so as to explore the interaction of imposed or 'received' colonial law with customary or communal legal systems. In Africa, the indirect rule or dual mandate ideology of British colonialism enforced the separation of State or individual land title systems from tribal or customary tenure. In Trinidad, a history of colonial rule by a succession of European powers, and a role as an 'experimental colony', affected land tenure, creating historical patterns which included family land, absentee ownership of estates, settlement of freed African slaves and land grants to East Indian indentured labourers.

The researchers went into the informal settlements of peri-urban areas in Gaborone (Botswana), Port of Spain (Trinidad) and Kitwe (Zambia): all places where people live with unclear land titles. In Botswana, rapid growth in and around the Gaborone capital territory has engaged with a consequence of the colonial dual land tenure system: high prices and slow delivery of public sector serviced land within the municipal area combined with the availability of cheap peri-urban land nearby, weakly managed by the tribal land boards. The government has applied tough anti-squatting measures (a 'zero-tolerance' policy), but with limited success, and the transmutation of tribal tenure practices has made the peri-urban area of Mogoditshane a particularly high profile and productive location for study. In

Zambia, the Copperbelt town of Kitwe (home of the Copperbelt University) was selected for study. A stable urbanised population has existed here since the 1930s, but economic collapse with the decline and privatisation of the copper mines and related industries has dramatically increased poverty levels. Trinidad, with much higher population densities, has a less defined peri-urban zone but has similar problems of squatting on State land, which recent land title programmes have attempted to regularise.

The researchers conducted lightly structured, face-to-face, in-depth interviews with a total (across all three countries) of over 200 plot-holders, selected by a physical assessment of poor standards of housing structures within the peri-urban areas. Some interviews were tape-recorded and transcribed in full, allowing quotations that reflect the vivid use of vernacular language. The interviews explored a range of topics: the life histories of respondents, household status, employment patterns, history of plot use, acquisition and improvements, family relationships, access to services and attitudes to credit. As well as talking to the residents in informal settlements, the researchers undertook interviews with other key players or stakeholders: professionals, government officers, community leaders, formal and informal credit providers (government and private) and project leaders. Group discussions were also held, allowing information sharing, and presenting an opportunity for participants to develop each other's contributions and reveal common experience.

In this book, each of the three country case studies is covered in a chapter, in alphabetical order, placing emphasis upon the 'voices of the poor' themselves (their lives, property relations and attitudes to credit). Three preceding chapters address some self-selected, over-arching themes: Home on historical perspectives of colonial land law, policy and regulation; Fourie on tribal land tenure and the potential of land readjustment methods for the planned improvement of peri-urban areas (with particular reference to Botswana); and Lim on the important but neglected theme of inheritance and HIV/AIDS (with particular reference to Africa).

## References

Asp, D (2003) 'Argentina's mystery of capital: why the international monetary fund needs Hernando de Soto' *Minnesota Journal of Global Trade* 12: 383

Ayiga, N and others (1997) 'Causes, patterns, differentials and consequences of AIDS mortality in Northern Uganda' in Bond, GC and Vincent, J (eds), *AIDS in Africa and the Caribbean*, Boulder: Westview Press

Barnes, T and Win, E (1992) *To Live a Better Life: An Oral History of Women in the City of Harare, 1930–70*, Harare: Baobab Books

Bourbeau, H (2001) 'Property wrongs: how weak ideas gain strong appeal in the world of development economics' *Foreign Policy*: 78–79

Burgess, R (1982) 'Self-help housing advocacy: a curious form of radicalism. A critique of the work of John FC Turner' in Ward, P (ed), *Self-Help Housing: A Critique*, London: Alexandrine Press

Chamberlayne, P and others (eds) (2001) *The Turn to Biographical Methods in Social Science: Comparative Issues and Examples*, London and New York: Routledge

Christensen, SF and Hojgaard, PD (1997) *Innovative Land Surveying and Land Registration in Namibia*, London: Development Planning Unit Working Paper No 93, University College London

Clinton, W (2001) *The Struggle for the Soul of the 21st Century*, London: Dimbleby Lecture, BBC

de Soto, H (2000) *The Mystery of Capital: Why Capitalism Triumphs in the West and Fails Everywhere Else*, London: Black Swan

de Waal, A (2003) 'Why the HIV/AIDS pandemic is a structural threat to Africa's governance and economic development', *Fall Fletcher Forum World Affairs* 27: 6

Dean, H (2001) 'Poverty and citizenship: moral repertoires and welfare regimes' in Wilson, F, Kanji, N and Braathen, E (eds), *Poverty Reduction*, London and New York: Zed Books

Deininger, K and Binswanger, H (1999) 'The evolution of the World Bank's land policy: principles, experience, and future challenges' *World Bank Research Observer* 14(2): 247–76

DFID (2001) *Strategies for Achieving the International Development Targets: Meeting the Challenge of Poverty in Urban Areas*, London: Department for International Development

Durand-Lasserve, A and Royston, L (eds) (2002) *Holding their Ground: Secure Land Tenure for the Urban Poor in India, Brazil and South Africa*, London: Earthscan

Fernandes, E (2002) 'The Influence of de Soto's *The Mystery of Capital*', *Land Lines: Newsletter of the Lincoln Institute of Land Policy* 14(1): 5–8

Fernandes, E and Varley, A (eds) (1998) *Illegal Cities: Law and Urban Change in Developing Countries*, London: Zed Books

Gilbert, AG (2002) 'On *The Mystery of Capital* and the myths of Hernando de Soto: what difference does legal title make?' *International Development Planning Review* 24(1): 1–20

Guha, R (1987) *Subaltern Studies V: Writings on South Asian History and Society*, Delhi: OUP

Gubrium, JF and Holstein, JA (2003) *Postmodern Interviewing*, London: Sage

Hindson, D and McCarthy, J (eds) (1994) *Here To Stay: Informal Settlements in KwaZulu-Natal*, Daldridge, South Africa: Indicator Press

Landry, D and Maclean, G (1996) *The Spivak Reader*, London: Routledge

Larsson, J and Elander, I (2001) 'Consensus, democracy and the land surveyor in the Swedish Cadastral Executive Procedure' *Planning Theory & Practice* 2(3): 325–42

Lea, D (2002) 'Tully and de Soto on uniformity and diversity' *Journal of Applied Philosophy* 19(1): 55

Lim, H (2001) 'The waqf in trust' in Scott-Hunt, S and Lim, H (eds), *Feminist Perspectives on Equity and Trusts*, London: Cavendish Publishing

McAuslan, P (2000) 'Only the name of the country changes: the diaspora of "European" land law in Commonwealth Africa' in Toulmin, C and Quan, J (eds), *Evolving Land Rights, Policy and Tenure in Africa*, London: IIED and NRI

Manji, A (2001) 'Land reform in the shadow of the State: the implementation of new land laws in Sub-Saharan Africa' *Third World Quarterly* 22(3): 327–42

Manji, A (2003) 'Capital, labour and land relations in Africa: a gender analysis of the World Bank's Policy Research Report on Land Institutions and Land Policy' *Third World Quarterly* 24(1): 97–114.

Narayan, D and others (eds) (2000) *Voices of the Poor: Crying Out for Change*, New York: OUP

Narayan, D and Petesch, P (2002) *Voices of the Poor: From Many Lands*, New York: OUP

Otto, D (1999) 'Subalternity and international law: the problems of global community and the incommensurability of difference' in Fitzpatrick, P and Darian-Smith, E, *Laws of the Postcolonial*, Ann Arbor: Michigan UP

Payne, G (ed) (2002) *Land, Rights and Innovation: Improving Tenure Security for the Urban Poor*, London: ITDG

Rai, SM (2002) *Gender and the Political Economy of Development*, Cambridge: Polity

Scott, J (1990) *Domination and the Arts of Resistance: Hidden Transcripts*, New Haven, NJ: Yale UP

Sparkes, P (2003) *A New Land Law*, 2nd edn, Oxford: Hart Publishing

Spivak, GC (1994) 'Can the subaltern speak?' in Williams, P and Chrisman, L (eds), *Colonial Discourse and Postcolonial Theory*, New York: Columbia UP

Toulmin, C and Quan, J (eds) (2000) *Evolving Land Rights, Policy and Tenure in Africa*, London: DFID/IED/NRI

Trinh T Minh-ha (1989) *Woman Native Other*, Bloomington and Indianapolis: Indiana UP

Turner, JFC (1976) *Housing by People: Towards Autonomy in Building Environments*, London: Marion Boyars

UNAIDS (2002) *Report on the Global HIV/AIDS Epidemic*, UNAIDS

USAID (2002) *Promoting Effective Property Rights Systems for Sustainable Development*, Washington, DC: US Agency for International Development

Walker, C (2002) *Land Reform in Southern and Eastern Africa: Key Issues for Strengthening Women's Access to Rights in Land*, Harare, Zimbabwe: FAO

Wengraf, T (2001) *Qualitative Research Interviewing: Biographic Narrative and Semi-Structured Methods*, London: Sage

# Chapter 2
# Outside de Soto's Bell Jar: Colonial/Postcolonial Land Law and the Exclusion of the Peri-Urban Poor

*Robert Home*

## Introduction

Hernando de Soto, in one of those vivid images which bring a potentially rather dry topic alive, compared capitalism in the colonial and postcolonial world to a bell jar, sealed off from the rest of society:

> Inside the bell jar are elites who hold property using codified law borrowed from the West. Outside the bell jar, where most people live, property is used and protected by all sorts of extralegal arrangements firmly rooted in informal consensus dispersed through large areas ... The bell jar makes capitalism a private club, open only to a privileged few, and enrages the billions standing outside looking in ... This capitalist apartheid will inevitably continue until we all come to terms with the critical flaw in many countries' legal and political systems that prevents the majority from entering the formal property system (de Soto 2000: 66–80 and 164).

The current encouragement of land tenure regularisation for the urban poor in developing countries, popularised by de Soto and the Habitat Global Campaign for Secure Tenure, is drawing attention to the historical role of colonialism and its exclusionary land laws in creating illegality. Within the academic community, new cross-disciplinary work in critical legal geography is now exploring the influence of the colonial and postcolonial state upon physical and jurisdictional landscapes (Kedar 2002).

As Max Weber put it, modern officialdom functions through the principle of 'fixed and official jurisdictional areas which are generally ordered by rules, that is, by laws or administrative regulations ... concerning the coercive means, physical, sacerdotal, or otherwise, which may be placed at the disposal of officials' (Gerth and Wright Mills 1991: 196). Territorial jurisdictions can be an instrument of State power, controlling what people are allowed to do within defined spatial boundaries. Not only is the modern nation-State partly defined through its territorial claims to sovereignty, but the construction and exercise of State power takes place within this territory, giving spatial geography a heightened significance in most of the State's activities. 'Space is by its very nature, full of power and symbolism, a complex web of relations of domination and subordination, of solidarity and co-operation' (Doreen Massey, quoted in Blomley and Delaney 2001: 16). An important attribute of State/society relations is what has been called the 'internal territorialisation characteristic of modern State rule', which creates and maps land boundaries, allocates ownership and use rights to land, and regulates where people live and work (Robinson 1996: 21). Urban jurisdictions allow the State to control population, land use and activities more closely than outside the town, and it can exclude unwanted people, uses and activities, banishing them beyond municipal boundaries. Similarly, the laws protecting private property confer upon the owner the right of exclusive possession within the physical limits of his or her land.

This chapter will place the State's relationship to landed property within a historical context, relating colonial and postcolonial constructions of land rights to the present debate about land titling and development. First, it explores the historical case of the English enclosures movement at the time of the Industrial Revolution, which reinforced private, individuated property rights at the expense of common or customary rights, increasing landlessness and poverty for many. The transfer of individuated property rights and the associated devices of social control to the British overseas colonies brought about the restriction and devaluation of the customary, usually communal, land rights of the colonised, particularly through the dual mandate or indirect rule ideology of colonial administration as practiced in Africa and elsewhere. Secondly, colonial land policy is explored through the formation and development of a new cadre of technocrats, the cadastral land surveyors, whose job it was on behalf of the colonial State to map and record through 'scientific survey' those land rights which the State chose to recognise through the Torrens system of land registration. This development is also related to a revival of communal or customary land tenure in partial reaction to the Torrens idea. Finally, the concept of the peri-urban is deconstructed, representing an intermediate space between urban and rural, where the dual construction of land rights under colonialism came to be hybridised, uncertain and open to renegotiation.

## 'The Magic of Property Turns Sand to Gold': Exclusionary Land Law and the Creation of Illegality

'The magic of property turns sand to gold' is an aphorism that aptly encapsulates the de Soto thesis and current policies of the World Bank, USAID and other aid agencies. To put it in modern policy-makers' language, a framework of secure, transparent and enforceable property rights is a critical precondition for investment, economic growth and poverty alleviation (Deininger and Binswanger 1999). But the aphorism is not new. It predates de Soto by two centuries and was written in 1787 by Arthur Young, an eminent English agricultural economist of the day and supporter of enclosures, who was travelling at the time in pre-revolutionary France (Young 1917).

Hernando de Soto supports his thesis of a link between the formalisation of property rights and the creation of wealth with the historical example of the United States. Indeed, he devotes a whole chapter of *The Mystery of Capital* to celebrating the settlement of the American West, which involved the acceptance by federal and State governments of large-scale squatting. He identifies the Pre-emption Act (1841) as 'the legal breakthrough' which allowed squatters (or 'pioneers'), who had settled on public lands before they could be surveyed and auctioned by the government, to stake a claim to 160 acres and, after 14 months' residence, to buy from the government at a preferential price. The Homestead Act (1862) further developed the provisions, allowing anyone to gain title after five years if they had built a house, dug a well, broken or ploughed ten acres, fenced a specified amount, and actually lived on the land. Pre-emption and homesteading came about because the United States had acquired vast tracts of territory, by purchase, treaty or conquest from native Americans and from European colonial powers, but lacked the land management capabilities to keep pace with the growth and inexorable westward movement of its people. De Soto makes little mention of the devastating impact of white settlement upon native American land rights, for homesteading was also for the State a cheaper alternative to direct military force against the native Americans whom it wished to supplant (Allen 1991). For de Soto, this wholesale land-grabbing can be justified by the argument that land is a precious resource and should be given to those who can put it to the most productive use – and they were not the native Americans.

De Soto also dismisses the contribution to the legal history of land made by the British experience, a section of his book being headed 'Leaving behind antiquated British law'. Yet Britain has its own history of land-grabbing sanctioned by the State, particularly the century of enclosures in England and Wales around 1750–1840. During that period, private Acts of Parliament, justified by arguments of agricultural efficiency and the need to increase food supplies, extinguished what was perceived as an inefficient traditional system of customary, communal land rights. The enclosures movement reduced the holders of such rights (the commoners or peasantry) from some level of independence and self-sufficiency to dependency upon a wage, and restructured much of the rural landscape for a post-feudal society. By the end of the enclosures, the remote prospect for the dispossessed commoners of ever owning their own land was encapsulated in the poignant English working-class slang expression 'to become a land-owner', which meant 'to die' (and occupy your grave) (Partridge 1951). The history of enclosure, concentrating land-ownership in exclusive large private estates (identified by Macpherson (1962) as 'possessive individualism' and associated with the philosophical writings of John Locke), has lessons for the present-day discourse around tenure regularisation in the developing world.

What makes Arthur Young, who wrote 'The magic of property turns sand to gold', interesting and relevant to present land policy debates is that, having been an ardent advocate of enclosure, which he saw as the best route to economic strength and full employment, he recanted of his convictions when he saw how enclosure did not alleviate poverty, but increased it among those who lost their common or customary land rights. He was shunned by the powerful for his apostasy in exposing the poverty of those villages whose land had been enclosed and how, in his words, 'the rich ate up the poor'. By 1800, he was writing of the need to soften the social impact of enclosures: 'what have not great and rich people to answer, for not examining into the situation of their poor neighbours?' (quoted in Neeson 1993: 48–50). The Hammonds, in their classic study of the effect of enclosures upon the English village labourer, put it like this:

> This movement, assumed by the enlightened opinion of the day to be beneficent and progressive, was none the less a gigantic disturbance; it broke up the old village life; it transferred a great body of property; it touched a vast mass of interests at a hundred points. A governing class that cared for its reputation for justice would clearly regard it as of sovereign importance that this delicate network of rights and claims should not be roughly disentangled by the sheer power of the stronger: a governing class that recognized its responsibility for the happiness and order of the State would clearly

regard it as of sovereign importance that this ancient community should not be dissolved in such a manner as to plunge great numbers of contented men into permanent poverty and despair (Hammond 1966: 34).

Recent research has examined the changes of ownership and increased poverty (child mortality being a potent indicator) that followed the enclosure movement. Neeson quotes the 'village poet' of the time, John Clare, 'vile enclosure came & made a parish slave of me' (Neeson 1993: 297).

Enclosures affected the poor by removing their access to land where, and off which, could live under secure tenure. A particular casualty of enclosures was the tradition of the 'one-night house', which in the feudal, pre-enclosure 'open' village allowed the poorest to build a home on common or manorial waste land (Hammond 1966: 24–25; Beckett 1991). If they could erect a structure overnight, with a roof in place or a functioning fireplace by sunrise, then their right to stay might be conceded, subject to the payment of appropriate rent. Modern legal commentators have described this pre-modern means of acquiring secure tenure as a 'tenuous if picturesque practice ... shrouded in the mists of the past', and assert that its clandestine nature would prevent its legal sanction under the modern rule of law (Everton 1971). The term used for the present-day squatter settlements of Turkey has the same meaning (*gecekondu* = to find lodgings in a night) (Karpat 1976), and the anarchist writer Colin Ward has celebrated the history of this self-help approach to housing (Ward 2002). Squatters in the 18th century were described as 'encroachers' onto land, and the term survives in present-day India, where it is applied to efforts by the poor to house themselves on public land. Legally tolerated squatting by the poor in England, however, largely disappeared with the 19th century enclosures, which gave the enclosers or 'engrossers' of land increased legal powers against often undocumented communal use rights, along with tougher sanctions against trespass. One who already had title could expand his boundaries through the rules of adverse possession, and the landless poor were denied such access to land as they might previously have enjoyed under the 'one-night house' tradition. While it is the enclosers' view that has hitherto largely shaped the historical record, recent radical critiques of land law have recognised the inequalities and exclusionary effects that strengthening individual land-ownership can create (Green 1998: 230).

Those whose common rights were threatened by enclosure resisted it. The physical means of enclosure – the fences and surveyors' equipment – could become symbolic 'sites of struggle' between the competing land tenure systems. The Hammonds wrote of the disturbances at Otmoor in Oxfordshire, for instance, where in 1830 five hundred residents perambulated the bounds of the parish, pulling down fences erected by the enclosers and defending their ancient rights even against State-sanctioned violence from the yeomanry. 'So long and so bitter was the civil war roused by an enclosure which Parliament had sanctioned in absolute disregard of the opinions or traditions or circumstances of the mass of the people it affected' (Hammond 1966: 83–92). Young and others argued that commoners should at least be better compensated, in money or land, for the loss of their historic rights, and compensatory land would have allowed the poor to maintain what today's policy-makers would call 'sustainable multiple livelihoods'. Allotments or vegetable gardens (called 'provision grounds' on the Caribbean planter estates) were one remedy, which was justified by reference to colonial practice in a report on the state of Hampshire's poor in the 1790s: 'it is chiefly this practice which renders even the state of slavery in the West Indies tolerable, what an advantage it would be to the state of free service here!' (quoted in Hammond 1966: 151–57).

Enclosures were also associated with increased State control over the free movement of the poor, who were by Poor Law reforms restricted to their enclosed parishes under the Speenhamland system of relief. Harsh laws of settlement and vagrancy regulated movements by poor people between parishes (Beier 1974; Landau 1988; Hammond 1966: 108–16). Vagrants could be punished and even deported, while poor relief was only to be claimed in the legal place of settlement, which often meant forced transfer of claimants from parish to parish (Charlesworth 1999).

The parallels between the enclosures movement (with its related processes of social control), the methods of British colonial settlement, particularly from the mid-19th century, and the present-day squatter or informal settlements seem to have been largely overlooked by academic researchers (but for Canada, see Spry 1976). When Europeans colonised overseas, they imposed their legal systems, took the best land into their ownership and devised various legal devices and jurisdictional forms with which to establish, maintain and defend a hierarchy of social and spatial controls, and dominate the indigenous populations. Recent reappraisals by geographers, lawyers and historians have explored how colonial legal and regulatory systems have shaped urban landscapes and the land claims of different social groups (Abramson and Theodossopoulos 2000; Yeoh 1991; Robinson 1996; Home 1997) and the place of differentiated territorial jurisdictions in regulating social relationships (Blomley and Delaney 2001; McAuslan 2003). Recurrent themes in colonial and postcolonial theory have been those of duality and exclusion, concepts and processes which express the tensions between coloniser and colonised, with the latter subordinated and defined as the 'subaltern' other (Sibley 1995; Spivak 1994). In the words of Peter Fitzpatrick, a leading critical legal theorist, colonialism and postcolonialism share the 'recurrent, overlaid dualities of universality and particularity, inclusion and exclusion, sameness and difference' (Fitzpatrick 2001: 147).

Colonialism created and maintained boundaries through dualistic or pluralistic legal structures, especially boundaries in physical space which were defined and managed by land laws and regulations. Customary or communal land tenure was territorially distinguished, systematically misinterpreted and undermined by the judiciary, manipulated by administrators and overlooked in legislation. The Lugardian ideology of British colonialism between the two World Wars encouraged a dichotomy of systems of law and government under the so called 'dual mandate'. Lugard (writing of Nigeria, where he shaped his theories of indirect rule and the dual mandate) expressed the ideology thus:

> The British role here is to bring to the country the gains of civilisation by applied science (whether in the development of material resources, or the eradication of disease, etc), with as little interference as possible with Native customs and modes of thought (Lugard 1919: 9).

The dual mandate required a strategy of separate development, most famously expressed in *apartheid* South Africa (Dubow 1989). The dualistic construction was problematised where the 'native' population was heterogeneous, or where immigrant racial groups were introduced (such as the Chinese in Malaya, the Indians in East Africa, or the Zionist Jews in Palestine) whose aspirations the British both encouraged and sought to curb in the interests of protecting the 'natives' (Home 2003). Territorial jurisdictions were differentiated through the indirect rule system, which distinguished between the plantation estates and townships of the European colonisers and the tribal areas where customary land tenure was maintained and codified by social anthropologists (rather than lawyers).

A policy of separation and exclusionary boundaries implied restriction upon the free movement of people, especially of the non-white colonised (such as slaves, freed slaves, indentured and migrant workers), through travel and work documents. Plantation owners and mining companies had to stop their workers from absconding, and State officials managed the migration of workers between and within colonies, in a transition from private to State control over movement that was part of the transition from feudalism to capitalism. Infamous examples of controlled population movement are indentured labour (promised free land or a ticket home at the end of their indentures, but with the workers in practice often getting neither) and the South African pass laws, which managed the supply of mine labour and denied access to racially segregated areas for Africans lacking the correct pass (Hindson 1987; Torpey 2000; van den Boogart and Emmer 1986). It does not take much to find the roots of these controls in the colonial power's home experience of land consolidation through enclosures, the strengthening of private property rights and the enforcement of exclusionary social controls. In the Caribbean after emancipation, for example, tough controls over the movement of freed slaves were maintained through the adoption of a version of British vagrancy laws (see Hall 1997 on Barbados).

The territorial exercise of internal State power in *apartheid* South Africa has been conceptually mapped by Robinson (1996) and others. The so called Stallard doctrine regarded South African towns as European cultural creations and restricted African access to those whose labour was needed, forcing Africans to live in 'locations' or the inappropriately named 'townships' (racially segregated housing on the edge of town, usually outside the city limits). Successive legislation (eg, the Group Areas and Influx Control Acts) struggled with the growing pressures of African population growth and rural–urban migration. As rural impoverishment grew, those tribal or communal lands near urban areas became places where Africans could settle in unregulated, unserviced settlements and gain access to urban employment opportunities. When *apartheid* State power was no longer able to manage these areas, the 'squatter camps' were relabelled as 'informal settlements', designated for upgrading rather than clearance – 'here to stay' (Hindson and McCarthy 1994).

The case of *apartheid* South Africa, like that of the enclosures movement in England, was replicated with variations in the management of colonial lands across the Empire. When freed slaves, former indentured labourers or rural–urban migrants (today reconceptualised as 'the poor') settled on land without permission from the State or land-owners, they lived at risk of eviction (or 'summary ejectment', to use the term preferred in jurisdictions following the English common law). The essentially temporary housing structures that they built for themselves reflected not only their poverty and limited access to building materials, but also the threat of demolition that usually loomed. In the Caribbean, the impermanence and insecurity of such housing was expressed in the tradition of the 'chattel house', so called because it was regarded as a moveable rather than permanent structure, and a legacy of the landless emancipated slave who still depended upon his former master for a 'spot' to stay (Watson and Potter 1993; Glenn and Toppin-Allahar 1997; Home 1997: Chapter 5). Official disapproval and harassment of the poor, labelled as squatters, thus has deep roots in the colonial experience, and has only begun to soften in recent years. Part of de Soto's achievement has been to help lift the threat of demolition and eviction from the poor, treating them as settlers or homesteaders rather than squatters, and restoring to them a greater measure of human dignity. Similarly private or State controls over the internal movement of people have largely disappeared, although exclusionary land rights and building controls may remain. Further research into the largely hidden legal history of the relationship of the poor to land rights can help to inform present debates over law and policy by contributing a richer and more nuanced contextualisation.

## 'Land was Made to be Registered': The Torrens System in British Colonialism

This statement occurs in a recent book on land law, investigating what the author calls the 'seismic effects' of the new Land Registration Act 2002 in England and Wales (Sparkes 2003: 1). Although not referring to de Soto, he emphasises the importance of fixing assets in a formal property system for a capitalist market economy to function efficiently and effectively. Registering land requires a Weberian-style bureaucracy, keeping records in a public agency. Across much of the world, the process is known as the cadastre, based upon a survey showing accurately the extent and measurement of every plot of land (Greek *kata stichon* = line by line).

State registration of land title in Britain was historically slower to emerge than on the European mainland, but in the British colonies existed under the Torrens system. Mentioned only in passing by de Soto, this was the 'jewel in the crown' of land management in both the 'old' and the 'new' Commonwealth. With origins in the North German towns of the Hanseatic League and in the registration of shipping, the system was introduced by Torrens into South Australia in 1858 and spread to much of Australasia, North America, the Middle East and Africa (Thom 1912; Shick 1978; Whalan 1982). Largely superseding deeds registries, a Torrens register incorporated six main attributes: security, simplicity, accuracy, expedition, cheapness and suitability. State survey departments mapped the colonial territories, and lands departments allocated the leases and title deeds to private or corporate owners, overriding indigenous land rights in the process. The State guaranteed the accuracy of the record, which comprised an unambiguous definition of the land parcel, owner details, and legal interests affecting the parcel. The Torrens system followed three main principles (the so called Hogg's tests):

(1) The mirror principle – it should reflect accurately and completely current facts material to the title, with adverse claims, rights and qualifications recorded.
(2) The curtain principle – it represents the sole source of information for prospective purchasers.
(3) The insurance principle – it guarantees that any defects in the title subsequently discovered will be compensated to the person suffering the loss.

Property rights over land acquire a bundle of characteristics, particularly exclusivity, inheritability, transferability, enforcement mechanisms and possible time limitations. The owners can exclusively use land, enjoy the income and capital gains that accrue and transfer, lease, mortgage or pledge it (Hogg 1920; Simpson 1976).

The procedure of first-time registration captures new or existing rights to a land parcel, based upon an adjudication procedure and a physical survey by State-recognised land surveyors. Adjudication, the authoritative ascertainment of existing rights to land, can be undertaken either on transfer, when a land-owner requests it (sporadic adjudication), or through a process of compulsory and systematic adjudication by the State for an area. Boundaries, which are often disputed, can be defined either as general boundaries (physical features determined on the ground) or 'fixed' geodetic co-ordinates. Cadastral survey delimits the land parcels and determines boundaries on the ground, either on initial formation of a parcel, when subsequent boundary changes are made (eg, subdivision, assembly or consolidation), or to re-establish missing boundaries (Simpson 1976: 16–17; Larsson 1991; Kain and Baigent 1992).

The mapping of new territories and property rights was central to the colonial project. From the mapping, or 'geographical construction' (Edney 1997), of India and the survey of Ireland (Andrews 2002), the work of 'scientific survey' was spread through the British empire by a cadre of dedicated land surveyors. The Empire Conference of Survey Officers, first held in 1928 at Cambridge, was held again in 1931 and then at four-yearly intervals, and still survives as the Cambridge Conference, a global event for national mapping organisations. The spread of the Torrens system of survey and registration across the dominions, colonies and protectorates of the British Empire in Africa, Asia and the Middle East was facilitated through the *Empire Survey Review* and various specialist textbooks. The leading British colonial advocate of cadastral survey, Sir Ernest Dowson, produced the standard textbook upon invitation by the Cambridge Conference, funded by the Colonial Office and subsequently revised (Dowson and Sheppard 1956). As the British Empire was dismantled, further textbooks followed to ensure that the postcolonial States were equipped with surveying expertise (Dale 1976; Simpson 1976; Dale and McLaughlin 1988 and 2000). International professional organisations, such as the Commonwealth Association of Surveyors and Land Economists (CASLE) (based in London) and the International Federation of Surveyors (FIG), which supported the Habitat Campaign for Secure Tenure in its so called 'Bathurst declaration' (Bathurst 1999), have maintained the global mission. The current transnational exchange of approaches and legal instruments continues a historical feature of colonialism and globalisation (eg, Land Policy 2003).

The proponents of such modern cadastral systems have usually subscribed to a Darwinian evolutionary approach, seeing land registration as part of an inevitable historical process 'towards a greater concentration of rights in the individual and a corresponding loss of control by the community as a whole' (Simpson 1976: 225). Land registration, Simpson claimed, offered four advantages for developing countries ('continuous finality of the register', an unambiguous brief definition of the land, easier conveyancing, and an official certificate of title), and the British enclosures movement offered a model for systematic adjudication, producing a 'stable pattern of landholdings defined by durable fencing' (Simpson 1976: 163–68).

For Dowson, land registration would defend the peasantry against exploitative landlords and promote agricultural efficiency through smallholdings (Bunton 1999). The idea of an evolutionary process, where land rights 'evolve' from communal to individual forms, is also implicit in de Soto's thesis (although he shies away from an explicit endorsement) and remains a sensitive issue in debates about African land tenure (Platteau 1996).

Cadastral survey within a State-guaranteed land registration system is the key to de Soto's 'integration' of property rights, intended to facilitate global investment in property, and is the aim of many nation-States, encouraged by donor agencies. It has been promoted not only for the Third World, but also for the 'Second World' of countries emerging from socialism as an essential prerequisite for free market systems. The UN Economic Commission for Europe created in 1996 a group (initially called MOLA, subsequently WPLA) to address issues of tenure and real estate markets for countries in transition and to promote co-operation and exchanges of experience (UNECE 2003). This defined land administration as 'the process of recording and disseminating information about the ownership, value and use of land and its associated resources', a rather limited and technical definition which disguises the potentially wide array of functions and agencies that comprise land administration in the modern nation-State. Land registries record property rights, and surveying and mapping agencies provide the cartographic base (or, in the era of digital technology, the spatial data infrastructure). State and public lands must be managed in their various forms (eg, local government, national parks, heritage areas, defence installations and communal/customary land). Land dispute resolution may involve specialised courts and administrative tribunals with enforcement and appeals machinery. Valuation agencies (both public and private) appraise property for taxation, securitisation and mortgage purposes. A land use planning system regulates development and land use change within a framework for future spatial development and environmental protection. Environment agencies protect the natural environment, managing water resources and promoting, for example, sustainable development of coastal zones and wildlife habitats. The amalgamation, subdivision and reconstitution of land, and acquisition by the State, require expropriation and compensation rules. The very complexity of these multifarious activities furthermore creates a need for mechanisms of periodic review and reform. Such a national land management infrastructure can be viewed as technical and apolitical, a classic Weberian record-keeping bureaucracy which is capable of accommodating changing policy aims and objectives. For example, there are many ways to tax land, intervene in land markets and reform land-ownership, and the choices will be politically determined, but all require an institutional capacity if they are to be effective delivered.

A Torrens-style land registry is costly enough, however, let alone the rest of the State land administrative structure outlined above. Even in the wealthy UK, the Land Registry is under pressure to reduce its costs: 'The root problem is cost, coupled with delay. If this can be overcome, particularly with the introduction of computerisation, then land registration may be regarded as successful' (Smith 1986). The procedures of land management by the State are time-consuming and demanding, and require specialist staff to undertake a myriad tasks: to survey, examine plans, prepare legal documents, keep records, update valuation and rating lists, manage tenancies, execute enforcements and evictions, correct errors in past records and resolve land appeals and disputes. A review of cadastral systems in developing countries found that up to 90% of land parcels had no documentary evidence of title, and only 1% of sub-Saharan Africa was covered by any kind of cadastral survey (Fourie and Fluck 1999). Improved hardware and software for processing geo-spatial data could potentially change the situation through a spatial data infrastructure that integrates GIS, GPS, remote-sensed digital photogrammetry and online public access. In practice, however, cadastral records in most developing countries remain paper-based, dependent upon a small specialist cadre (these days often depleted by the ravages of AIDS), and the data conversion process is expensive and difficult. Attempts during the last decade to modernise land information in developing countries have produced disappointing results, questioned by both the potential beneficiaries and the cadastral specialists. The degrading of State land administration has contributed to the so called 'failing State', increasing rather than reducing tenure insecurity and destructive disputes over land.

If full land titling is becoming perceived as too complex and expensive, one much promoted alternative is some form of intermediate tenure, with incremental tenure regularisation linked to the physical upgrading of plots and infrastructure (Glenn and Belanger 2002; McAuslan 1985). There are precursors in the colonial experience. Self-build housing and the sites-and-services schemes promoted in the 1970s had their colonial origins in 'aided self-help' (Harris 1998). British colonial officials, especially in Africa, used the term 'temporary occupation licence' (or 'permissions to occupy') for some form of paper intermediate title in situations where the formal system of leases was not in place but new settlements were being laid out and occupied. Such licences did not usually distinguish residential from business use and were widely used to speed up settlement, for example, when railway-building was creating demand for trading areas but the lands officials were too few to draw up proper leases. Such licences were then passed from hand to hand to subsequent occupiers (Home 1974: 221–35).

A leading development lawyer, Patrick McAuslan, remains sceptical, however, about the potential for change:

> The diaspora of land law from Europe to Africa was to facilitate the grabbing of land from Africans by colonial officials and settlers. The idea that the law relating to land was also part of the law relating to governance, and existed for the benefit of the ruling classes, was embedded in the culture of colonialism. But it was also part of the culture of many African societies, so that there was an easy transfer of the colonial approach to the new independent governments. Liberalising the law, removing the central organs of the State from management of land, and allowing a market in land to develop thus pose fundamental governance and power challenges to African governments. Both liberal market reformers and those espousing reforms aimed at conferring land-owning rights on the people may then be disappointed as, whatever the form of the new laws, the temptations of the old approach will be too powerful for governments to resist completely (McAuslan 2003: 95).

## The Revival of Communal Tenure

Managing land, that most basic of natural resources, in the national and public interest (however constructed) carries its contradictions and contestations, especially under the conditions of postcolonialism that affect most developing countries. During the 1990s, it became recognised that land titling was less effective than had been thought, while communal tenure had benefits for maintaining social stability. In some former colonies, such indigenous land rights (and indeed populations) might have been completely extinguished, as occurred in most of the Caribbean islands, but on the larger land masses of Africa, Asia and Australia, they survived in tribal, customary or communal systems as a residual land tenure category.

Colonial law functioned as an instrument of control, and as an arena for inter-community and class struggle, and engendered a process of legalisation and professionalisation through which such struggles were mediated (Darian-Smith and Fitzpatrick 1999). The informal local property systems which de Soto calls 'extralegal' were usually communal or tribal, managed by different communities and organisations as private, autonomous systems serving a homogeneous social group, based on oral traditions and supported by communal sanctions. Such autonomous legal systems may be seen as foreign to, and competing with, the laws of the nation-State, and the process of integrating them into a single system may devalue their complexities, reducing them to 'subaltern' or folk-lore status (Weyrauch 2001). They often support surviving pre-colonial societies, which may be variously characterised as 'indigenous', 'aboriginal', 'native', or 'chthonic' (= in harmony with the earth; see Glenn 2000: Chapter 3). Colonial culture typically excluded and marginalised such unwanted social groups (Sibley 1995; Jacobs 1996), but in a postcolonial, pluralist world they are increasingly pursuing legal challenges and human rights arguments to reassert their claims, for example, in Australia post-*Mabo* (Stephenson and Ratnapala 1993) and in North America (Singer 1994; Brody 2001).

Communal or informal land tenure traditions can thus re-emerge to contest State-dominated hegemonic land dispensations. Autonomous sub-national land systems can allow distinct communities to survive, embedded within the territorial nation-State but with minimal recourse to the official institutions of the host society and State. 'Custom is consensual, while law is imposed: and, while custom is a part of social reality, law is a part of the secondary interpretive reality' (Mansell and others 1999: 45). The State is not the only source of law, since many private systems of law can co-exist, with characteristics more akin to tribal than State-structured societies: based upon strong oral traditions, giving less emphasis to due process but with robust rules of evidence, concentrating on protecting shared values and communal peace rather than individual rights. Such extralegal systems, as de Sousa Santos (1977) found in the *favelas* of Brazil, are non-professional, accessible, participatory and consensual, and exist alongside and within hegemonic national systems of law, protecting their members from external and internal threats. Private community-based law-making may indeed have the capacity to prevail over and influence official State law, refusing to be downgraded to 'folk-lore' status or labelled as primitive 'extralegal' forms of social regulation. A recognition of diversity in cultures and legal systems can provoke a mutual interrogation and challenge and offer perspectives on relationships between global and national, State and local, land and people.

One of de Soto's six property effects is what he calls 'integrating dispersed information into one system', requiring an expansion of the role of land registration.

He likens an integrated, formal property system to 'a bridge, if you will, so well-anchored in people's own extralegal arrangements that they will gladly walk across it to enter this new, all encompassing social contract' (de Soto 2000: 182). His optimistic language conceals, however, the likelihood that such a system – converting oral into written, informal into formal, local into national – will not be uniformly benign, neutral or free of power relationships and exploitation. The beneficiaries of informal systems may not wish to be integrated, preferring to preserve values and defend themselves against the penetrative forces of global capitalism and the modernising nation-State. Integrating plural and informal property rights into one unified system under State control may facilitate the spread of global capitalism and 'open' land markets and has become an aim of many nation-States, encouraged by donor agencies, but the process is not without risk or resistance.

De Soto is promoting formal property systems at a time when the dominance of individualised land tenure in policy prescriptions by donor agencies is increasingly seen as having negative consequences for the poor. The process devalues secondary, derived or delegated rights, concentrates ownership, promotes inequality and contributes to landlessness (Toulmin and Quan 2000). Communal property may provide a form of social security for the poor, old and disabled, and the process of integration and codification has its practical difficulties and costs (Shamir 2001). As assets become more closely administered, and individual property rights erode obligations to other community members, holders of secondary rights, especially women, may lose out, with land markets and formal property systems operating to concentrate ownership and accelerate landlessness. Identification with land can be a vital component in retaining cultural identity, and the deliberate withholding of land from State land-titling processes may become a means of preserving family and community cohesion and continuity. This is exemplified by the role of family land in the post-emancipation Caribbean and its survival into the postcolonial present (Crichlow 1994; Besson 2002).

The example of sub-Saharan postcolonial Africa shows the strength and resilience of communal or extralegal social contracts under pressures of population growth, environmental change and often oppressive land policies (Platteau 1996; Manji 2001). Tribal or customary land tenure has retained an important welfare function and indeed served as a reservoir of cheap, unserviced land in peri-urban areas (Hindson and McCarthy 1994). The revival of interest in customary or communal tenure is not, however, just a story of the continuing resilience and survival of motley overlapping systems of land-ownership, which defy both national law and formalised colonial legal pluralism. More recently, it is also a story of initiatives, for example, in sub-Saharan Africa, that are designed quite consciously to reclaim philosophical, legal and value systems including various local level practices of land management.

One alternative to formal registration of individual rights is the registration of collective or common property rights, potentially a simpler, cheaper and more equitable process. It requires respect for the values and aspirations of society, stakeholder participation and partnerships with civil society, as well as the building of capacity of local institutions for decentralised land management (Toulmin and Quan 2000: 5). New flexible property systems could record non-parcel land information, regularise informal occupation, apply new information technologies, assist with conflict management and adjudicate overlapping tenure types (Christensen and Hojgaard 1997). Common property resource knowledge attempts to secure the claims of the poorest in the face of competitive consumptive pressures from local, regional, national and international stakeholders (Shivji 2002) and can emerge in the hybrid conditions of peri-urban areas.

## Peri-Urban, the 'New Conceptual Landscape'

In de Soto's striking image of the bell jar, formal property rights are concentrated among the colonial and postcolonial elites, usually located physically within municipal areas and the plantation estates. Just outside the limits of urban areas lies the peri-urban, which has been seen as 'a new conceptual landscape' (Adell 1999) in the discourse on development and donor policies. Peri-urban areas can be defined as those areas surrounding towns and cities, within a daily commuting distance from the core and characterised by high interaction with it; they often concentrate along transport corridors as ribbon development, connecting a large city core to smaller town centres. As a city expands in area, the peri-urban zone shifts and grows, being in a constant state of rapid change. Land that earlier met the definition of 'peri-urban' becomes 'urban', while rural land becomes peri-urban, embracing villages where agricultural and non-agricultural uses compete for land. With rapid population growth, peri-urban areas typically outstrip the capacity of official agencies to map, record, monitor, service and regulate them, although new geo-spatial technologies are developing to meet the challenge of data capture through remote sensing and digital data analysis.

The peri-urban has been the subject of much recent research, which was reviewed in Adell (1999). For Laquinta and Drescher (2000), the peri-urban is less a geographical location but rather represents a state of mind or change in mental orientation. The UK DFID funded a major research programme in 1996–2001 into the peri-urban interface, analysing it as a zone of interaction between different systems (urban and rural), with flows of natural, human and financial resources, and proposed improvements in natural resource management and agricultural production (Brook and Davila 2000). The peri-urban may be a state of mind or a zone, but it is also a physical place: it is landscape, territory and space and should be conceptualised as such. The modern nation-State defines itself by territorially-based claims to sovereignty, and the construction and exercise of State power creates and maps boundaries, clearly seen at the boundary between urban jurisdictions and that which lies outside, unincorporated.

The concept of 'peri-urban' erodes a deep-rooted dichotomy in human affairs: that between the urban and the rural. Over 3,000 years ago, the Judaic land code, as set out in the Old Testament Book of Leviticus, distinguished between individual property rights (associated with the town) and communal rights (in the country):

> Anyone who sells a house inside a walled city has the right to redeem it for a full year after its sale ... But if it is not redeemed within a year, then the house within the walled city will become the permanent property of the buyer ... But a house in a village – a settlement without fortified walls – will be treated like property in the open fields. Such a house may be redeemed at any time and must be returned to the original owner in the

Year of Jubilee ... After all, the cities reserved for the Levites are the only property they own in all Israel. The strip of pastureland around each of the Levitical cities may never be sold. It is their permanent ancestral property (*Leviticus* 25: 29–34).

These Biblical rules endorsed the creation of property markets within urban areas, where limited space created a scarcity of land, and the protection of communal rights outside, but were silent about how processes of urban expansion and peri-urban land should be managed (Mutale 1996).

This differentiation between urban and rural matters has also created an academic and professional division of labour, with the literature on land markets being developed by urban and agricultural economists more or less independently of each other. Modern land use planning also distinguishes between urban and rural: the British system of 'town and country' planning, for example, defines settlement boundaries for urban areas, outside which a range of separate countryside protection policies apply, with land release for new urban development tightly controlled. A recent DFID-sponsored workshop on land rights and sustainable development in sub-Saharan Africa was content to address only rural issues to the exclusion of the urban (while admitting to the failing) (Toulmin and Quan 2000).

Not all human societies and cultures, however, recognise such a rural–urban dichotomy. The peri-urban may be on a conveyor belt from the rural to the urban, but it is not inevitably so, nor is it necessarily locked into yet another allegedly inevitable evolutionary process. West African societies combined urban and rural activities in 'close-settled zones', and the recent interest in 'urban agriculture' is rediscovering an ancient pattern of activity (although the SARS epidemic has exposed the risks of mixing humans and animals at high densities). Dwyer has invented a theoretical model of Indonesian settlement patterns, which he calls *desakota* (*desa* = village; *kota* = town), to describe mixed agricultural and non-agricultural activities (Wang 1997).

Peri-urban areas are as old as towns and cities, lying just outside the urban jurisdiction, relatively free from tax and controls and following their own particular dynamics. They are the places where travellers and traders could pause, and livestock could be fattened, before entering the regulated and taxed confines of the town. Waste disposal and noxious processes declared as 'non-conforming' (ie, unacceptable in a densely occupied area) could be banished beyond the municipal limits to the peri-urban, which could also be a place of intensive water management and horticulture, supplying water, fresh fruit and vegetables to the town-dwellers.

The 20th century saw urban populations increase dramatically, cities burst their walls and motor vehicles open up hinterlands. As urban expansion came to consume more land than the urban area, it was usually labelled as 'suburban', and in recent years concepts of the 'new urbanism', the 'compact city' and 'the 24-hour city' have attempted to reinvent urban cultural values. Planning codes are being revised to reflect the change, with single-use planning zones being superseded by policies to encourage mixed uses. Developed countries have largely pre-empted the concept of suburban development, while the term 'peri-urban' has become associated with unregulated development and with developing countries of the Third World. The global rise, both of human population and of the urban proportion within that population, has been most marked in the developing countries and has caused a physical expansion of towns and cities, sometimes through planned development, but more often through unregulated expansion at the urban fringe or within the peri-urban zone. The peri-urban can be characterised by various attributes: intermediate between urban and rural (and interacting with both), institutional fragmentation, mixed land uses, opportunities for multiple livelihoods, fragmented land holdings and social structures, rapid change, and places of risk and of opportunity.

The institutional fragmentation is often reflected in the uncertain legal position of the land itself. Ownership may be disputed, with squatters on State, communal or private land, and improvements to land may go unauthorised because of the lack of effective regulation. Land-grabbing and speculation thrives, spurred by the availability of cheap land with the hope of future development value. As rural impoverishment and population grows, tribal or communal land close to urban areas converts into unregulated, unserviced settlements, accommodating those people and activities which urban territories, jurisdictions and regulations exclude but which are not absorbed by the surrounding rural territory. Thus, peri-urban areas are the physical expression of a divided and fragmented institutional landscape, in a condition of limbo, neither urban nor rural. As a consequence, they often lack the utilities and infrastructure which urban systems are supposed to provide: properly designed and constructed roads, piped water supply, surface and foul water drainage, the energy utilities of gas and electricity, and telecommunications. They lack the institutional infrastructure of local or municipal government, such as physical and economic planning (and property taxes). Rental markets are unregulated, entailing insecurity and risks for both landlord and tenant, but more usually for the tenant.

Fragmentation characterises not only the cloudy property rights and institutional framework but the physical condition of the land itself, which may be subdivided or 'parcellated' into plots varying in size and shape. Subdivided plots are generally of a size intermediate between the smaller, denser urban plots and the larger rural farm-holdings, ranging typically between 500 and 5,000 sq m. The subdividers may have attempted a regular layout, but more typically plots are unplanned and poorly related to the road network. The uses to which plots are put may be classifiable as both urban and rural and are typically mixed in a mosaic of natural, productive and urban processes and sub-systems. Techniques of land pooling and readjustment offer the opportunity for reshaping unplanned peri-urban areas for incorporation into the planned area, but the knowledge, will and sustained effort to implement such schemes are rarely employed.

Peri-urban areas also show fragmented, heterogeneous and changing social patterns. Farmers and villagers may accept (willingly or not) the immigrants and the poor who have been excluded from or priced out of the adjoining urban jurisdiction. Thus, a mixture of the former occupiers, migrants from the remoter countryside, perhaps refugees displaced by conflict, the unwanted from the town, and down-raiding land speculators may all find themselves jostling to get land and the opportunities that possession of land creates. The peri-urban poor have the opportunity to pursue 'multiple livelihood strategies', a term which better describes the reality of their lives than the traditional distinctions made by academics between formal/informal or farming/non-farming activities. Peri-urban agriculture often has to compete for available land with urban activities while fulfilling an important function in feeding local poor populations, waste recycling and reducing unemployment.

Thus, the peri-urban areas researched in this book are zones of transition, places of uncertainty and change, creating opportunities and attracting risk-takers, both the poor and speculators. For low-income households, they can offer access to an individual plot, large enough to live on and make a living from renting rooms, vehicle repairs, food or livestock raising, petty trading, etc. They arise opportunistically in advance of government schemes for planned urban expansion and therefore pose particular challenges for governance and policy. Their challenge to governance is not just land dispute resolution and the regularisation of title, but the difficulties and costs of infrastructure provision (water, roads, drains and other services), the inefficiencies of land use including high transport costs, and the problems of establishing and maintaining the rule of law and fostering democratic political processes.

## Conclusions

Hernando de Soto has contributed to a rediscovery of the importance of land as a basic resource, whose effective and sensitive management by the State is crucial, not only for economic development, but for sustainable development and social justice. The challenge of providing secure tenure for the poor in a world of rapid population and urban growth requires an awareness of differing legal cultures and traditions, particularly in postcolonial and pluralist societies, as they relate to the problems of urban and peri-urban development. Tenure upgrading and integrated property rights are not new initiatives for the State, nor is entrepreneurial activity and aided self-help by the poor.

This chapter has sought to interpret de Soto's thesis within the historical context of British colonialism, for his account of pre-emption and homesteading in the United States has its parallels in the English enclosures movement. It is not fanciful to draw a comparison between the dispossession of the native Americans from their land by the farmers and cattlemen of expansionist American capitalism and the English enclosures movement, which allowed the enclosers and engrossers of land to exclude and dispossess the holders of common rights in the cause of extracting greater productivity from the land. Thus, the State's protection of property rights often reinforces inequalities in land-ownership and adds to the insecurity, indebtedness and landlessness of the poor. The processes of enclosure, including control of population movement and the guarantee of exclusive possessory title, were transferred to Britain's overseas colonies, with the dual mandate system maintaining individual settler rights alongside residual tribal or customary rights for the indigenous or 'native' peoples.

The British colonies devised the Torrens system of State-guaranteed land registration, which could serve as a model for sustaining de Soto's vision of small capitalists secure in their property rights. The land surveyors and land registry executives became the agents of a global network of technical knowledge, spread by media such as the Cambridge Conference, the *Empire Survey Review* and textbooks, and through advocates like Dowson and Simpson. But the Torrens system was expensive, and the difficult task of integrating common or customary property rights creates a challenge that the 'failing nation-State' is often unable to manage. The value of customary, more flexible and localised land rights systems is being increasingly recognised, and the peri-urban areas have become 'sites of struggle' between competing legal cultures and property rights systems and hybridised places of risk and opportunity, which the rest of this book explores further.

# References

Abramson, A and Theodossopoulos, D (eds) (2000) *Land, Law and Environment: Mythical Land, Legal Boundaries*, London: Pluto

Adell, G (1999) *Theories and Models of the Peri-Urban Interface: A Changing Conceptual Landscape*, London: DPU

Allen, DW (1991) 'Homesteading and property rights; or "how the West was really won"' *Journal of Law and Economics* 34: 1–23

Andrews, JH (2002) *A Paper Landscape*, Dublin: Four Courts Press

Bathurst (1999) *Bathurst Declaration on Land Administration for Sustainable Development*, FIG/UN Workshop on Land Tenure and Cadastral Infrastructure, Bathurst, Australia, available at www.fig.net/figtree/figun/sessions/session1/bathurstdec.pdf

Beckett, JV (1991) 'The disappearance of the cottager and the squatter from the English countryside: the Hammonds revisited' in Holderness, BA and Turner, M (eds), *Land, Labour and Agriculture, 1700–1920*, London: Hambleton Press

Beier, AL (1974) 'Vagrants and the social order in Elizabethan England' *Past & Present* 64: 3–29

Besson, J (2002) *Martha Brae's Two Histories: European Expansion and Caribbean Culture-Building in Jamaica*, Chapel Hill and London: UNC Press

Blomley, N and Delaney, D (eds) (2001) *The Legal Geographies Reader*, Oxford: Blackwell

Brandao, ASP and Feder, G (1995) 'Regulatory policies and reform: the case of land markets' in Frischtak, C, *Regulatory Policies and Reform: A Comparative Perspective*, Washington, DC: World Bank

Brody, H (2001) *The Other Side of Eden: Hunter-gatherers, Farmers and the Shaping of the World*, London: Faber and Faber

Brook, R and Davila, J (eds) (2000) *The Peri-Urban Interface: A Tale of Two Cities*, London: DPU

Bunton, M (1999) 'Inventing the status quo: Ottoman land-law during the Palestine mandate, 1917–1936' *International History Review* 21(1): 28–56

Charlesworth, LJ (1999) 'Why is it a crime to be poor?' *Liverpool Law Review* 21: 149–67

Christensen, SF and Hojgaard, PD (1997) *Innovative Land Surveying and Land Registration in Namibia*, London: DPU Working Paper 93

Crichlow, MA (1994) 'An alternative approach to family land tenure in the Anglophone Caribbean: the case of St Lucia' *New West Indian Guide* 68(1 & 2): 77–99

Dale, PF (1976) *Cadastral Surveys within the Commonwealth*, London: HMSO

Dale, PF and McLaughlin, JD (1988) *Land Information Management: An Introduction with Special Reference to Cadastral Problems in Third World Countries*, Oxford: OUP

Dale, PF and McLaughlin, JD (2000) *Land Administration*, Oxford: OUP

Darian-Smith, E and Fitzpatrick, P (eds) (1999) *Laws of the Postcolonial*, Ann Arbor: Michigan UP

Deininger, K and Binswanger, H (1999) 'The evolution of the World Bank's land policy: principles, experience, and future challenges' *World Bank Research Observer* 14(2): 247–76

de Soto, H (2000) *The Mystery of Capital: Why Capitalism Triumphs in the West and Fails Everywhere Else*, London: Black Swan

de Sousa Santos, B (1977) 'The law of the oppressed: the construction and reproduction of legality in Pasargada' *Law and Society Review* 12(1): 5–126

Dowson, E and Sheppard, VLO (1956) *Land Registration*, London: HMSO

Dubow, S (1989) *Racial Segregation and the Origins of Apartheid in South Africa 1919–36*, Oxford: Macmillan

Edney, MH (1997) *Mapping an Empire: The Geographical Construction of British India 1765–1843*, Chicago: Chicago UP

Everton, AR (1971) 'Built in a night' *Conveyancer* 35 (NS): 249–55

Fitzpatrick, P (2001) *Modernism and the Grounds of Law*, Cambridge: CUP

Fourie, C (1998) 'The role of local land administrators: an African perspective' *Land Use Policy* 15(1): 55–66

Fourie, C and Fluck, NO (1999) 'Cadastre and Land Information Systems for Decision-Makers in the Developing World', Joint UN-FIG Conference on Land Tenure and Cadastral Infrastructures for Sustainable Development, Bathurst, Australia

Gerth, HH and Wright Mills, C (eds) (1991) *From Max Weber: Essays in Sociology*, London: Routledge

Glenn, HP (2000) *Legal Traditions of the World: Sustainable Diversity in Law*, Oxford: OUP

Glenn, JAM and Belanger, V (2002) 'Informal law in informal settlements' in Holder, J and Harrison, C (eds), *Law and Geography*, Oxford: OUP

Glenn, JAM and Toppin-Allahar, C (1997) 'Chattel houses and mobile homes: fixtures in Caribbean and Canadian law' *Caribbean Law Review* 7(1): 368–91

Green, K (1998) 'Citizens and squatters: under the surfaces of land law' in Bright, S and Dewar, J (eds), *Land Law: Themes and Perspectives*, Oxford: OUP

Hall, CG (1997) 'A legislative history of vagrancy in England and Barbados' *Caribbean Law Review* 7(1): 314–67

Hammond, JLB (1966) *The Village Labourer*, London: Longman

Harris, R (1998) 'The silence of the experts: "aided self-help housing", 1939–1954' *Habitat International* 22(2): 165–89

Hindson, D (1987) *Pass Controls and the Urban African Proletariat in South Africa*, Johannesburg: Ravan Press

Hindson, D and McCarthy, J (eds) (1994) *Here to Stay: Informal Settlements in KwaZulu-Natal*, Daldridge, South Africa: Indicator Press

Hogg, JE (1920) *Registration of Title to Land Throughout the Empire*, Toronto: Carswell

Home, RK (1974) 'The influence of colonial government upon Nigerian urbanisation', unpublished PhD thesis, London School of Economics, University of London

Home, RK (1997) *Of Planting and Planning: The Making of British Colonial Cities*, London: Spon

Home, RK (2003) 'An "irreversible conquest?": colonial and postcolonial land law in Israel/Palestine' *Social and Legal Studies* 12(3): 291–310

Jacobs, JM (1996) *Edge of Empire: Postcolonialism and the City*, London: Routledge

Kain, RJP and Baigent, E (1992) *The Cadastral Map in the Service of the State: A History of Property Mapping*, Chicago: Chicago UP

Karpat, K (1976) *The Gecekondu: Rural Migration and Urbanization in Turkey*, New York: CUP

Kedar, S (2002) 'On the legal geography of ethnocratic settler states: notes towards a research agenda' *Current Legal Issues* 5: 401–41

Land Policy (2003) 'Land policy in the Caribbean', report of a workshop held in Port of Spain, Trinidad

Landau, N (1988) 'The laws of settlement and the surveillance of immigration in eighteenth-century Kent' *Continuity and Change* 3: 391–420

Laquinta, D and Drescher, AW (2000) *Urban and Peri-Urban Food Production: A New Challenge for the Food and Agriculture Organization (FAO) of the United Nations*, Rome: FAO

Larsson, G (1991) *Land Registration and Cadastral Systems*, New York: Longman

Lugard, FD (1919) *Revision of Instructions to Political Officers on Subjects Chiefly Political and Administrative 1913–1918*, London: Waterlow

Macpherson, CB (1962) *The Theory of Possessive Individualism*, Oxford: OUP

McAuslan, P (1985) *Urban Land and Shelter for the Poor*, London: Earthscan

McAuslan, P (2003) *Bringing the Law Back In: Essays in Land, Law and Development*, Aldershot: Ashgate

Manji, A (2001) 'Land reform in the shadow of the State: the implementation of new land laws in Sub-Saharan Africa' *Third World Quarterly* 22(3): 327–42

Mansell, W and others (1999) *A Critical Introduction to Law*, London: Cavendish Publishing

Mutale, E (1996), 'A biblical view of land policy' *South African Journal of Surveying and Mapping* 23: 325–32

Neeson, JM (1993) *Commoners: Common Right, Enclosure and Social Change in England, 1700–1820*, Cambridge: CUP

Partridge, E (1951) *A Dictionary of Slang and Unconventional English*, London: Routledge Kegan Paul

Platteau, J-P (1996) 'The evolutionary theory of land rights as applied to sub-Saharan Africa: a critical assessment' *Development and Change* 27(1): 29–85

Robinson, JB (1996) *The Power of Apartheid: State, Power and Space in South African Cities*, London: Butterworth-Heinemann

Shamir, R (2001) 'Suspended in space: Bedouins under the law of Israel' in Blomley, N (ed), *The Legal Geographies Reader*, Oxford: Blackwell

Shick, BC (1978) *Torrens in the United States*, Lexington, Mass: Lexington Books

Shivji, I (2002) *Village Governance and Common Pool Resources in Tanzania*, Common Pool Resource Paper, Department of Geography, Cambridge University

Sibley, D (1995) *Geographies of Exclusion: Society and Difference in the West*, London: Routledge

Simpson, JR (1976) *Land Law and Registration*, Cambridge: CUP

Singer, JW (1994) 'Well settled? The increasing weight of history in American Indian land claims' *Georgia Law Review* 28: 481–532

Smith, R (1986) 'Land registration: white elephant or way forward?' *Current Legal Problems* 39: 111–30

Sparkes, P (2003) *A New Land Law*, Oxford: Hart

Spivak, GC (1994) 'Can the subaltern speak?' in Williams, P and Chrisman, L (eds), *Colonial Discourse and Postcolonial Theory*, New York: Columbia UP

Spry, I (1976) 'The great transformation: the disappearance of the commons in Western Canada' in Allan, R (ed), *Man and Nature on the Prairies*, Regina

Stephenson, MA and Ratnapala, S (1993) *Mabo: A Judicial Revolution*, Brisbane: Queensland UP

Thom, DJ (1912) *The Canadian Torrens System*, Calgary: Burroughs

Toulmin, C and Quan, J (eds) (2000) *Evolving Land Rights, Policy and Tenure in Africa*, London: DFID/IED/NRI

Torpey, J (2000) *The Invention of the Passport: Surveillance, Citizenship and the State*, Cambridge: CUP

UNECE (2003) *Working Party on Land Administration*, available at www.unece.org/env/hs/wpla/welcome.html

van den Boogart, E and Emmer, PC (eds) (1986) *Colonialism and Migration: Indentured Labour Before and After Slavery*, Dordrecht: Martinus Nijhoff

Wang, MYL (1997) 'The disappearing rural-urban boundary. Rural socio-economic transformation in the Shanyang-Dalian region of China' *Third World Planning Review* 19(3)

Ward, C (2002) *Cotters and Squatters: Housing's Hidden History*, Nottingham: Five Leaves Publications

Watson, IB and Potter, RB (1993) 'Housing and housing policy in Barbados: the relevance of the chattel house' *Third World Planning Review* 15(4): 373–95

Weyrauch, WO (ed) (2001) *Gypsy Law: Romani Legal Traditions and Culture*, Berkeley: California UP

Whalan, DJ (1982) *The Torrens System in Australia*, Sydney: Law Book Co

Yeoh, BS (1991) *Municipal Control, Asiatic Agency and the Urban Built Environment in Colonial Singapore 1880–1929*, Oxford: OUP

Young, A (1917) *Travels in France*, London: G Bell

# Chapter 3
# Land Readjustment for Peri-Urban Customary Tenure: The Example of Botswana

*Clarissa Fourie*

## Introduction

Gaborone, the capital of Botswana, is experiencing large-scale urbanisation, much of it taking place in peri-urban areas on tribal land. One such area is Mogoditshane, where different approaches have been tried to manage large-scale urban growth, and which will be used here as an illustration. It is argued that lessons learned over the last decade indicate that, in countries where customary land tenure is a national symbol (as is the case with Botswana), so called 'modern' systems of property rights, spatial planning and so on are unlikely to work as anticipated in the peri-urban context. This is because the customary way of doing business includes the manipulation of land tenure rules, flexibility, uncertainty, ambiguity and coalition formation linked to entrepreneurship. 'Modern' land titling systems, by comparison, aim at certainty built around formal rules. (The term 'modern' as opposed to 'customary' is used here to engage with the debate that is taking place in Africa and does not imply any superiority of 'modern' to 'customary'.)

In areas like Mogoditshane, therefore, land law reform, including schemes to integrate dual legal systems, should not be the main concern. Instead, it is recommended that legal land instruments that can facilitate conflict management should be prioritised for land delivery. This focus is also more likely to deliver sustainable tenure security for the poor, as it addresses a structural tension present in the society, expressed here in social anthropological terms as being between 'hierarchy formation' and 'egalitarian behaviour' (following Comaroff 1982). Currently, elite groups are being strengthened by the hierarchical tendencies present in the society, but conflict management strategies could bring back some balance by encouraging more egalitarian behaviour. It is suggested that an adapted form of the land readjustment technique is the most useful, and pro-poor, mechanism that could be deployed for this.

This chapter attempts to pull together a range of themes and approaches, and to rethink approaches to land delivery in customary peri-urban areas. It is structured in terms of a number of analytical layers and begins with a brief contextual description of the issues and problems in Mogoditshane and Botswana, as well as the position of the urban poor in the Gaborone area. A conceptual framework for the analysis of land and property rights systems in peri-urban customary areas, and specifically Mogoditshane, is then outlined, drawing on comparative socio-political work in south-east Botswana and in informal settlements in South Africa. Comaroff's analysis in Botswana showed that rules change over time, being a 'cultural repertoire' which people manipulate for their own gain, within the 'contradictory tendencies' of hierarchy and egalitarianism (Comaroff 1982). His approach has been applied to the analysis of land tenure in informal settlements in South Africa (eg, Fourie 1994; Davies 1998; Barry 2000). It has been confirmed that land tenure rules in customary/informal areas are manipulated over time by different entrepreneurs and coalitions for their own political and financial gain, and in response to external developments in the wider society, such as urbanisation, government policy and the actions of government ministers. It will be argued here that an analysis of Mogoditshane over the last decade shows Gaborone-based elites manipulating the land tenure rules, based on customary behaviour, to introduce new peri-urban tenures in return for financial gain. As with some South African settlements studied by the author, tenure rules became ambiguous, but a constant in these customary/informal communities is the contradictory tendency of integration and fission.

This manipulation of tenure rules applies in other parts of the property rights system. The narrow focus on land tenure in the customary/modern debate has meant that the systems linked to 'modern' land management are taken for granted and given relatively less attention, such as planning layouts, land use controls, spatial information systems, and enforcement at local government level. The history of land tenure reform in Mogoditshane indicates that tenure rules come to be manipulated under customary peri-urban conditions. The ambiguity associated with peri-urban settlements arises because they are neither formal nor informal, legal nor illegal, but a complex combination of these (Doebele 1994; Davies 1998).

To replace customary tenure and ambiguous rules with so called 'modern' approaches would require a revolution in the society's view of customary tenure and is not seen as a practical land management option. In pursuing other possibilities, a brief review is made of recent recommendations about peri-urban land tenure, including the integration of dual legal systems (de Soto 2000; Farvacque and McAuslan 1992), and the promotion of customary approaches (McAuslan 1991 and 1992; Durand-Lasserve and Royston 2002).

The priority for places like Mogoditshane is, it is here argued, less the implementation of national land law reform than the development of instruments for land dispute resolution (Adelman and Paliwala 1993; Trubek and Galanter 1974; Manji 2001). Potential types of land-related conflict are discussed, followed by an assessment of conventional instruments for land development, with land readjustment suggested as the most promising. Some conflict management strategies associated with land readjustment are then identified, drawing upon the relevant international literature. A set of good technical practices is presented and a more appropriate form of land readjustment suggested. Many of the good practices that are suggested emanate from general pro-poor strategies, which are here embedded within practical land management approaches.

## Mogoditshane: A Case Study in Peri-Urban Land Conversion

In Botswana, urban land is classified as State land, with most of the country (aside from national parks) classified as tribal land under the jurisdiction of Tribal Land Boards (TLBs) (Mphathi and Modisagape 1998). Since independence, the Botswana government has strongly supported the retention of customary land rights and any changes for new ('modern') purposes have been incremental, rather than fundamentally affecting the underlying principles (ROB 1983; Modisagape 1998). Under the pressures of rapid urbanisation, the supply of land and formal housing stock under the so called 'modern' systems has failed to keep pace with demand, creating high prices and shortages and increasing the pressure upon peri-urban customary areas, including Mogoditshane, where customary land is being sold. Under government policy, only developments on land can be sold, not the land itself, and compensation is paid by the government based upon an official valuation which can be at a level as much as 40 times below open market value.

The government has tried to address the results of urbanisation in peri-urban customary areas, specifically in Mogoditshane. In 1991, the Presidential Commission found that:

> ... the owners of ploughing fields (*masimo*) had been subdividing and selling land to individuals without the consent of their Land Boards. Such informally allocated plots created unplanned and haphazard developments that were subsequently difficult to provide with infrastructure (Kgabo Commission 1991).

There were unauthorised changes of use from *masimo* to residential that had not been approved by the Land Board or the planning authority. Kgabo adds that, 'Land Board ... officials were selling plots, issuing fraudulent ownership certificates and without planning permission. The participants in these extralegal practices were uncontrite and defiant in their evidence to the Presidential Commission'. A High Court ruling gave field owners the right to dispose of their fields to whomever they wished (applied to allocations before 1994), and a Cabinet Minister (as a personal favour) overturned a petition by a TLB to the High Court for an eviction.

In 1992, the government tried to address the problem with various approaches, including creating a task force of police officers to monitor illegal land developments, mapping land rights, creating a subordinate TLB and a Land Tribunal with better record-keeping capacity and preparing a detailed layout plan. The results were dismal. When surveyors tried to place the beacons according to the plans, they discovered non-conforming subdivisions, unauthorised structures (houses, fences, etc) and land occupiers denying them access. A mandatory P5,000 fine was imposed by the government for cases of illegal occupation, but this also became part of the negotiations and manipulation that took place between government, owners and claimants who were buying the subdivided land.

The TLB records were found to be either non-existent or at least inadequate, especially for the definition of plot boundaries and site area, and the Board could allocate the same piece of land to more than one party. The TLB is being sued with increasing success, costing the government money, and capacity with regard to land record creation, maintenance and keeping records updated has been weak. While the TLBs may record some description of land rights, there is no description of types of land use. This in turn means that there is no detailed spatial information on existing land uses to inform spatial planning and zoning decisions, which often then do not fit existing and historical *de facto* use. Mphathi and Modisagape (1998) also indicate that the TLBs are often not sufficiently consulted in the process of preparing physical plans by the Town and Country Board, and yet they are expected to implement these plans.

The problems continue, as a South African newspaper reported:

> Haphazard settlement complicates the provision of services ... electricity, water and sewerage. Also ... towards the late 1990s attention became focused on about 5,000 'illegal squatter' households in Mogoditshane, ... last year the government commenced with demolitions of the homes of these squatters ... [and] half ... have been demolished (*Mail and Guardian* 2002).

These demolitions took place even though about half of the households had pending applications for land with the local Land Board.

Despite Botswana's impressive economic growth, the national poverty rate was still 47% in 1994, a decline of only 12% from 1985 (SARPN 2001). The government is scaling back earlier pro-poor urban land strategies, such as the Self-Help Housing Agency Scheme (SHHA), and encouraging conversion of SHHA plots to full urban services linked to cadastral surveys and registration, even though the price of housing is among the highest in the Southern African region, and in consequence the poor are generally forced to rent backyard accommodation where they cannot get land of their own.

The current debate about Mogoditshane is less about solutions to the problems of the poor, and their access to land and tenure security, but rather about customary tenure versus 'modern' approaches. Many of the 5,000 squatter houses demolished in Mogoditshane were brick-and-tile middle class houses, and a potential 'squatter' interviewed was a middle-class civil servant with plans for a house appropriate to his social station. The conceptual framework that follows attempts to locate this discourse among the land elites, and identify how robust poverty alleviation strategies could be introduced into land delivery.

## The Manipulation of Rules in Customary Tenure and Peri-Urban Areas

While customary/informal systems may seem to compete with the laws of the modern nation-State, the process of integrating them into one formal representational system (in de Soto's terminology) may devalue the complexities of the customary/informal systems, and present technical/legal approaches may make it impractical for formal and customary tenures to cohabit within the same property rights system.

The arguments presented here draw from anthropological work on Botswana and South Africa (eg, Fourie 1994; Davies 1998; Davies and Fourie 2002; Barry 2000; Barry and Fourie 2002), which shows that in customary areas, land tenure rules may not be fixed, but rather ambiguous and open to manipulation. By contrast, modern property rights systems are expected to give certainty and homogeneity, remain fixed over long periods of time, and not easily tolerate manipulation (McLaughlin and de Soto 1994: 308). Local customary communities, like Mogoditshane, are not isolated and insulated from outside factors such as urbanisation, and structural tensions within the community will interact with these factors to produce new ways of doing things. If Mogoditshane had conformed to modern land management prescriptions, it might have become a well-planned area, while, if customary tenure was a closed system, no peri-urban development would have occurred. The reality of Mogoditshane is something else: a hybridised situation allowing alternative outcomes, and this happened because of the internal dialectic or structural tension, both within the community and at national level, around customary tenure issues, and its response to external factors.

Comaroff argues that the constant in the society (his study was in south-east Botswana), rather than being the rules associated with political processes, is what he terms the internal dialectic or contradictory principles of 'hierarchy/aggregation: egalitarianism/individuation' (Comaroff 1982: 150–58). These contradictory principles are always present and manifest themselves in different ways. For example, the attempt by the Botswana government to control Mogoditshane's development without moving away from customary tenure shows the hierarchical and centralised tendency in operation, while the role of the Minister in giving special dispensations to friends undertaking 'illegal' land development also manifests hierarchical/aggregation behaviour, related to coalition formation. On the other hand, the informality in Mogoditshane, and the claims by field-owners that they own the land and have a right to subdivide and sell it can be seen as manifestations of the egalitarianism/individuation tendency. Thus, the constant internal dialectic has different manifestations over time, and the rules are manipulated to facilitate them.

Comaroff (1982) was concerned with political processes at national and community level in Botswana, while this author (Fourie 1994) has shown that his conceptual framework can also be applied to African land tenure systems, including informal settlements, with her original field work being on the Zulu tribe of South Africa. The structural tension in Zulu land tenure is defined as being between integration and fission, coalition formation and entrepreneurship. Land tenure rules do not determine the behaviour of people in customary areas but embody the ideational and organisational framework within which the process of competition for land and status takes place (Fourie 1994: 20, quoting Comaroff 1982: 12). Rules are part of the cultural repertoire that people use to manipulate events and so obtain power, land and influence. Davies (1998) and Barry (2000) showed that this approach to land tenure in informal settlements had wider application in South Africa, and it also appears to have potential in analysing land tenure in Mogoditshane.

Within the integration tendency, coalitions are formed to protect traditional rural customary tenure, just as coalitions are formed by entrepreneurs to introduce new forms of tenure (such as informal settlement) into customary areas. Both tenure types and coalitions represent the same contradictory tendency of fission/integration. In Zululand, traditional rural coalitions successfully prevented the growth of informal settlements, until an entrepreneur led a breakaway coalition to facilitate the development of one. When the person in charge of KwaZulu, and a leader in the hierarchy of Zulu land tenure, stated that informal settlers could not be removed in that community, the coalition supporting new tenure types was strengthened, affecting the local community and setting a precedent for other communities to come into existence.

The behaviour related to coalition formation is a key to understanding African land tenure systems and customary rights. Hierarchical behaviour in African land tenure systems does not follow European allodial systems of land rights, where lesser rights or interests are abstracted from the title, but rights are distributed among society members, with competing coalitions existing within the hierarchy, both vertically and horizontally. There may be competition over the same piece of land by different social units, such as the extended family, the headman, the chief, or (as in the case of Mogoditshane) between the field owner and claimant of residential rights, and between TLB officials and the planning office which allocates land according to the layout plan (representing the 'modern' property rights system). The manipulation of land tenure rules is part of this competition and reflects new economic opportunities created by external factors, such as urbanisation or a favourable court case. This manipulation of rules introduces ambiguity and uncertainty around land rights, status and values, which have therefore to be constantly renegotiated. New economic opportunities encourage entrepreneurs to fission away, develop coalitions, manipulate the rules and introduce new ways.

One could argue, for a settlement such as Mogoditshane, that customary tenure no longer exists, but instead there is a variation of modern tenure, which allows individualisation of tenure, the sale of customary land, land-holding by women, and nuclear rather than extended family control. But there is not necessarily an irreversible 'natural' evolution, from community to individual, or from customary to something else, which automatically leads to the emergence of a modern system of property rights (Fourie 1994; Davies 1998; Barry 2000). The studies in South Africa showed that if the internal dialectic of fission/integration continues, customary law still applies, and only when either of the contradictory tendencies has disappeared can one conclude that the area is no longer customary. If there was no longer integration (coalition formation) within the hierarchy of land tenure and politics, it could be concluded that customary tenure had been eradicated, but the Mogoditshane case shows customary tenure behaviour (rule manipulation) as still important at both local and national levels, operating within the internal dialectics of hierarchy/aggregation and egalitarian/individuation, and coalition formation and entrepreneurship, which are still part of the discourse around land. Mogoditshane is not (or not yet) an example of an individualised tenure system ready to be absorbed into the modern system (as de Soto would have it), nor can it be regarded as an isolated case in the Gaborone area. The Botswana government's policy on customary tenure relates to the operation of the land development business at many levels within the country. Other large developments around Gaborone, which could be considered as legal and customary anomalies or aberrations, are not aberrations within this analytical framework but a natural consequence of the internal dialectic and structural tensions within the customary tenure system.

Comaroff found that, where the tendency towards hierarchy/aggregation is dominant over time, it can increase elitism and create a greater distance between rich and poor. He showed (for south-eastern Botswana) that various factors made the tendency towards aggregation dominant, leading to a centralised and elitist political formation, that monopolised resources. These factors included national attempts to improve production through capital investment, the transition from subsistence to commercial farming, and the creation of the area as a separate chiefdom, all linked to the structural tensions or internal dialectic within the society (Comaroff 1982: 163–68, quoted in Fourie 1994: 23). Similar conclusions could probably be reached for Mogoditshane, with the voice of the poor being stifled by the manifestation of the hierarchy/aggregation tendency city, associated with entrepreneurship and coalition formation in land dealings.

The ambiguity of the formal/informal status of peri-urban settlements varies over time in relation to the internal dialectic in the community and the plans put in place by government, national and local. The urban management programmes of governments are a key external factor for peri-urban settlements, because they define the rules of the game, whether a settlement is considered legal or illegal, formal or informal, which can then be manipulated. For example, in Mogoditshane, the government decided to impose a fine of P5000 on illegal subdivisions, only for these to become part of the negotiation between buyers and sellers of residential plots in the fields.

A reason for this ambiguity is the lack of a clear distinction between legal development and that taking place within the framework of informal law (UNCHS (Habitat) 1991: 7). Rather than a simple duality of 'legal' and 'illegal', the real world contains complex mixtures of formal and informal systems, with many variations in between, so that informal settlements cannot simply be defined as legal, illegal, spontaneous, planned, formal or informal, but rather in terms of a continuum model (Doebele 1994: 48). Varley (2002), writing of the process of Mexican agrarian reform, rejects a simple dichotomy between legality and illegality, which she sees more as evidence of the power of dualisms in Western thought than a meaningful explanatory tool.

Davies takes the argument further for local government. As a municipal land surveyor of informal settlements in East London (South Africa), he found that informal settlement could be 'any settlement that exists on a continuum of development, and is jointly managed by the local community and the local authority', and its position may change over time with respect to the relationship of government (and its activities) and the particular settlement (Davies 1998: 104). This analysis can be applied both to national and local government programmes and recognises that an informal settlement is a complex mix of formality and informality, with the activities of government (including local government) affecting and altering this continuum over time as it interacts with the informal settlement. Understanding this continuum is important for property rights systems, and their application in peri-urban areas, because such systems tend to be national but have to be implemented locally. National government departments in Botswana have been directly engaging with the Mogoditshane area for over a decade through a range of urban management interventions and rules, many of which have been manipulated to secure personal, political and financial gain by both small and large entrepreneurs.

This way of doing business in Botswana generally follows the customary system, both within Mogoditshane and nationally, and a high level of ambiguity around land-related rules, uncertainty and the manipulation of rules, including urban management rules, are to be expected. This uncertainty is exacerbated in peri-urban areas, because they are not simply illegal or legal but lie upon a continuum of land development, depending on the position and role of government, whether national or local. In this situation, the voice of the poor may be lost and pro-poor strategies may be difficult to implement. Possible ways forward are, first, to replace customary tenure with modern forms, or, secondly, to develop land through customary practice and behaviour, which requires embracing ambiguity and uncertainty, the manipulation of rules by entrepreneurs, coalition formation, and competition for land and use rights and financial gain.

The first option would require a revolution in social thinking, eliminating unpredictable outcomes of the rules in peri-urban areas and integrating them within a modern system of property rights in order to achieve orderly land development. Urban land reform can be seen as resulting from changes in society, not the other way around (UNCHS (Habitat) 1991: 178). The customary values of the society, and policies of the existing national government, would have to change to create a more certain system of property rights. The second option offers a better opportunity to work with customary approaches, has implications for the type of land instruments and strategies that should be adopted, and provides the background for recommendations in this chapter on land readjustment.

Property rights systems are linked to a range of systems, which are likely to become part of the manipulative and competitive processes discussed above. The links between these systems are especially evident when undertaking land readjustment, the land instrument which seems most suitable for the Mogoditshane situation. A range of systems are engaged in the process of readjustment, including spatial information management, land records and land titling, valuation, enforcement, land use planning and control, service delivery for urban areas, and adjudication, dispute resolution and conflict management. Following from the proposition, the property rights system will not be made more certain or effective by building capacity into other associated systems. Secondly, the rules of these other systems are also manipulated, so that it is not just tenure rules that become ambiguous and uncertain. Thirdly, given the manipulation of system rules and consequent ambiguities and uncertainties, appropriate instruments for urban land management need to address the realities.

Cadastral information is often used as the basis for these systems, leading to the concept of a cadastral or land information infrastructure, which consists of the aggregate of hundreds of generally contiguous cadastral parcels as is found in the developed world (UN/FIG 1999), and is used as the basis for other systems, to facilitate programme implementation on a national scale (Fourie 2002). Customary areas, where there is either no cadastral or land administration infrastructure or they are incomplete (as in Mogoditshane), either lack experience or have a legacy of these other systems. Because such areas lack this infrastructure, they also lack the technical personnel usually associated with property rights systems, who are often licensed and disciplined by a statutory body/government with education requirements for entry.

Botswana attempted land tenure reform in its customary areas but focused predominantly upon land tenure rights to individual parcels of land. In the last decade in Mogoditshane, a land administration infrastructure has been attempted, but with limited success because of insufficient understanding and resourcing, and has as a result become uncertain and ambiguous, just as is the case with land tenure rules. Whatever capacity the urban management system has, the rules will still be manipulated. In Mogoditshane, the rules have been used tactically to transact land matters, whether by ordinary people, TLB officials, or even Ministers, and these entrepreneurs manipulate not only the land tenure rules but also those associated with other parts of the property rights system, such as planning layouts, land use controls and enforcement. There is thus competition, uncertainty and ambiguity affecting all the urban land management systems implemented in the area.

To conclude, it is not just land tenure rules that are subject to manipulation under customary conditions, but also the rules of the other linked mechanisms. Any land instrument for urban land management needs to recognise this situation. Given that land readjustment does not only focus on land titling, but interacts with other systems associated with property rights, it will be subject to even greater manipulative pressures. Indeed, it lends itself to strategic manoeuvres because of its multiple systems and facilitates conflict management in ways that are not possible with other instruments.

## Land Readjustment for Conflict Management

The approach outlined above differs from other schools of thought, which are associated with de Soto (2000), McAuslan (2003) and Durand-Lasserve and Royston (2002). McAuslan sees extralegal tenures reflecting the subordinate status of customary relative to statutory tenure. For him, 'the inheritance of law for many countries is deleterious; alien, authoritarian, divisive and incomprehensible' (UNCHS (Habitat) 1991: 173), and he argues that urban law reform should not seek to complete 'the process, started by the former colonial powers, of replacing traditional with modern law', but should acknowledge the dual legal systems, and create more balanced law reform which is sensitive to customary tenure (UNCHS (Habitat) 1991: 45–46). He sees the way forward as being 'integration between formal and informal systems of tenure', using traditional landholders and others as 'the first line of management of urban land' (Farvacque and McAuslan 1992: 87). This argument is growing in strength, with Durand-Lasserve, for instance, urging research into 'neo-customary tenure' to deal with urban extralegality, raising the status of customary/informal/extralegal systems, largely because 'modern' systems are seen as imported colonial systems, and creating a single legal system which integrates the range of evidence used to defend property rights. According to this argument, the Mogoditshane situation could be largely solved by creating a single decentralised legal system that would be cheaper and more accessible, and that recognised customary tenure, but this approach fails to address the ambiguity and uncertainty of such systems where playing with, and negotiating around, the rules is the usual way of doing business. The use of customary legal evidence and approaches, the integration of formal and informal systems and the introduction of decentralised and affordable property rights systems are attractive policy options in appropriate circumstances. Nevertheless, if peri-urban land management approaches are only developed as legal-political issues, along the lines suggested by de Soto and McAuslan, they may create more problems and emphasise the wrong priorities for action. The Mogoditshane case shows that an attempt to integrate modern property rights systems with a high-status customary system in an incremental fashion for the purposes of urban land management (following the de Soto/McAuslan proposition) may not succeed because of the manipulation of rules and the obscurity, doubt and confusion which are part of customary tenure in the modern world.

The reform of land law could attempt to integrate dual legal systems, and land readjustment cannot be successfully undertaken without a measure of certainty and clarity in the legal system. The Mogoditshane case suggests that legal clarity may have to be set aside, and that land management strategies and instruments should be assessed against their ability to resolve disputes and manage conflict, which would make land readjustment the most promising instrument available. Before implementing the approaches advocated by de Soto, McAuslan and Durand-Lasserve, further research is needed. Can uncertain and ambiguous evidence of land rights and the manipulation of rules, as are found in customary systems, be successfully integrated into a formalist property rights system? In so called modern systems, which derive much of their authority from their supposed immunity from social processes, certainty is valued and uncertainty is not. Research could explore what has to be done to either the customary/extralegal system and/or the modern property rights system to manage this certainty/uncertainty conundrum. Only when these fundamental issues have been addressed will it be possible to integrate the formal and informal, the customary and the 'modern' into a single legal system.

Based on the conceptual framework developed here, any appropriate land instrument should concentrate upon socio-political complexity rather than law and process, according priority to conflict management and dispute resolution strategies. A first priority for land development in Mogoditshane would thus be to manage the conflicts that already exist, including those engendered by the development process itself. Conflicts will occur at various levels and have to be managed on various levels. For instance, they might arise on the ground between field-owners and claimants, or between claimants and government (such as national departments or the TLB), or between national departments themselves, or between the TLB and branches of local government.

There will also be clashes between customary and modern rules and practices, which must be treated even-handedly as appropriate to the situation, with no system being automatically treated as superior to the other. A structural tension or internal dialectic has already manifested itself in Mogoditshane over the last decade, as occurs within most systems of customary tenure. Other conflicts may be engendered among rival coalitions, and new relations emerge, as individuals compete for land and benefits from the new economic opportunities opened up by land development. Many such alliances are linked to those with political and economic power. The divergence between the fixed laws and procedures of government departments and the *de facto* ways of doing things on the ground through rule manipulation offers a further potential source of discord. Local entrepreneurs may negotiate the rules outside of the existing national laws and procedures, making it impossible for officials to implement them.

Land readjustment can incorporate a number of the systems linked to property rights, such as land-use planning, valuation, land records, and spatial information management and enforcement, which take time to implement (UNCHS (Habitat) 1999; Fourie 1999). The conflicts associated with land readjustment will be increased by the number of systems associated with it, and will continue over a medium to long-term timeframe. In Mogoditshane, for example, land readjustment might be expected to generate medium to long term manipulative pressure over a two to five year period. There is already conflict over valuation and compensation for land in this peri-urban area, which would continue in any land readjustment programme. Land development in Mogoditshane has largely been affected by powerful socio-economic and political interests, and an explicit pro-poor element is needed, with the internal dialectic managed so as to accommodate the needs of the poor, adding a new dimension of socio-political interaction.

In the Mogoditshane situation, large-scale professional management capacity, particularly conflict management capacity, is likely to be required as well as technical skills. Sufficient resources, both finance and management, would need to be allocated and the right technical choices made of instruments for land development which manage rather than exacerbate conflict. There are a number of land instruments commonly used for peri-urban land development, such as compulsory land acquisition, development of vacant land, resettlement, upgrading and land readjustment. The most suitable choice would be land readjustment, which is here described, with the most appropriate forms identified and applied from international best practice.

The evidence from transnational studies is that land acquisition in peri-urban areas is not delivering sufficient land in time for urban management. This is because of bureaucratic delays, litigation, disputes over ownership, poor records, inadequate financial capacity, tension between government and customary owners/authorities and the increasing political unacceptability of eviction (Fourie 1999: 53). Peri-urban areas are becoming much more densely populated and urbanised, but rarely are suitable urban management programmes successfully installed in advance, especially in Africa. With the general failure of governments to undertake land acquisition on the scale demanded by the pressures of urban growth, green field development (where vacant land is developed and then settled) is rare and is not considered useful in terms of the conceptual framework presented here. Another land instrument no longer considered politically viable is the mass resettlement of squatters (see Barry 2000 for a case study). Resettlement is not considered viable for Mogoditshane, because it generates unacceptable levels of confrontation and conflict between individuals, and between individuals and government. Informal settlement upgrading has become the method that has replaced resettlement throughout the developing world (Fourie 1999), under which most homes (and associated uses) are upgraded from informal to formal, with little change from the informal to the formal planned layout. Upgrading can be applied to land rights (including use rights) and services.

The land readjustment technique, which can include, but goes beyond, upgrading, involves wide-ranging change to the layout and people's rights. It has a range of forms and is known by various terms, which include land sharing, land pooling, consolidation and land assembly. A number of upgrading projects have been undertaken in Africa which might have benefited from land readjustment procedures (Akrofi 2000), but there is still too little experience of land readjustment in peri-urban areas in Africa, aside from those attempted in West Africa (UNCHS 1999), and best practice approaches need to be developed and disseminated.

The land readjustment or consolidation approach rearranges land-ownership and land use in order to provide land for development purposes and increase environmental quality. It aims to upgrade slum areas, secure orderly development of rapidly growing existing and new areas, achieve planned development of relatively vacant areas expected to develop (Oetomo and Kusbiantoro 1998: 111), and rationalise the use of existing residential space (FIG/Habitat 1998: 5). Essentially it involves the readjustment of adjoining parcels held in fragmented ownership. First, the fragmented parcels are consolidated, and the area is then developed and partitioned into serviced plots in a rational and planned manner. Usually, the original land-owners contribute some portion of their land to finance the basic infrastructure and other development costs (Lee 1998: 145).

Based upon international experience, schemes for low-cost housing are more successfully negotiated with land-owners where government purchases part of the land in the project area and participates in the readjustment as a land-owner. Government then has more leverage to increase the pace of building activity and ensure provision for the poor (Fourie 1999: 58). Munro-Faure (1998: 226–27) states that land readjustment typically follows four steps:

(a) an inventory of rights on the land affected and the valuation of the land affected;

(b) the drafting and confirmation of a reallocation plan which indicates the new land rights and owners (in urban areas this would be linked to the development of a structure plan for the area);

(c) the implementation of the reallocation plan and the structure plan;

(d) financial arrangements.

Critical issues that require solution include the value of the land, rather than just the size, and the reallocation should be based on value rather than just size, especially in dense urban areas.

Thomas (1998: 250) indicates that a major purpose of land readjustment is to resolve conflicts over land. While dispute resolution is a routine part of land readjustment procedures, it is little mentioned by the technicians undertaking the work. Connellan (2002), reviewing lessons for the UK with respect to land readjustment, states that confrontation between owners and the State must be avoided, otherwise lengthy delays result, and indicates that a mediation forum is required to help land-owners to accept the valuation of their property. He further states that a major problem is local governments' weak financial and human resource capacity. Derlich (2002), with practical knowledge of the French experience, states that the preliminary planning phase should include a forum for dispute resolution through a public inquiry, recognising that identification of land for readjustment is not simply a technical exercise and should be an open and public process incorporating best practices in participatory planning (Farvacque and McAuslan 1992: 90; UNCHS (Habitat) 1996: 6–8). Uimonen (2002), drawing upon experience in Finland, indicates that during this phase owners should be able to assess the financial implications of alternative decisions on the size and location of their final land holding.

Andersen, drawing upon land consolidation experience in Denmark, states:

To ensure the required local support it is necessary to supply precise, punctual and invariable information. This information should by supplied at a fitting moment, as a lack of information can, at any time, lead to rumours and subsequently to a atmosphere of distrust and condemnation. ... It is important that the local population feels that the central steering authorities take notice of their wishes before they agree to a certain solution. This has ... been one of the main areas of interest in many of the preliminary investigations (Andersen 1998: 268–69).

UNCHS (Habitat) (1999), drawing from examples in peri-urban West Africa, confirms that best practice allows regularisation to take place at the same time as land readjustment, taking account of the interests of customary owners, government and those occupying the land illegally. UNCHS (Habitat) adds the need for transparency regarding the taking of land for public purposes, because corruption can often result in its transfer for private purposes by elite groups, and recommends a range of financing mechanisms, including the creation of private-public and public-public partnerships.

These lessons from international experience suggest that, for land readjustment in Mogoditshane, a number of issues need to be addressed and strategic tools devised. Stakeholders in the process should include not only the government and field-owners, but tenants in the area and those with other claims, such as people whose houses have been demolished or are threatened with demolition. Secondly, a range of conflict management approaches need to be implemented including a mediation forum, together with dispute resolution and due process mechanisms, an information campaign and the facilitation of partnerships between the various stakeholders. Officials must be accountable and the process transparent. Thirdly, top-down planning with zoning applied from above will not deliver results without participatory methods to involve all stakeholders in the decision-making process (UNCHS (Habitat) 1996: 6–8).

Conflict between government and field-owners about the valuation of land and compensation payable is almost inevitable and can result in delay and even withdrawal from participation. Clarity on valuation negotiations and compensation levels between government and owners will be needed, both at the outset and throughout the exercise. Finally, it is important to build sufficient financial and human capacity to undertake the project, specifically in conflict management skills. Further, public-public and public-private partnerships need to be developed. All these strategies could be critical to the success of land development in Mogoditshane, yet they require extensive resources in terms of management skills, time and money. Without prioritising these strategies and resourcing them correctly, Mogoditshane will not move forward and the needs of the poor will not be addressed.

The land readjustment mechanism will need modification to meet the types of conflicts likely to surface, many of which are associated with customary practice of land tenure. International experience in conflict management and land readjustment can provide valuable lessons, but land adjustment strategies from the developed world, which are underpinned by costly systems rooted in accuracy, certainty and behaviour focused on the individual, should not be followed too closely. In the peri-urban context of Mogoditshane, the process of evidence creation can be as important as the product, incorporating an emphasis upon participation, empowerment and flexibility rather than codifying laws or rules. Local land records should be created which are accessible and in a format that all stakeholders can understand and, where possible, should be transferred into a modern digital system that assists dissemination and information retrieval. Any land readjustment programme should improve transparency, so that all stakeholders understand what is involved. As Akrofi argues (based upon his experience in a South African peri-urban area), there needs to be emphasis upon transfer of knowledge and information at all stages. The declaration of the area for adjustment as a special zone, outside of national law, for a period of time can avoid confrontation between the national legal framework and local processes. Santiago describes for the Philippines how urban land reform zones were created to increase low-income access to housing (Santiago 1998: 110), and Junior (2002) describes similar interest zones in Brazil, urban areas primarily destined for social housing and already containing informal settlements, collectives, illegal subdivisions and vacant or under-utilised areas. These areas typically have a high number of land/housing ownership conflicts and carry the risk of forced eviction of the poor.

Claims to land (including overlapping claims, not just registered or recorded rights) need to be mapped. Experience in customary areas demonstrates also that it is a waste of time and money-making official plans and establishing planning and surveying mechanisms without an iterative process of adjudication and a transfer of resources (Fourie and Hillerman 1997). Iterative adjudication can produce records which can be deployed in planning the area, and allow the incorporation of existing uses into plans (Haldrup 1996). A land information system can record the details of existing and planned land uses at the local level, and planning should take place on-site, integrating the transfer of knowledge. The South African experience suggests that communities experience difficulty in relating plans to the ground, unless it is done on-site at the same time as adjudication and planning takes place. Aerial photographs showing land use, or off-site workshops, are likely to be of little use, so capacity-building in government planning departments should address participatory site-based processes rather than top-down planning.

Earlier projects in customary peri-urban areas have shown that cadastral evidence held centrally is ineffective without adequate courts and police being in place to protect property rights (Fourie and Hillerman 1997). Appropriate enforcement of land use control should be adaptable to the evolving local governance structure, and any forum created for such enforcement or adjudication should integrate the various dynamic cultures at play (urban/rural, customary/modern, certain/ambiguous) in order to create local rules, build new knowledge and change attitudes. The governance function should be split from the technical function for better conflict management. Experience in other customary peri-urban areas shows that a critical factor in dispute resolution is capacity within the relevant community or communities, developed through informed and knowledgeable non-governmental and community-based organisations (NGOs and CBOs) and negotiated with government and other bodies (FIG/Habitat 1998; Fourie 1999: 77). Certain lessons have emerged from West Africa (UNCHS (Habitat) 1999). First, develop public-public and public-private partnerships that enhance conflict management and diminish confrontation by, for example, including Land Boards and national government within the same development body. Secondly, decentralise as many land-related functions as possible when undertaking land readjustment. Finally, protect the technicians involved in the land development, so that they do not become the scapegoats in what is largely a political process.

Since many of these approaches are innovative, they cannot be simply lifted from one context, project or community and slotted into another context, project or community. They require adaptation to the conventional technical systems already in operation and to specific local conditions. They are, however, considered appropriate for areas under customary tenure, confirm a more appropriate land readjustment approach and can be pro-poor in effect. A review of the pro-poor land literature (particularly UNCHS (Habitat) 1996, Farvacque and McAuslan 1992, Akrofi 2000) shows that some of the strategies of urban management are the same as those advocated above for conflict management and land readjustment, through which a space can be created for the poor to make their voices heard and have their tenure security and service needs met.

## Conclusions

Attempts to deal with land development problems in Mogoditshane have not met with much success and have ranged from doing nothing at all to introducing incremental change to customary land tenure. The way forward cannot simply replace customary with modern approaches, to bring certainty to land rights and land use rights, because customary tenure is a national symbol, not to be lightly overthrown. Reforming urban land law to accommodate customary tenure will also not deliver results, because modern property rights systems, emphasising clarity and predictability, are unlikely to strengthen tenure security and access to land. Using law to advance the position of the disadvantaged can be hazardous. As Smart states, it is wise to avoid 'the siren call of law' (Smart 1989: 160). Law tends to be imperialistic, especially when it encounters alternative understandings of the world (such as the internal dialectic of customary tenure), and sets itself above other knowledge, disqualifying other truths. The power of law is its ability to exclude or distort those understandings that cannot be rebuilt in its own image, and using the law to bring about change may, therefore, have profoundly disempowering and unexpected consequences. Attempts to reform land law to address issues in peri-urban areas are likely to have these undesirable effects.

An alternative way forward is suggested, namely to use land instruments that can accommodate the customary approach, which is about the manipulation of rules, ambiguity, uncertainty, coalition formation and entrepreneurship, to maximise access to land, its use and for financial gain. In assessing the land instruments which might best fit this mode of practice, an appropriate form of land readjustment was found to be the most promising, linked to conflict management strategies and pro-poor stakeholder involvement. Recrafting urban land laws to emulate pro-poor customary tenure will not solve tenure security problems for the poor. The focus should rather be upon the larger issue, namely managing the hierarchy/aggregation tendency inherent in the society and in customary tenure, which can strengthen the economic position of the powerful, and using land readjustment and conflict management techniques to reposition the poor in the debate. In other words, instruments such as land readjustment should be used to encourage what Comaroff calls (rather awkwardly) the 'egalitarianism: individuation contradictory tendency', to balance the hierarchical tendency which presently facilitates the elites and stifles the voice of the poor.

Comaroff showed that the hierarchical tendency became dominant in his Botswana case study area because of the availability of new resources resulting from changes in national policy, agricultural production methods and the local political system, linked to the operation of the contradictory tendencies (Comaroff 1982: 150–58). Applying this to Mogoditshane, seeking to balance the contradictory tendencies and create a place for the poor, careful management of the land readjustment exercise will be needed through resource allocation (land, use rights and financial compensation), adaptation of the political system and changes from farming to 'growing houses'.

Comaroff showed that the customary system can be anti-poor, as is the case in Mogoditshane, but under other conditions customary tenure can be pro-poor (Fourie 1994). Land readjustment and conflict management strategies through the customary tenure system can deliver land to the poor if a serious attempt is made to alter the dialectic inherent in the society, encouraging the democratic processes associated with customary land tenure as well as sharing resources among a wider group of people, including the poor. A range of tools and strategies are suggested to do this, many already considered as pro-poor.

Sufficient professionals with appropriate technical knowledge, and participatory rather than conventional planning skills will be required, as well as managers and leaders who are politically sensitive and have expertise in dispute resolution and conflict management. All will have to be able to deploy non-conventional technical tools and be open to new ways of doing things. The whole project will require time and money on process, as part of the goal, allowing the voice of the poor to be heard and for them to benefit from land development.

# References

Adelman, S and Paliwala, A (eds) (1993) *Law and Crisis in the Third World*, London: Hans Zell

Akrofi, EO (2000) 'Upgrading security of tenure for the peri-urban poor in Africa', unpublished MSc thesis, School of Civil Engineering, Surveying and Construction, University of Natal

Andersen, SL (1998) 'Establishment of wet meadows and extension of cultivated wetlands', paper presented to FIG XXI Congress, Brighton, UK, 20–25 July

Barry, M (2000) 'Evaluating cadastral systems in periods of uncertainty: a study of Cape Town's Xhosa-speaking communities', unpublished PhD thesis, Faculty of Engineering, University of Natal (Durban)

Barry, M and Fourie, C (2002) 'Evaluating cadastral systems in uncertain situations: a conceptual framework based on soft systems theory' *International Journal of Geographical Information Science* 16(1): 23–40

Bathurst (1999) *Bathurst Declaration on Land Administration for Sustainable Development*, FIG/UN Workshop on Land Tenure and Cadastral Infrastructure, Bathurst, Australia, available at www.fig.net/figtree/figun/sessions/session1/bathurstdec.pdf

Comaroff, JL (1978) 'Rules and rulers: political processes in a Tswana chiefdom' *Man* 13(1): 1–20

Comaroff, JL (1982) 'Dialectical systems, history and anthropology: units of study and questions of theory' *Journal of Southern African Studies* 8: 143–72

Connellan, O (2002) 'Land assembly for development – the role of land pooling, land re-adjustment and land consolidation', FIG XXII Congress, Washington, DC, 19–26 April

Davies CJ (1998) 'Land management of an informal settlement in East London', unpublished MSc thesis, Dept of Surveying and Mapping, University of Natal

Davies, CJ and Fourie, C (2002) 'A land management approach for informal settlement in South Africa' in Durand-Lasserve, A and Royston, L (eds), *Holding their Ground. Securing Land Tenure for the Urban Poor in Developing Countries*, London: Earthscan

de Soto, H (2000) *The Mystery of Capital: Why Capitalism Triumphs in the West and Fails Everywhere Else*, London: Black Swan

Derlich, F (2002) 'Land consolidation: a key for sustainable development, French experience', FIG XXII Congress, Washington, DC, 19–26 April

Doebele, WA (1994) 'Urban land and macro economic development: moving from "access for the poor" to urban productivity' in Jones, G and Ward, PM (eds), *Methodology for Land and Housing Market Analysis*, London: UCL Press

Durand-Lasserve, A and Royston, L (eds) (2002) *Holding their Ground: Secure Land Tenure for the Urban Poor in India, Brazil and South Africa*, London: Earthscan

Farvacque, C and McAuslan, P (1992) *Reforming Urban Land Policies and Institutions in Developing Countries*, Washington, DC: Urban Management Program, World Bank

FIG/Habitat (1998) *Informal Settlements, Security of Tenure, Urban Land Management and Local Governance: Experiences in Implementing the Habitat Agenda*, Draft Report of the Durban Conference, August 1997

Fourie, C (1994) 'A new approach to the Zulu land tenure system: an historical anthropological explanation of the development of an informal settlement', unpublished PhD, Rhodes University, Grahamstown, South Africa

Fourie, C (1999) *Best Practices on Access to Land and Security of Tenure*, Nairobi: Habitat

Fourie, C (2002) 'Designing viable land administration systems: options and challenges', paper presented at World Bank Regional Workshop on Land Issues for Africa and the Middle East, Kampala, Uganda, 29 April–2 May

Fourie, C and Hillerman, R (1997) 'The South African cadastre and indigenous land tenure' *Survey Review* 34(265): 174–82

Habitat/UNDP (1991) *Institutional/Legal Options for Administration of Land Development, Background Paper*, Nairobi: Urban Management Programme

Haldrup, NO (1996) 'Adjudication – a way of coping with incomplete information in developing countries' *Survey Review* 33(262): 504–17

Home, RK (2001) 'Eating farmland, growing houses: peri-urban settlements and customary land tenure in Botswana, Southern Africa' *Trialog* 69: 30–35

Junior, NS (2002) 'Forms of protection of the right to housing and to guarantee the security of tenure in Brazil' in Durand-Lasserve, A and Royston, L (eds), *Holding their Ground. Securing Land Tenure for the Urban Poor in Developing Countries*, London: Earthscan

Kgabo Commission (1991) *Report of Presidential Commission of Inquiry into Problems in Mogoditshane and Other Peri-Urban Villages*, Gaborone: Government Printer

Lee, T (1998) 'Improving urban land management in Korea' in Ansari, JH and von Einsiedel, N (eds), *Urban Land Management Improving Policies and Practices in Developing Countries of Asia*, New Delhi: OUP

McAuslan, P (1991) 'The objectives of planning legislation in Africa', unpublished paper to Swedeplan First International Conference on Planning Legislation in Africa (ICPLA 1), Maseru, Lesotho

McAuslan, P (1992) 'Institutional legal arrangements for the improved administration of land development' *Regional Development Dialogue* 13(1): 14–32

McAuslan, P (2003) *Bringing the Law Back In: Essays in Land, Law and Development*, Aldershot: Ashgate

McLaughlin, J and de Soto, H (1994) 'Property formalization: the proforma solution', *Geomatica* 48(4): 307–14

*Mail and Guardian* (2002) 'Land hits the black market' *Mail and Guardian newspaper*, 24–30 May, 32

Manji, A (2001) 'Land reform in the shadow of the State: the implementation of new land laws in sub-Saharan Africa' *Third World Quarterly* 22(3): 327–42

Modisagape, DO (1998) 'Botswana customary land tenure system' in Kirk, M and others (eds), *Land Tenure and Policy Issues in Land Use Planning, with Special Reference to Southern and Eastern Africa*, Zschortau, Germany: DSE and ZEL

Mphathi, M and Modisagape, DO (1998) 'Land tenure and land policy issues in relation to land use planning in Botswana' in Kirk, M and others (eds), *Land Tenure and Policy Issues in Land Use Planning, with Special Reference to Southern and Eastern Africa*, Zschortau, Germany: DSE and ZEL

Munro-Faure, P (1998) 'A Report on the Activities of the Commission 7 Working Group: Land Management' in *Proceedings of the XXI International Congress: Developing the Profession in a Developing World*, Brighton, UK, 19–25 July

Oetomo, A and Kusbiantoro, BS (1998) 'Improving urban land management in Indonesia' in Ansari, JH and von Einsiedel, N (eds), *Urban Land Management: Improving Policies and Practices in Developing Countries of Asia*, New Delhi: OUP

ROB (Republic of Botswana) (1983) *Report of the Presidential Commission on Land Tenure*, Gaborone: Government Printer

Santiago, AM (1998) 'Law and urban change: illegal settlements in the Philippines' in Fernandes, E and Varley, A (eds), *Illegal Cities Law and Urban Change in Developing Countries*, London: Zed Books

Simpson, JR (1976) *Land Law and Registration*, Cambridge: CUP

Smart, C (1989) *Feminism and The Power of Law*, London: Routledge

Southern Africa Regional Poverty Network (SARPN) (2001) *Botswana Poverty Reduction Tender*, Newsletter 4

Thomas, J (1998) 'Non-polluting land use and sustainable development on rural regions: support through land regulation and village renewal' in Proceedings of the FIG XXI International Congress: Developing the Profession in a Developing World, Brighton, UK, 19–25 July

Trubek, D and Galanter, M (1974) 'Scholars in self-estrangement: some reflections on the crisis in law and development studies in the United States' *Law and Society Review* 4: 1062–1102

Uimonen, M (2002) 'New tools and processes for land consolidation' FIG XXII Congress, Washington DC, 19–26 April

UNCHS (Habitat) (1991) *Report of the Workshop on Land Registration and Land Information Systems*, Nairobi, Kenya (15–18 October 1990)

UNCHS (Habitat) (1996) *New Delhi, Habitat II Global Conference on Access to Land and Security of Tenure as a Condition for Sustainable Shelter and Urban Development*, New Delhi, India: 17–19 January

UNCHS (1999) '*Amenagement et gestion fonciere urbaine et Gouvernance locale en Afrique francophone*', draft report of the Meeting, *Colloque des professionnels de l'Amenagement urbain en Afrique francophone*, Ouagadougou: April

UN/FIG (1999) *The Bathurst Declaration on Land Administration for Sustainable Development*, Frederiksberg, Denmark: FIG

Varley, A (2002) 'Private or public: debating the meaning of tenure legalization' *International Journal of Urban and Regional Research* 26(3): 449–61

# Chapter 4
# Inheritance, HIV/AIDS and Children's Rights to Land in Africa
*Hilary Lim*

## Introduction

De Soto's thesis that securing formal property titles for the poor provides a good, perhaps the best, chance of releasing their capital, enabling them to access credit and thereby emancipating them from poverty 'in the grubby basement of the capitalist world' (de Soto 2000: 20), has inspired a wide range of critiques. Several commentators have pointed to what they regard as the spaces or absences in de Soto's rhetoric, which potentially distort any assessment of the benefits or otherwise from legalisation of land tenure (Varley 2002; Lea 2002). One perceived absence in de Soto's argument, for instance, is a lack of differentiation within the category of people who are central to his thesis, namely 'the poor', or indeed in the categories of 'migrants' and 'extralegals' to which he makes less frequent reference.

De Soto rightly wants to dispel the pictures that feed the Western imagination of the poor as sorrowing, powerless and dependent on aid, replacing them with what he perceives as a realistic representation of the poor as entrepreneurial heroes. He urges also getting outside the bell jar, adopting the perspective of the poor, walking in their shoes around their dwellings and 'listening to the barking dogs'. However, is it possible to speak of the poor and their perspective as if the human beings involved were like a great lake? To take the obvious example, it is widely accepted now as part of established international development policy that poverty is gendered, with respect to both its causes and its effects. Few commentators would now attempt to envisage women as a homogenous group. Nevertheless, as Walker recently stated, 'gender plays a crucial role in shaping, differently and differentially, how men and women are constituted as social groups, the opportunities available to them and their access to resources, including land' (Walker 2002: 6). There are detailed assessments of the limitations in these gender analyses, including those adopted at institutional, particularly international, levels (Manji 2003), but that does not detract from the basic critique of de Soto. Gender is in any event not the only, or even the most important, differentiating factor.

A further perceived deficiency is de Soto's failure to look beyond the market or the simple human need for shelter. He does not acknowledge, or appear to recognise as important, the meanings, including emotional meanings, which a house, or the land on which it sits, may have for individuals or families. This is hardly surprising, given de Soto's central argument that formal property interests have the ability to transform people into accountable individuals divorced from their historical, and perhaps detrimental, reliance on local relationships. Varley has argued, in the context of her own research in urban Mexico, that ignoring the domestic and private sphere, 'locating all explanatory power in the public' (Varley 2002: 458), can hide both positive and negative effects of formalisation. She points out, in a discussion linked firmly to her specific research, that an over-emphasis on the public sphere misses the importance of informal networks amongst friends and family. These connections supply resources and informal credit that is invested in the development of homes. It is a theme that emerges also in several contributions elsewhere in this book.

Furthermore, a major benefit of the provision of secure titles may be missed in the focus on market rationale, that is, the simple public confirmation of the effort and work involved in building a home. Legality also provides an assurance that children and kin can be enabled to succeed to that human and financial investment in the home. Children are, in fact, conspicuous by their absence from de Soto's discourse, while inheritance, presumably located in the private sphere and governed by family law, is of little interest. A further aspect of this failure to attend to the domestic is that security of tenure is envisaged as security against eviction by government or public authorities, overlooking the threats closer to home from neighbours and other family members intent on land-grabbing. Where de Soto breaks down the category of the poor and pays some attention to the private sphere, however, it is to record briefly the motivations and behaviour of 'the migrant and his family' as a unit in gradually establishing, building and developing their shelter (de Soto 2000: 205). However, the family is not, as suggested above, an unproblematic concept, not least because it may be difficult to define. Neither the interests nor the wishes of family members will necessarily coincide.

The purpose of this chapter is to argue that the laws and practices surrounding the inheritance of land should not be viewed as semi-detached from general debates about security of tenure, land rights and land reform or regularisation, particularly in the context of poverty alleviation. The right to inherit land has widely been seen, at best, as secondary in any strategies or policy formation surrounding land and land tenure. De Sousa Santos has pointed to the ideological projection that can be detected in legal systems, which is similar to that in the production of maps, whereby each legal order has a centre and a periphery. The centre of bourgeois State legality, he argues, is always occupied by contracts. The formal registration of titles must also lie close to the centre, where he asserts that 'the space is mapped in greater detail and absorbs greater inputs of institutional resources (legal professions, courts, etc) and symbolic resources (legal science, legal ideology and culture, etc)' (de Sousa Santos 1987: 292).

Family law, on the other hand, including inheritance law, is easily located on the periphery of such a map (Lim 1996). There are commentators who argue that the laws of inheritance have always warranted greater attention (Butegwa 1991), but it will be tentatively suggested that the effects of the HIV/AIDS epidemic provide an impetus to thinking anew about this field. Specifically, the inheritance rights of children to land and security of tenure have been highlighted by the social and economic circumstances of those children who have been orphaned through AIDS. A recent report, prepared for the International Aids Conference in Barcelona in July 2002, suggested that 'all orphans have essential needs irrespective of parental death but ... [o]ne thing is clear from this study: HIV/AIDS is causing the most significant and worrisome changes' (UNAIDS 2002: 5). The comment was made in a general context, but can be applied without difficulty to the more particular issue of inheritance. It could be wrong 'to single out children orphaned by AIDS', when such children are sometimes already the subject of stigma and discrimination. At the same time vulnerable children who are not orphans may be excluded by such a focus. Nevertheless, it is the case that 'AIDS does create unique circumstances' (UNAIDS 2002: 134), particularly for children affected by the epidemic, and these are circumstances which debates about land tenure and formalisation need to address.

This chapter is not based on specific fieldwork, nor does it purport to provide a literature review of the area; rather, its intention is to draw attention to issues of comparatively recent research and discussion. First, there will be a brief outline of the epidemic's, or perhaps more correctly epidemics', growing reach and its toll upon children, through the use of statistics, estimates and official forecasts. Secondly, the social, economic and familial support systems for children affected by HIV/AIDS will be explored, together with the strains, sometimes dislocation, placed upon these systems as a consequence of the epidemic. The pressures placed upon bureaucratic systems as a consequence of the effects of HIV/AIDS will also be noted. Thirdly, it will be argued that the gender focus on AIDS, which is part of the development paradigm used at an official level in the analysis of the disease, combines with the gender approach to property rights. The consequence is that, where inheritance issues are discussed, the interests of children are usually subsumed in, or adjuncts to, the rights of women. While there is widespread argument that it does not benefit women, or extend their human rights, to link them in a dyad with children, it will be argued here that the discursive link may not be in the interests of some children or promote their rights. Finally, research on inheritance issues in the context of the HIV/AIDS epidemic, which does concentrate on children's rights and interests, will be explored and suggestions made for future research.

## The Scope of the HIV/AIDS Pandemic

The statistics and estimates, which mask the deep personal tragedies at their heart, are well-documented and often repeated. Global figures for people affected by HIV/AIDS vary a little, but together express clearly the scale of the epidemic. The most recent estimates available from UNAIDS are that 40 million people around the globe are living with HIV/AIDS and that there were five million new infections in 2003. Three million deaths during 2003 are attributed by UNAIDS to HIV/AIDS (UNAIDS/WHO 2003). It is further recorded that 22 million people had died of AIDS since 1981 in the sub-Saharan region of Africa alone (UNAIDS/WHO 2003). A report released in July 2002, before the 14th International AIDS Conference in Barcelona, suggested that AIDS could kill nearly 70 million people worldwide over the next two decades. Peter Piot, Director of the UN Aids programme, stated at the time this report was launched that:

> ... we have grossly underestimated how bad this was going to be ... It is now clear to me that we are only at the beginning of the AIDS epidemic in historic terms. It's also clear to me when we look at Eastern Europe and Asia, and even in the case of southern Africa ... we don't see a leveling off (quoted in Donnelly 2002).

In Botswana, well over a third of the adult population is estimated to carry HIV (UNAIDS 2002: 190). HIV prevalence among pregnant women in urban areas grew from 38.5% in 1997 to 44.9% by 2001. There can be very few families, if any, in Botswana that are wholly unaffected by AIDS (Upton 2003: 315). A UNDP (2000) Report on Botswana suggested that, as a consequence of HIV/AIDS, every income-earner in Botswana could expect to care for four people in addition to his or her immediate family. Research carried out for UNICEF-Zambia, published in 1999, revealed that 44% of Zambian households were looking after orphans (Guest 2003). Average life expectancies across the sub-Saharan region, which without AIDS would have stood at 62 years, now stand at 47 years (UNAIDS 2002: 44). The higher rates of infection amongst women are also frequently highlighted. There are two million more women than men who are HIV positive in the sub-Saharan region. The overall male to female infection rates in Botswana, for instance, are roughly 1:1, but young women are more likely to be infected than young men, and the HIV prevalence rate in young people is much higher amongst the female population than the male population (UNAIDS 2002: 191).

Extreme care must be taken with the publication and use of statistics and, in particular, forecasts or estimates (Whiteside and others 2003). It should be stated clearly and repeatedly that 90% of people in Africa are *not* HIV positive. The devastating effects of other diseases such as malaria and measles, not to speak of hunger and malnutrition, should not be repressed. The effects of HIV/AIDS are magnified themselves by their interaction with poverty and other epidemics (Baylies 2002). Furthermore, the efforts to reduce the prevalence of new infections with HIV, or to alleviate the suffering of those with AIDS or AIDS-related illnesses, must be recognised. A recent BBC report cites research which indicates that in South Africa, which has a greater number of people carrying HIV than any other country, the annual rate for new infections has gone into a marked decline (*BBC News*, 21 October 2003). In 1997, the new infection rate in the crucial 15–49 age group stood at 4.1% of the population, but by 2002 had decreased to 1.7%. However, despite this change, the researchers involved point out that the proportion of the population that is HIV positive will remain fairly constant, with life expectancy continuing to fall. The experience of Uganda, which is in the so called third wave of the disease, is important in this regard (Bond and Vincent 1997), with an average period of 10 years between infection and death of an individual. In Uganda, the high point of infection rates was reached at the end of the 1980s of approximately 40% and then declined dramatically to approximately 5% at the beginning of the new century. One effect was that the number of new orphans to AIDS continued to climb and only recently began what is anticipated to be a slow decline.

UNICEF estimates that 14 million children had been orphaned through AIDS by the end of 2001, the majority of them living in sub-Saharan Africa (UNICEF Press Release, 21 October 2003). Forecasts produced before the Barcelona Conference in July 2002 indicate that the global figure could rise to more than 25 million by 2010 out of a total figure for all children projected to lose one or both parents of 106 million (UNAIDS/UNICEF/USAID 2002: 3). The same report indicates that of 42 million orphans who are forecast to live in Sub-Saharan Africa in 2010, AIDS will have orphaned 20 million (2002: 6). It is the view of UNICEF that if it were not for HIV/AIDS, the number of orphans in sub-Saharan Africa would be decreasing (UNICEF Fact Sheet 2003). However, orphans as a category of vulnerable children are in many ways a new phenomenon in Africa. Given that children who lost one or both parents were supported traditionally within the safety net of the wider family, it was possible to argue that 'there was no such thing as an orphan in Africa' (Foster 2000: 56). International and other responses to the HIV/AIDS epidemic have served to constitute orphans and particularly 'AIDS orphans' as a group warranting particular concern and intervention, although some researchers and analysts have warned that targeting orphans is counter-productive and based on false assumptions (Guest 2003: 122–23; Grainger and others 2001: 44–46).

According to UNICEF, in Botswana, where there has been great progress in terms of health and education, 64% of deaths of children under the age of five were, by 2000, as a consequence of AIDS. The rate at which children were orphaned quadrupled in just three years between 1994 and 1997 (*New York Times*, 22 July 1999). In Zambia, where 80% of the population is estimated to be living in poverty, 9% of children under the age of 15, in 1997, were deemed to be orphans (UNICEF 1999: 15) and, according to the latest figures from UNAIDS, by 2001, 570,000 children in Zambia had been orphaned through AIDS. By the end of 2001, at least half of the orphans in Botswana and Zambia were as a result of AIDS and it is estimated that 75% of all the orphans living in Zambia in 2010 will be orphaned to AIDS (UNAIDS 2002: 7). Finally, it is forecast that, by 2014, one in every 12 of the Zambian population will be an orphan (Jackson and Lee 2002: 210). However, as Guest (2003: 122) points out, basing her argument on research in Zambia, it should not be inferred that these figures, because of their magnitude, necessarily mean that orphans form an underclass which may be distinguished from other vulnerable and needy children, or that orphans are peculiarly subject to discrimination.

Until recently, the definition of an orphan in this context as used by the international agencies, such as UNAIDS, UNICEF and WHO, was a child who had lost its mother to the disease before the age of 15. As UNICEF commented, total figures may, therefore, have underestimated the effect of the epidemic on children, since the data ignored paternal orphans. However, the global statistics produced for the Barcelona Conference in July 2002 attempted to encompass all those children orphaned through AIDS, whether maternal orphans, paternal orphans or double orphans. It is the case that children orphaned by AIDS are more likely to lose both parents than other orphans. The loss of one parent through disease or an accident does not imply that a child will lose the other parent in the near future. Unfortunately, where a family is affected by HIV/AIDS, there is a high likelihood that the loss of one parent will be followed shortly afterwards by the loss of the other. Moreover, a child who loses one parent to a disease unconnected with HIV/AIDS, or for some other reason, is in many parts of the world quite likely to lose the other parent to AIDS (UNAIDS 2002: 6–7).

A range of programmes designed to supply affordable anti-retroviral drugs to those who could benefit from them have begun or are planned in a number of countries, including Botswana and Zambia. However, only a relatively small percentage of those who could benefit from these drugs are receiving them. In particular, there are many successful projects to supply drugs to prevent mother-to-child transmission of HIV, sometimes combined with the supply of anti-retroviral drugs, which in Botswana are extensive particularly in urban areas (Tlou and others 2000). There is experience in Brazil of the use of both kinds of programmes, which have raised life expectancies amongst those with HIV/AIDS to levels similar to those in North America (Reardon 2002). The most effective way to prevent a child becoming an orphan is to keep the child's mother and/or father alive. The WHO has stated that three million people will receive treatment by 2005, but it is unlikely that these programmes will be rolled out fast enough to make an appreciable effect on the numbers of children orphaned to AIDS in the near future. Moreover, as a recent BBC Report (Hale 2003) recorded, the health workers may not be available to implement these strategies. Botswana began a programme to offer anti-retroviral drugs to all those who would benefit free of charge about 18 months ago, but the report indicates that a shortage of skilled health workers, social workers, counsellors and administrators is reported by hospital doctors and charitable foundations even in Gaborone, which is hampering attempts to reach all those who need treatment.

Stephen Lewis (2003), the UN Secretary General's Special Envoy for HIV/AIDS in Africa, made clear in a recent conference speech that 'Africans know HIV/AIDS in all its manifestations and requirements [and] ... Africa has vastly more experience of orphans than the rest of us'. He continued: 'we should simply stop barracking, and provide the resources for Africa to find solutions.' In any event, all that statistics can do is express the size of the problem but not the tragedies that lie behind them. Statistics cannot reflect the consequences of the epidemic for individuals, families and communities but, as de Waal has argued, in the context of lowered life expectancy 'land tenure systems may be critically important in order to protect the rights of widows and orphans' (de Waal 2003: 10).

## Social and Economic Impacts upon Families and Households

In reviewing 'the first decade' of HIV/AIDS in Uganda, Bond and Vincent argued that the 1980s saw a gradual shift from a medical paradigm to a community paradigm, from 'curing' to 'caring', from a concentration upon 'the victim of the disease' to 'the social dislocation caused by his or her death' (Bond and Vincent 1997: 91). Just as it is currently being argued that the numbers of people affected by HIV/AIDS have been under-estimated, so it is also being suggested that the social and economic impacts of HIV/AIDS have not been fully appreciated (Lisk 2002). Jackson and Lee recently noted the widely held view of many researchers that 'AIDS deaths often have a greater impact on livelihoods than deaths by other causes'. Deaths from AIDS or AIDS-related illness 'usually occur earlier and after a long period of illness and decline and ... they are often associated with illness or death of the spouse' (Jackson and Lee 2002: 210).

The 'HIV/AIDS pandemic consists of multiple and overlapping epidemics, each with its own distinctive dynamics and character' (Mane and Aggleton 2001: 23). However, it has been suggested that the Ugandan experience may be indicative of the effects of HIV/AIDS upon households elsewhere. As one of the first countries in Africa to open itself up to research on the social and economic effects of the pandemic, a number of relatively extensive and long-term research projects have reported their findings. Studying data from a survey of 1,206 households, Ayiga and others (1997: 150) concluded that all households that had experienced an adult death suffered 'financial ruin, followed by household conflict and depression'.

However, the effects from death through AIDS or AIDS-related illness were greater than, for instance, deaths from either malaria or violence. The researchers suggested that it is the slowness of the development of the disease, and the long deterioration of those who suffer from AIDS or AIDS-related illness, that leads to financial ruin. HIV/AIDS causes poverty (Whiteside 2002). It also exacerbates existing poverty and can trigger a rapid shift from relative wealth to relative poverty (Nampanya-Serpell 2000).

All households that experience an adult death suffer grief and financial difficulty, but the long deterioration associated with AIDS leads to a particularly steady drain on resources, including the depletion of savings and distress sales of land or other assets (Ayiga and others 1997: 151; UNAIDS 2002: 48). In addition, both medical care and the cost of funerals prove a considerable burden for families. As one international report on the global epidemic in 2002 records, HIV/AIDS 'strips the family of assets and income-earners, further impoverishing those already poor' (UNAIDS 2002: 47). In Zambia, one peri-urban study showed that, in two-thirds of households where the main breadwinner died from AIDS, there was an 80% drop in income (UNAIDS 2002: 47). There are indications, however, that the effects of the death of a woman in a household may be particularly detrimental. Research conducted in western Kenya, which included interviews with orphans and their carers, supports this view (Nyambedha and others 2003). In Ayiga and others' study, 'the financial, depression and family-conflict effects of AIDS mortality on the household were greater for female mortality than for male mortality' (Ayiga and others 1997: 150). The researchers suggest that this finding is particularly important for an area like northern Uganda, where women head significant numbers of households, as is the case in, for instance, Botswana and Zambia. Any concentration, however, upon so called 'female-headed households' should recognise that the notions of household and headship are dynamic and women in 'male-headed households' should not be excluded (Walker 2002).

*Children on the Brink 2002* provides a useful brief summary of some possible consequences of being orphaned to AIDS or AIDS-related illness:

> As parents and other family members become ill, children take on greater responsibility for income generation, food production and care of family members. They face decreased access to adequate nutrition, basic health care, housing, and clothing. Fewer families can afford to send their children to school, with young girls at particular risk of being denied education. In both urban and rural areas, many orphans are struggling to survive on their own in child-headed households. Many more are forced to live on the street (UNAIDS/UNICEF/USAID 2002: 9).

Nor does AIDS only affect children who have lost one or both parents:

> In heavily affected countries, for each child who has lost a parent to AIDS, there are one or two children of school age who are caring for an ill parent, acting as breadwinners for the household, or otherwise unable to attend school because of AIDS. Children who are not orphaned are also affected when orphans are brought into their homes or, obviously, when they themselves are infected. Thus, AIDS-affected children comprise a much larger population than just orphans (Human Rights Watch 2001: 6).

The family and local communities still carry the main burden of caring for orphans, although these networks are under strain and are not always able to provide support (Foster 2000; Ntozi 1997). The extended family safety net, which traditionally absorbed orphans into the homes of their fathers' extended family or clan, may be weakened in some contexts, although it must be appreciated that coping mechanisms vary widely depending on the particular social, geographic and economic climate. Commenting on the effects of the pandemic in Uganda as early as 1992, Barnett and Blaikie argued that 'there is one important misconception to put aside, [which is] that Uganda is a "traditional society" in which "the extended family" will always pick up the pieces when disaster strikes' (Barnett and Blaikie 1992: 111). Ntozi and Nakawiya analysed data extrapolated from a multi-phase study, conducted in six districts in Uganda, between 1991 and 1996, which had as one of its objectives to study the population's coping mechanisms in the face of the epidemic. The extended family on the paternal side would in the past have been obliged to care for orphans, at least where the father had been married to their mother. They conclude that this is no longer the case, since the family can no longer meet the needs of the numbers of AIDS orphans (Ntozi and Nakawiya 1997: 156–57). Ntozi and Nakawiya comment: 'The general picture is that the burden of orphan care was increasingly on grandmothers, probably upon the death of the surviving mothers. Uncles were also found to care for AIDS orphans in 1995 more than in 1992/3. This may be due to the death of both parents in the inter-survey period' (Ntozi and Nakawiya 1997: 167–68).

In many instances, it is not so much that the family safety net has broken, but that it has been rewoven in a process that was underway quite apart from the particular pressures associated with HIV/AIDS (Foster 2000: 56). Recently, Jackson and Lee, commenting upon the whole sub-Saharan region, reiterated the frequently expressed view that the majority of orphaned children were, in fact, taken in by their extended families and concluded that 'the strains are beginning to show in many communities' (Jackson and Lee 2002: 210). A similar statement is made in *Children on the Brink 2002* (UNICEF/UNAIDS/USAID 2002: 9). It appears to be the case that the majority of children in Botswana are still cared for by the extended family (UNICEF 1999), although their carers are usually women who are often amongst the poorest people in society. In Zambia, grandparents 'foster' more than a third of orphans (Deininger and others 2003: 1213) and some estimates suggest that 85% of families living in poor peri-urban settlements in Lusaka are looking after orphans (Nampanya-Serpell 2000: 8).

Research conducted by Baylies (2000) in clusters of villages close to Lusaka and the township of Petauke found that most individuals interviewed would take orphans into their households. For some of the respondents, it seems also that the need to care for orphans affects family size preferences. A large number of those willing to discuss the matter indicated that 'they would have fewer or no more of their own children if they took in orphans' (Baylies 2000: 79). The economic impact on households of fostering orphans was also revealed in data gathered in Uganda from 1992–2000, which suggests that annual income and the annual rate of 'business' investment in families that received a foster child under the age of 14 were considerably lower than the levels found in families with no foster child (Deininger and others 2003: 1206).

As suggested already in this chapter in the context of de Soto's analysis, it is not the case that the concepts of either the family or the household are fixed, stable and unproblematic. A study of families in Botswana, under the auspices of the WLSA, argued that:

> ... the family extends beyond the unit of analysis of the dwelling. It expands and contracts, depending on the issues or events that it has to contend with. Events that signify important rites of passage such as weddings and funerals expand the family to its outward limits, whilst it contracts for purposes of day to day life and decision-making (Kidd and others 1997: 24).

The researchers identified two levels of family amongst their respondents. On the first level were the people associated with by the respondents on a day-to-day basis, including partners, children and siblings, while on the second level were those relations who were involved in important events or provided some kind of assistance with life's difficulties. While blood links were important elements in some relationships, the researchers found, for instance, that it was often unclear whether the children who were the basis of the largely multi-generational families were biologically related to the adults. They observed that 'it did not seem to matter' (Kidd and others 1997: 24). Family relationships did appear to be rooted in economic capacity, education, power and authority. Despite the fact that other members of his family were making considerable contributions to the management and running of his homes, an elderly male respondent unhesitatingly and 'immediately identified himself as the head of the family' (Kidd and others 1997: 25).

HIV/AIDS impacts upon familial relationships, particularly the power relationships, in a variety of not always predictable ways. Sebina-Zziwa (1998) in Uganda highlighted that widows in AIDS-affected households lost their status in the family and were vulnerable to property-grabbing, but a study in Zambia found 'evidence of AIDS affecting the balance of power within households in ways that actually enhanced the status of women' (Walker 2002: 31). The role of these women as breadwinners was being recognised, giving them enhanced rights to family property. Walker concludes that research needs to be conducted at both broad and micro-levels in order that these complexities may be revealed and understood. Further, she points out that the idea of the household as a target for planners and a unit for research, which is sometimes treated as synonymous with the family and sometimes not, raises its own difficulties. The nature of a household will shift over time, sometimes over quite short periods (including a project cycle). However, while Walker acknowledges the difficulties with the idea of the family, the household, the female-headed household and the child-headed household, she does not suggest that these concepts can be abandoned: 'Household and families remain basic components of social organisation, even if their variety, mutability and structure are more complex than often thought' (Walker 2002: 51).

Child-headed households are not uncommon and are an obvious indicator that traditional patterns of care in the extended family are not available or are being denied. Such households are often formed when the eldest child takes over responsibility from a dead grandparent (Foster 2000: 59). It is estimated that in Zambia there are at least 130,000 children under the age of 14 who are running households (AFXB, *Aids Orphans Alert*, 19 May 2000). While some orphans struggle to survive in child-headed households, caring for siblings younger than themselves, others will become street children (Guest 2003). Some children will find their way onto the streets, living by begging, stealing or, particularly in the case of girls, as sex workers. The effects on children are multi-faceted and highly complex, including both psychological distress and material hardship, intensified sometimes by the stigma and discrimination associated with HIV/AIDS.

Governments, religious groups and NGOs rightly give high priority to interventions geared to the basic survival of orphans and protection from malnutrition, exploitation and abandonment (Upton 2003: 320). Support systems concentrate on the fostering of children. School vouchers have, for instance, been provided in Lusaka to families caring for orphans who are at risk of being withdrawn from school. Schemes providing health vouchers, income generation for foster families and family tracing services are widespread. Botswana set up a National Orphans Programme, drawing together a range of organisations to provide support and monitor interventions (Deininger and others 2003: 1215). Despite the relatively high costs of care, orphanages have been created on a fairly large scale in Zambia (Deininger and others 2003: 1216; Upton 2003: 320).

It is hardly surprising in the above context that the recent report, *Children on the Brink 2002*, having outlined some of the social and economic consequences of the epidemic, adds, almost as an afterthought, that 'orphans and widows can face loss of inheritance, which impoverishes them further' (UNICEF/UNAIDS/USAID 2002: 9). Strengthening inheritance rights may not appear crucial when the effects of AIDS for many children are so profound and in many households there is unlikely to be any property, let alone land, for a child to potentially receive. Indeed, it may be the case that parents who die young hand on debts to children (de Waal 2003: 8). However, it will be argued in succeeding sections that the vulnerability of some children to 'property-grabbing', and the importance of 'their inheritance and property rights [as] ... major sources of income and food' (UNICEF 1999: 32), makes disinheritance an important matter for consideration.

As Mullins has argued, 'HIV/AIDS is a massive development issue ... that ... fundamentally affects any land reform process in Southern Africa which is intended to reduce poverty' (Mullins 2001: 1). He contends that severely affected families will be unable to make use of their land or invest in it, resorting to renting it out informally or formally, selling or abandoning it. These families may also be excluded altogether from any land reform process. In addition, HIV/AIDS affects the personnel running the institutions connected with land reform, whether they be managers, drivers, surveyors, members of land boards or cleaners (Mullins 2001: 4; Whiteside 2002). Similar arguments are made by Drimie (2002), based on case studies from Kenya, Lesotho and South Africa, again highlighting the impact of HIV/AIDS on land administration capacity. He emphasises also that 'those households with a stronger economic safety net and a wider range of options [including land] to draw upon during the crisis are less vulnerable at each stage of the continuum of HIV/AIDS illness than their poorer counterparts' (Drimie 2002: 4).

Where children's rights to inheritance have been discussed, it is usually (as in *Children on the Brink 2002*) as an adjunct to women's rights. The discursive connection is understandable. It can be easily explained in two ways. First, the connection between women and children is embedded, at a general level, in international human rights and development discourse, and a range of 'categories of child' is used in expressing that connection. Women are connected with 'children', 'young adults', 'girls', 'girls and boys' and 'other vulnerable groups'. Secondly, at a more specific level, it has been said that 'as the rights of children are inextricably linked to those of the surviving parent, laws and practices that deny widows their rights and property have devastating consequences for children after their father's death' (UNICEF 1999: 33). The gender perspectives on HIV/AIDS and inheritance will be explored, but it will be suggested in the final part of this chapter that there is an argument to strategically 'decouple' women and children in order fully to realise the rights of the child.

## Gender Perspectives, HIV/AIDS and Inheritance

Women's low social status in terms of inheritance and possible 'land-grabbing', while not regarded as the most prominent of their difficulties in relation to the effects of HIV/AIDS, is also the subject of comment, discussion and recommendations for change. For instance, Ackroyd argues:

> Women are still legal minors in many countries or have only recently been granted full adult status and the personal, social, political and economic concomitants of this may be critical in understanding the impact of HIV/AIDS. Their position under customary law is often unfavorable; and even where they are married in accordance with statute law they may still have their personal property removed by a deceased husband's heirs ... (1997: 24).

Such statements combine the developing gender sensitive approach to the HIV/AIDS pandemic with the well-established gender focus on property rights, including questions of land tenure, land reform and inheritance (Agarwal 1994; Owen 1996; Fortmann 1997; Gray and Kevone 1999).

The demand for a gender-sensitive lens to be focused on the HIV/AIDS pandemic has been made at many levels, whether nationally, regionally or internationally (Amaratunga 2002). There are commentators concerned as to whether 'the vulnerability of women' should be deployed as the basis for the development of strategy and public policy, either in relation to the HIV/AIDS pandemic or other activities, and the gender analysis is well-established on the international plane (Cohen and Reid 2002). However, as already recorded, there is little doubt that women as a group are particularly vulnerable to HIV/AIDS, and within that group girls and young women are at specific risk. A series of overlapping paradigms has emerged at different stages and locations in attempts to explain the HIV/AIDS epidemic, of which perhaps the most important is the development paradigm. For example, Jayasuriya (2001) identifies the messages from the UN General Assembly Special Session on AIDS in 2001 as rooted in this analytical model and, despite differences in emphasis between commentators, it is widely used by international organisations, governments and NGOs. A gender dimension is central to this paradigm, as evidenced by (to take just one example) the Declaration of Commitment on HIV/AIDS, which resulted from the UN Special Session. It is noted in the introductory sections to the Declaration that 'women, young adults and children, in particular girls' are the most affected and most vulnerable to the virus. Elsewhere in the Declaration, a target of 2005 is set to implement national strategies to empower women in relation to their sexuality in order to enhance their ability to protect themselves from infection. There is also a section carrying a commitment to implement strategies, policies and programmes that address 'the gender dimension of the epidemic', which is entitled 'Reducing Vulnerability'.

The importance of the pursuit of gender equity to the development paradigm is explicit also in the *HIV/AIDS and Human Rights: International Guidelines*. Guideline 8 states as follows:

> States, in collaboration with and through the community, should promote a supportive and enabling environment for women, children and other vulnerable groups by addressing underlying prejudices and inequalities through community dialogue, specially designed social and health services and support to community groups

The role of women as the carers who assume responsibility for relatives with HIV, and orphans left behind by parents who have died from AIDS, is also widely noted (Machipisa 2001).

The gender focus on HIV/AIDS mingles with the gender analysis of property rights. The core of the latter is summarised by Tlou, speaking of the Southern African Development Community (SADC), thus:

> In most countries, the legal systems and cultural norms reinforce gender inequality by giving men control over productive resources such as land, through marriage laws ... and inheritance customs that make males the principal beneficiaries of family property (Tlou 2001: 2).

This broad stance can be found in official documents and the Botswana Human Development Report 2000, to take one example, notes that:

> ... gender-based ascription of roles to men and women on the basis of tradition and custom is still pervasive. It has discernible effects on material outcomes and rights of citizenship for men and women ... both common and customary laws still have clauses that discriminate against women and limit their decision-making rights (UNDP 2000: 8–29).

However, such broad statements do not express the complexity of the situation of women with respect to property rights. Kalabamu (1997) highlights the number of female-headed households in Botswana and records that many of these women, at least in an urban context, live in owner-occupied houses developed on plots held under Certificates of Rights, which were part of a government-led strategy to provide the poor, both men and women, with affordable but secure tenure. In fact, Kalabamu demonstrates that female heads living in such houses outnumber those headed by men (Kalabamu 1997: 5), as was confirmed by interviews undertaken for this research in Botswana. Nevertheless, she concludes that there remain gender disparities in access to housing, not least because 'there still exist in Botswana ... numerous laws and legislations which hinder women's access to, and decision-making on, land resources' (Kalabamu 1997: 7), including the fact that a married woman's name cannot be registered alongside that of her husband, and that she cannot borrow money without his consent. On the other hand, in the context of HIV/AIDS, a recent 'Think Tank' meeting on Land Reform in Southern Africa concluded that 'the record of Botswana in securing land rights is creditable [and] ... the impact of the ... pandemic on women's land and property rights is less severe than elsewhere, as land boards have been exceptionally sympathetic to the rights of widows and orphans' (FAO 2003: 10).

Another fairly recent report from the Zambian government to the UN Committee on the Elimination of Discrimination Against Women (CEDAW) indicates that 'traditional law' which governs personal law 'in practice is often discriminatory to women' and 'custom dictates that women cannot own land or livestock' (CEDAW 1999: 60–61). The need for many wives to obtain their husband's consent to enter into contracts in relation to loans, or to apply for a piece of land, is recorded (CEDAW 1999: 61), together with a reference to the fact that inheritance passes through the male line. The majority of women are married according to customary law, which largely governs family relations (Human Rights Watch 2002: 55). According to custom, Zambian wives could not inherit from their husbands. Ownership of the deceased's property would pass to a male relative, who in turn was expected to take on the responsibility of the widow and the deceased's children. The CEDAW Report, however, records that 'social and economic changes in the country' have undermined traditional support systems for widows and children.

The practice of women being evicted from their homes after the deaths of their husbands, including from AIDS or AIDS-related illness, either with or without their children, is common to many African societies (Machipisa 2001; Barnett and Blaikie 1992; Kirkpatrick 1993). In some kinship groups, the system of wife inheritance, where a widow is married by the male relative, often the brother, of her deceased husband, may have afforded protection to some women who would otherwise be without economic support for themselves or their children. However, 'in the era of HIV/AIDS', it may be considered 'undesirable to inherit a widow' and her in-laws 'may rather consider themselves entitled to claim his property' (WHO/UNICEF 1994: 42). One study in Zambia reports that wife inheritance may make 'property-grabbing' worse when widows and orphans are in families affected by AIDS (Human Rights Watch 2002: 58–60).

With the intention of ameliorating the position of widows and their children, the Zambian government enacted in 1989 the Intestate Succession Act, which provides some protection to the dependants of the deceased. Under the Act, the surviving spouse receives 20% of the estate and the children of the deceased, including those born out of wedlock, share 50% of the estate. While the CEDAW Report suggests that courts have punished violators of this legislation, it has a number of drawbacks, not least the fact that, in the words of Malungo, it has 'generated a lot of contention, debate and disharmony among many stakeholders' (Malungo 2001: 379; see also Machina 2002: 11). In the Report, it is stated that the provisions of the statute are 'not widely used', in part because they are 'not widely known' and 'because relatives of the deceased choose to ignore the law' (CEDAW 1999: 67).

The WLSA used somewhat stronger terms in their comments on the Intestate Succession Act, stating that 'earlier resentment at the passing of a law which usurps customary rights has blossomed into a blatant disregard of statutory law and a perpetuation of the distorted and evil practice of property-grabbing' (WLSA 1995: 83). The Legal Resources Foundation (LRF) in Zambia handles many thousands of cases each year, in part through seven legal advice centres in Lusaka, some of which are referred to lawyers and pursued through the courts. Amongst these cases, a significant proportion is concerned with inheritance, as evidenced by the highlighted cases in the LRF's monthly newsletter. For example, one paralegal working for the LRF in Kitwe is reported in the newsletter of October 2003, commenting after an individual case, but in general terms, that, 'despite the awareness campaigns on the law of Intestate Succession, many people ... continued to practice property-grabbing and a good number of these have unfortunately gone scot-free'.

Customary law disputes, including those relating to property and inheritance, will usually be heard in local courts, which are the lowest rung in the Zambian judicial hierarchy (Human Rights Watch 2002: 55). Fairly recent research in these courts was conducted for Afronet (1998) by means of interviews and observation of cases in local courts in both urban, peri-urban and rural contexts. The researchers concluded that the local courts are highly respected by litigants, who give weight to the ease of access, speed in providing an outcome to disputes and relative simplicity in terms of procedure. They suggested that 'contrary to popular beliefs, the local courts are often sanctuaries to learned and wise justices ... [who] provide a necessary fusion of modern concepts and positive values from the past'. While they took also the position that 'in the urban areas, particularly in Lusaka ... customary law is increasingly becoming a myth', the courts were still valued as dynamic institutions which could respond to change and promote harmony. No doubt their views reflect the tensions around the nature of Africa's legal pluralism and customary law (Manji 1999; Griffiths 2001; Whitehead and Tsikata 2003), which is discussed elsewhere in this book.

Where the Intestate Succession Act was concerned, the researchers' assessment was that courts 'gladly enforce' the claims of surviving spouses and others, but it is 'not the law that is defective' in this area 'but the conservative social forces'. Schlyter (2002) drew a similar conclusion in her research into the local courts in Matero, where she found that statutory law on inheritance was 'acknowledged and accepted' but that widows may not claim their rights in order to maintain good relations with their in-laws. Interviews conducted by her with a range of respondents suggested that many 'caring husbands were conscious about the vulnerability of a widow', with widespread acceptance that property-grabbing was common. However, the same interviewees were unable to view their wives as part of their family and rejected making their spouses into their heirs. Perhaps, as Palmer has indicated, with reference to the work of Ambreena Manji, in considering women's land rights 'we are in danger of putting a great deal too much faith in law' (Palmer 2002: 4).

The gender focus to the human rights discourse, which is firmly ensconced within the understanding and programming of both the UN and other organisations, and which also marks the debate surrounding inheritance laws and practices, does 'not for the most part' emphasise the 'children affected by AIDS and the way in which the epidemic threatens' their human rights (Human Rights Watch 2001). It is implicit that advances in gender justice, which enhance the position of women, will necessarily be in the best interests of children. To empower women is to empower children. However, it is suggested here that sometimes the picture may be less reassuring and comfortable. The authors of a Human Rights Watch (2002) report, entitled *In the Shadow of Death: HIV/AIDS and Children's Rights in Kenya*, for instance, are concerned with the numbers of children who, as consequence of the epidemic, have no family environment at all and their vulnerability, not necessarily connected to that of women, to land-grabbing and disinheritance.

Feminists have expressed concerns about the danger of women's autonomy being threatened by association with children and their 'dependency', a fear to which Goonesekere (2001) alludes in an issue of *Change and Development* devoted to the theme of children's and women's rights. She sees women and children as locked in a paradigm in which women's health and wellbeing is a 'conduit to reach children' but which does not necessitate any concentration on women's own rights and need for empowerment (Goonesekere 2001: 19). One of the most obvious and frequently cited links between women and children in the context of HIV/AIDS concerns the transmission of infection between mother and baby. This link is, however, in many ways the most difficult and open to critique from within feminism. In this context, the maternal link between woman and child casts the former as 'host' to the latter, as womb, breastfeeder and primary caretaker. The health, education and other basic human rights of women are either assumed to be synonymous with the rights of the child, or women are seen as the means to ensure the survival and wellbeing of children. For Goonesekere, this can mean that children's rights become women's burden. However, while campaigns designed to enhance the position of children, or ensure their survival, may intentionally or unintentionally have the effect of disempowering women, the women/children dyad may need to be problematised also from a child rights perspective. As indicated by the authors of *In the Shadow of AIDS*, some support for such a stance may come from discussions surrounding the often desperate situation of children orphaned by AIDS.

## Inheritance, Disinheritance and the Rights of the Child

The Human Rights Watch (2001) researchers conducted a small-scale project in Kenya during February–March 2001, and interviewed 26 AIDS-affected children, young adults or their guardians, together with NGO spokespersons, lawyers and four people who were guardians of children orphaned through AIDS. An AIDS-affected child in this context included those who had a parent or guardian living with AIDS, those whose parent or guardian had died from AIDS, those who were themselves living with AIDS, and children living in households which were fostering children orphaned by AIDS. The researchers also interviewed a youth group, teachers, school administrators and UN officials. They found that children affected by AIDS were at a high risk of sexual or physical abuse, often by their guardians, and were also at high risk of contracting HIV/AIDS, being withdrawn from school and ending up on the streets.

The research was also concerned to highlight the difficulties AIDS-affected orphans may have in claiming property, such as a family home. An interview with a children's law expert suggests that, in some communities, children will not just have lost their parents but all the 'siblings and cousins in the parents' generation'. As discussed earlier in this chapter, a child may have few, if any, relatives who will either take care of the child or protect his or her property rights. The Human Rights Watch (2001) researchers state that: 'Several of the children interviewed ... had the experience of having no one to turn to but a relative who was apparently more interested in their property than in taking care of them.' This situation is by no means confined to Kenya and, in *The State of the World's Children*, Yemisrach from Ethiopia, whose parents died from AIDS, is quoted as follows:

> They [our relatives] want to split us up. They want us to be their servants. No one has suggested a way to keep us together and help us. They have picked who they want to take – to make us work for them - not to help us. And we are not willing to be separated. We want to stay together. We would rather eat nothing but beans, as long as we are together (UNICEF 2002: 41).

The Human Rights Watch (2001) researchers recount the story of Susan B, a 10-year-old child, both of whose parents had died of AIDS and who was living with a neighbour:

> My father's relatives said that the property didn't go with me and my sister, and they said go back to Nairobi to what you're used to. They didn't help my mother when she was sick. We got no assistance. When we were there up-country with them, they made my mother sleep in the kitchen ... and not in the main house. We had to come back to the house my mother had here ... But then [after my mother's death] my uncle took the house and I have to live somewhere else.

Similar situations were confirmed by lawyers working on AIDS-related cases, who were 'unanimous in linking the increasing number of disinheritance cases to the AIDS epidemic'. While there were connections between this land-grabbing and the disinheritance of widows, which had apparently occurred even before the advent of HIV/AIDS, it was now 'a particular problem of children since surviving spouses usually do not live very long in AIDS-affected households'.

While great care must be taken between drawing connections between different cultures and communities, many of the stories recounted to Human Rights Watch (2002) researchers in Lusaka, Zambia are hauntingly similar. A 16-year-old, Patty B, stated that, on the death of her father, his relatives 'grabbed all our property, even my clothes' (2002: 59). Peggy R was six when her father died, and described how her father's sister 'took everything', while Matilda S said that, on the death of her father, his parents 'took chairs, the bed, license plates and cabinets' (Human Rights Watch 2002: 59).

The newsletter of the Legal Resources Foundation in Zambia recounts disputes that echo with the Human Rights Watch research, although making no link with the HIV/AIDS pandemic. The November 2003 newsletter recounts the experiences of Maybin Lungu, whose father was a police officer in Kitwe. Upon the father's death in 1996, when Lungu was in grade six, his uncle was appointed as administrator of his father's estate. Lungu managed to complete school with the help of the local Social Welfare Office and then sought help from his uncle in Lusaka because he wanted to get a job which would enable him to pay school fees for his younger brothers and sister. It was only at this stage, and after failing to find a job, that Lungu asked about any benefits that might have been paid after the death of his father. At first, his uncle said that the Pensions Board had lost the file, but later other relatives told Lungu that his uncle had withdrawn and presumably used part of the benefits for himself, rather than sharing it according to the required percentages. When he attempted to take up the matter again with his uncle, Lungu was chased out of the house, and, on the advice of the Foundation, Lungu pursued the matter through the Permanent Human Rights Commission and the Pensions Board.

In Kenya, Human Rights Watch (2001) encountered a number of relatives and guardians of AIDS orphans who wished to work on behalf of the children to safeguard the inheritance of their property but had run into difficulties. The informants described not being able to get the necessary papers to be acknowledged as the official guardian of the children, being sent from one government department to another on a 'wild goose chase' and even being told by local authorities to 'take the children and let us deal with the land'. It seems that, even where a child's guardian might wish to act in the best interests of the child, many are not aware of the legal system or come up against official barriers. The director of a legal aid service pointed out that children face even greater problems, since they have no standing:

> They need someone to seek a letter of administration on their behalf. For a letter of administration, there have to be identification documents and birth certificates. What child will know how to obtain a birth certificate? Sometimes by the time we obtain a letter of administration, the movable property has already been taken away ... The mechanism that is in place, the public trustee, doesn't do its work. The bureaucracy takes forever – it takes years to settle a case with adults, and it's worse with children.

Children's inheritance interests are located in a complex web of overlapping and multi-dimensional legal systems and a diffusion of power, not always with a clear hierarchy or role for a particular legal authority, including the court. Furthermore, there will be children whose parents' tenure may have been informal and largely depends for its security on continued occupation of the property, which may be difficult if not impossible for the child to maintain. Many child-headed households may be 'motivated' in part to try to retain occupation of land on which the parent had some kind of tenure, whether formal or informal.

Even if a child has the knowledge to assert his or her rights in a court, has the money to pay for a lawyer and an adult who will assume the role of administrator (all of which will be comparatively rare), there may be detrimental consequences from following such a course. Quick and Ziss (2001) recount the experiences of Alli Shikongo, living in Swakopmund, Namibia, who refused to accept the decision of her husband's brothers concerning the home in which she and her husband had lived until his death at 41. According to traditional inheritance rules, the brothers had the right to decide that the flat pass over to one of them, but, Alli, with the help of a local social project, pursued her case through the magistrate's court that dealt with inheritance matters. The court eventually decided that the house should be transferred to her, but, since 'she did not agree to her late husband's family decision, she is now an outsider and cannot expect the Shikongo family ever to help her' (Quick and Ziss 2001: 27). A child dependent upon the uncertain care of their relatives is in a much more vulnerable position and less likely to pursue an 'individual rights' course that could further destabilise his or her insecure situation. As Griffiths argues in the context of women's rights in Botswana, but in which the word children has been substituted here for that of women:

power is not confined to, or solely derived from, the formal legal settings in which it operates, but derives more generally from the broader domain of social life. Taking into account those considerations, which are absent from a legal centralist model of law associated with colonialism, enables a more accurate understanding of people's access to, and use of, law, which highlights the obstacles that [children] face in the legal arena and the interconnectedness between social and legal worlds (Griffiths 2001: 120).

## Conclusion

This chapter has made the case for inheritance laws and practices to be fully integrated into the debates around land rights and security of tenure. The lack of attention to the transmission of capital within the family or attention to the domestic context is a key absence from de Soto's thesis. Attempts to extend paper titles will be distorted without attention to inheritance, as will the assessment of any benefits accruing from such legalisation schemes. Further, it is contended that the HIV/AIDS crisis and its effects on children have brought to the surface the need to further investigate the problems for all orphans trying to realise their inheritance interests. It has been suggested that one should not assume that children's interests will necessarily be concomitant with those of women, and that empowering women will empower children. A number of recommendations for possible reform in this area were suggested by the Human Rights Watch researchers in Kenya, including:

(a) giving NGOs standing to act as guardians for children;
(b) to establish a larger pool of people to provide children with legal assistance;
(c) simplification of the succession system to improve access for children;
(d) better information relating to inheritance rights for children;
(e) a well-paid public trustee office which is not open to abuse.

Similar suggestions have been put forward in other contexts. The participants at the Copperbelt Land Workshop, held in Kitwe in 2002, took the view that the Department of Social Services should hold land in trust for child-headed households, provided it was with the consent of the relevant community, 'to avoid the problem of family administrators going behind the backs of the benefactors and selling the land/property without their knowledge and consent' (Copperbelt Land Workshop 2002: 4). Malawi was the first country in sub-Saharan Africa to develop National Orphan Care Guidelines, in 1992, which included a determination that the 'government will protect the property rights of orphans and that these rights should be widely publicized' (UNICEF 1999: 13). In the report on sub-Saharan Africa, *Children Orphaned by AIDS*, it is suggested that while 'laws may exist to protect children and women, ... these sometimes marginalized members of society may be unaware of the laws or have no channel to take advantage of them, making strong advocacy in this area essential' (UNICEF 1999: 32). The development of a system of child advocates, who would not need to be legally qualified and perhaps might themselves be children or young adults who have experienced being orphaned, may be a useful step in some social and legal contexts. Ensuring that children acquire life skills, including 'how to obtain information, advice and assistance regarding human rights, including legal rights such as inheritance' (UNICEF 1999: 33) is also important.

There are possibilities for the development of a human rights discourse in appropriate circumstances. For instance, the High Court in Botswana accepted a case concerning the citizenship rights of children, which it was argued were being violated by provisions in the Citizenship Act 1984. It was contended successfully that these provisions were unconstitutional, since they contravened Section 3 of the Constitution, which confers rights and freedoms on all individuals in Botswana, and Section 15, which provides for non-discrimination (Griffiths 2001: 120). It is possible that similar arguments might be used in suitable circumstances, as part of a legal strategy on behalf of children seeking to gain access to their inheritance, although, of course, the individual rights approach will be itself limited to an appropriate context. Whether any proposal for reform is likely to enhance the position of children requires further research, not least to discover the real problems that children encounter in trying to assert or even understand their property rights.

## References

Ackroyd, AV (1997) 'Sociocultural aspects of AIDS in Africa: occupational and gender issues' in Bond, GC and others (eds), *AIDS in Africa and the Caribbean*, Boulder, CO: Westview Press

Afronet (1998) *The Dilemma of Local Courts in Zambia*, www.oneworld.org.za/reports, accessed 29 November 2003

Agarwal, B (1994) 'Gender and command over property: a critical gap in economic analysis and policy in South Asia' *World Development* 22(10): 1455–78

Amaratunga, A (ed) (2002) *Gender Mainstreaming in HIV/AIDS: Taking a Multisectoral Approach*, London: Commonwealth Secretariat and Maritime Centre of Excellence for Women's Health

Ayiga, N and others (1997) 'Causes, patterns, differentials and consequences of AIDS mortality in Northern Uganda' in Bond, GC and others (eds), *AIDS in Africa and the Caribbean*, Boulder, Colorado: Westview Press

Barnett, T and Blaikie, P (1992) *Aids in Africa*, London: Belhaven Press

Baylies, C (2000) 'The impact of HIV on family size preference in Zambia' *Reproductive Health Matters* 8(15): 77–86

Baylies, C (2002) 'HIV/AIDS and older women in Zambia: concern for self, worry over daughters, towers of strength' *Third World Quarterly* 23(2): 351–75

Bond, GC and Vincent, C (1997) 'AIDS in Uganda: the first decade' in Bond, GC and others (eds), *AIDS in Africa and the Caribbean*, Boulder, CO: Westview Press

Butegwa, F (1991) 'Women's legal right of access to agricultural resources in Africa: a preliminary inquiry' *Third World Legal Studies: Special Edition*: 45–58

CEDAW, (1999) *Combined Third and Fourth CEDAW Report – Zambia*, CEDAW/C/ZAM/3–4

Cohen, D and Reid, E (2002) *The Vulnerability of Women: Is This a Useful Construct for Programming?*, www.undp.org/hiv/publications/issues/english/issue28e.html, accessed 20 October 2003

Copperbelt Land Workshop (2002) *Draft Position Paper and Recommendations*, Mindolo Ecumenical Foundation, Kitwe, 3–5 October de Soto, H (2000) *The Mystery of Capital: Why Capitalism Triumphs in the West and Fails Everywhere Else*, London: Black Swan

de Sousa Santos, B (1987) 'Law: a map of misreading: towards a postmodern conception of law' *Journal of Law and Society* 14: 279

de Waal, A (2003) 'Why the HIV/AIDS pandemic is a structural threat to Africa's governance and economic development' *Fall Fletcher Forum of World Affairs* 27: 6–18

Deininger, K, Garcia, M and Subbarao, K (2003) 'AIDS-induced orphanhood as a systemic shock: magnitude, impact and program interventions in Africa' *World Development* 31(7): 1201–20

Donnelly, J (2002) 'UN says AIDS deaths could near 70 million' *Boston Globe*, 7 March

Drimie, S (2002) 'The impact of HIV/AIDS on land: case studies from Kenya, Lesotho and South Africa', a Synthesis Report prepared for the Southern African Regional Office of the Food and Agricultural Organization of the United Nations (FAO)

FAO (2003) 'Seeking ways out of the impasse on land reform in Southern Africa: notes from an informal "think tank" meeting', Manhattan Hotel, Pretoria, South Africa

Fortmann, L (1997) 'Why women's property rights matter' *Capetown Conference on Land Tenure Issues* 19: 1–10

Foster, G (2000) 'The capacity of the extended family safety net for orphans in Africa' *Psychology, Health and Medicine* 5(1): 55–62

Goonesekere, S (2001) 'Realizing human rights of women and children: some reflections on law and policy' *Change and Development* 44(1): 15–22

Grainger, C, Webb, D and Elliott L (2001) *Children Affected by HIV/AIDS: Rights and Responses in the Developing World*, London: Save the Children

Gray, L and Kevone, M (1999) 'Diminished access, diverted exclusion: women and land tenure in Sub-Saharan Africa' *African Studies Review* 42: 15–39

Griffiths, A (2001) 'Gendering culture: towards a plural perspective of Kwena women's rights' in Cowan, J, Dembour, M and Wilson, R (eds), *Culture and Rights*, Cambridge: CUP

Guest, E (2003) *Children of AIDS*, London: Pluto

Hale, B (2003) *The Missing Medics in Botswana's Aids Battle*, http://news.bbc.co.uk/1/hi/business/3280735.stm, accessed 22 November 2003

Human Rights Watch (2001) *In the Shadow of Death: HIV/AIDS and Children's Rights in Kenya*, Nairobi: Human Rights Watch

Human Rights Watch (2002) *Suffering In Silence*, New York: Human Rights Watch

Jackson, H and Lee, T (2002) 'Sub-Saharan Africa' in McElrath, K (ed), *HIV and AIDS – A Global View*, Westport Connecticut and London: Greenwood Press

Jayasuriya, D (2001) 'HIV/AIDS and human rights in the third world' *Amicus Curiae* 38: 27–31

Kalabamu, F (1997) 'Effects of gendered land rights on urban housing by women in Botswana' *Capetown Conference on Land Tenure Issues* 34: 1–9

Kidd, PE, Mahgekgenene, K, Molokomme, A, Molamu, LL, Malila, IS, Lesetedi, GN, Dingake, K and Mokongwa, K (1997) *Botswana Families and Women's Rights in a Changing Environment*, Gaborone: Women and Law in Southern Africa Research Trust

Kirkpatrick, SM (1993) 'Living with the epidemic: the tragedy in Africa' *American Nurse* 3(20): 25

Lea, D (2002) 'Tully and de Soto on uniformity and diversity' *Journal of Applied Philosophy* 19(1): 55

Lewis, S (2003) *Address at the Official Opening of the XIIIth International Conference on AIDS and STIs in Africa*, Nairobi, 21 September

Lim, H (1996) 'Mapping equity's place: here be dragons' in Bottomley, A (ed), *Feminist Perspectives on the Foundational Subjects of Law*, London: Cavendish Publishing

Lisk, F (2002) *Statement to the XIV International AIDS Conference in Barcelona*, www.allAfrica.com, 11 July 2002

Machina, H (2002) *Women's Land Rights in Zambia: Policy Provisions, Legal Frameworks and Constraints*, Lusaka: Zambia National Land Alliance

Machipisa, L (2001) 'Women and girls bear the burden in Zimbabwe' *Choices*, 20–21 December

Malungo, JRS (2001) 'Sexual cleansing (*Kusalazya*) and levirate marriage (*Kunjilila mung'anda*) in the era of AIDS: changes in perceptions and practices in Zambia' *Social Science and Medicine* 53(3): 371–82

Mane, P and Aggleton, P (2001) 'Gender and HIV/AIDS: what do men have to do with it?' *Current Sociology* 49(6): 23–37

Manji, A (1999) 'Gender and the politics of the land reform process in Tanzania' *Journal of Modern African Studies* 36(4): 645–67

Manji, A (2003) 'Capital, labour and land relations in Africa: a gender analysis of the World Bank's *Policy Research Report on Land Institutions and Land Policy*' *Third World Quarterly* 24(1): 97

Mullins, D (2001) 'Land reform, poverty reduction and HIV/AIDS', paper presented at the SARPN conference on Land Reform and Poverty Alleviation in Southern Africa, Pretoria

Nampanya-Serpell, N (2000) 'Social and economic risk factors for HIV/AIDS-affected families in Zambia', paper presented at the AIDS and Economics Symposium, Durban, 7–8 July

Ntozi, JM (1997) 'AIDS morbidity and the role of the family in patient care in Uganda' *Health Transition Review* 1 (Supplement): 1–22

Ntozi, JM and Nakawiya, S (1997) 'AIDS in Uganda: how has the household coped with the epidemic' in Bond, GC *et al* (eds), *AIDS in Africa and the Caribbean*, Boulder, Colorado: Westview Press

Nyambedha, EO, Wandibba, S and Aagaard-Hansen, J (2003) 'Changing patterns of orphan care due to the HIV epidemic in western Kenya' *Social Science and Medicine* 57: 301–11

Owen, M (1996) *A World of Widows*, London: Zed Books

Palmer, R (2002) *Gendered Land Rights – Process, Struggle or Lost C(l)ause?*, London: Oxfam GB

Quick, B and Ziss, R (2001) 'The impact of AIDS and housing in Namibia' *Trialog* 69(2): 26–29

Reardon, C (2002) 'AIDS: how Brazil turned the tide', Ford Foundation Report, www.fordfound.org/publications, 23 July

Schlyter, A (2002) *Privatisation of Public Housing and Exclusion of Women. A Case Study in Lusaka, Zambia*, submitted for publication to the Institute of Southern African Studies, University of Lesotho

Sebina-Zziwa, AJN (1998) 'The paradox of tradition: gender, land and inheritance rights among the Baganda', PhD dissertation, Faculty of Social Science, University of Copenhagen

Tlou, SD, Field, M and Nyblade, L (2000) 'Community perspectives on mother to child transmission of HIV', abstracts of the 2nd National Conference on HIV/AIDS in Botswana, Gaborone, 14–18 February

Tlou, SD (2001) *Women, the Girl Child and HIV/AIDS*, www.un.org/womenwatch/daw/csw/tlou2001.htm, accessed 29 November 2003

UNAIDS (2002) *Report on the Global HIV/AIDS Epidemic*, New York: UNAIDS

UNAIDS/UNICEF/USAID (2002) *Children on the Brink 2002*, New York: UNAIDS/UNICEF/USAID

UNAIDS/WHO (2003) *Aids Epidemic Update*, Geneva: UNAIDS/WHO

UNDP (2000) *Botswana Human Development Report*, Gaborone: UNDP Botswana

UNICEF (1999) *Children Orphaned by AIDS*, New York: UNICEF/UNAIDS

UNICEF (2002) *The State of the World's Children 2002*, New York: UNICEF

Upton, RL (2003) '"Women have no tribe": connecting carework, gender and migration in an era of HIV/AIDS in Botswana' *Gender and Society* 17(2): 314–22

Varley, A (2002) 'Private or public: debating the meaning of tenure legalization' *International Journal of Urban and Regional Research* 26(3): 449

Walker, C (2002) *Land Reform in Southern and Eastern Africa: Key Issues for Strengthening Women's Access to and Rights in Land*, Harare, Zimbabwe: FAO

Whitehead, A and Tsikata, D (2003) 'Policy discourses on women's land rights in sub-Saharan Africa: the implications of the re-turn to the customary' *Journal of Agrarian Change* 3(1 and 2): 67–112

Whiteside, A (2002) 'Poverty and HIV/AIDS in Africa' *Third World Quarterly* 23(2): 313–32

Whiteside, A, Barnett, T, George, G and Van Niekerk, AA (2003) 'Through a glass darkly: data and uncertainty in the AIDS Debate' *Developing World Bioethics* 3(1): 49–76

WHO/UNICEF (1994) *Action for Children Affected by AIDS*, WHO/UNICEF

WLSA (1995) *Inheritance in Zambia: Law and Practice*, Lusaka: Women in Law in Southern Africa Research Project

WLSA (1997) *The Changing Family in Zambia*, Harare: Women and Law in Southern African Trust

# Chapter 5
# Botswana: 'Self-Allocation', 'Accommodation' and 'Zero Tolerance' in Mogoditshane and Old Naledi
*Chadzimula Molebatsi*

## Introduction

Among the nations of sub-Saharan Africa, Botswana offers a fruitful case study of the postcolonial tensions between communal and individual land tenure, seen through the prism of rapid peri-urban growth. The peri-urban space in Botswana provides the area at which indigenous land administration systems, creations of pre-capitalist formations, interface with received or capitalist and market-based systems found in the urban areas. In recent years, housing shortages and speculative land developers in urban areas have exerted intense pressure on Tribal Land Boards (TLBs) in adjacent tribal areas. The creation of TLBs can be viewed as indicative of the new nation-State's commitment to safeguarding access to land for its citizens in communal areas. It is the combined presence of land shortages in urban areas and the availability of relatively free land in communal areas that has created complex and disputed land transactions in the peri-urban space. Claims and counter-claims of 'self-allocation' have generated different responses from government, moving from tacit accommodation (as in the case of Old Naledi) to, more recently, 'zero tolerance' (as in the case of Mogoditshane).

Botswana covers an area of about 580,000 sq km, and is characterised by varied geomorphological features. Two-thirds of the country is covered by the Kalahari sands, a feature which has often earned the country a description of desert, although the Kalahari provides some of the country's most sought-after range lands. The eastern part of the country is less sandy, and it is within this area that most of the country's settlements are located. The last population census (2001) estimated Botswana's population at 1.7 million and the annual growth rate for the inter-census period 1991–2001 at 2.4%. It has been indicated that the more recent decline in the growth rate started in the pre-HIV/AIDS period and is attributed to declining fertility rates, increased participation in economic activities and access to better health facilities.

Formerly the British protectorate of Bechuanaland, at independence in 1966 Botswana functioned as a reserve of cheap labour for the neighbouring Republic of South Africa and was classed as one of the world's 10 poorest countries. The discovery of minerals, notably diamonds, copper and nickel deposits, combined with beef exports and tourism, transformed the country's fortunes, with the result that the World Bank now places it in the rank of lower middle-income economies, with an economic growth rate among the highest in the developing world. Despite this impressive record of sustained economic growth, the national poverty rate was still 47% in 1994, a decline of only 12% from 1985 (SARPN 2001). Poverty is widespread in both rural and urban areas, and an estimated 20% of the population in the capital city of Gaborone lives in poverty (DFID 1998).

**Figure 1: Tribal Land Boards in Botswana. This map shows the boundaries of main land boards. Population is concentrated to the east and south-east (Mogoditshane Subordinate Land Board at bottom right), Kalahari to the west, Okavango delta to the north (courtesy: DSM, Botswana 2002)**

## A Paradox of Political Economy

Botswana has been called a 'paradox of political economy': a capitalist economy with a multi-party democracy and little State intervention in industry, yet centrally planned, with decision-making concentrated in a small bureaucratic ruling class (Murray and Parsons 1990). Administratively, the country is divided into 10 districts and five urban councils. Local government now comprises the tribal administration, district administration, district councils and the TLBs. Botswana's political and administrative structures have been much studied (see, for example, Colclough and McCarthy 1980; Picard 1987; Molutsi 1989; Good 1993), and one of the most contested aspects is the characterisation of the administrative and planning system as centralised.

Adherents of the 'centralised planning' school of thought contend that this is realised mainly through the regular preparation of six-year national development plans through which the State sets development goals, which consequently form the basis for sub-national (district) and local (urban/settlement) planning. The replacement of traditional institutions by so called modern institutions is also cited as indicative of the centralising tendencies of the State in Botswana. Colonial indirect rule had left tribal administration largely unchanged, but the introduction of modern institutions in the postcolonial period substantially reduced the chiefs' functions and responsibilities, leaving them effectively only responsible for the customary courts and leading some of them to align with opposition political movements (Parsons 1990; Wiseman 1978). Centralisation has also been realised through the dependence of local government on central government for funding and manpower deployment. The appointment, transfer, dismissal and promotion of local government staff is co-ordinated from central government, thus separating the district authorities from their employees. This has led some observers to conclude that employees at local government have to be sympathetic to central government directions if they want career advancement (Noppen 1982: 31; Picard 1987: 197; Holm 1988: 189).

Centralisation is also realised by the retention of an office of the District Commissioner, a relic of colonial administrative practice. The District Commissioner, as the most senior local representative of central government, co-ordinates local development activities (ROB 1990b: 448) and dominates policy-making process at district level through chairmanship of the District Development Committee (DDC). The DDC comprises senior field officers of government ministries and representatives of council, TLBs, tribal administration and NGOs. DDCs were introduced in 1970 against protests from the district councils, who viewed them as 'neither elected nor appointed locally, yet [having] a decisive influence over development decisions' (a council secretary, quoted in Picard 1979: 282).

Measures to enhance centralisation were often presented as 'nation building' or 'effective planning'. The introduction of District Councils and TLBs exemplify this rhetoric of 'nation-building'; the establishment of the DDC that of 'effective planning'. The advent of District Councils and TLBs was seen by the State as introducing 'modern' and 'more democratic institutions' to overcome the parochialism of traditional tribal institutions. The need for more democratic institutions was articulated in the 1965 Election Manifesto of the Botswana Democratic Party (BDP), which has held power since independence: 'the BDP stands for a gradual but sure evolution of a national State in Bechuanaland to which the tribal groups will, while they remain in existence, take secondary place' (quoted in Parsons 1990: 103).

Centralised planning allows the State to control the society and neutralise areas of potential autonomy (Picard and Morgan 1985: 132). According to Reilly (1983:

144) a strong local government could threaten elite interests if controlled by the poor, hence the preference for 'weak local government institutions which are primarily bureaucratic rather than political and which are controlled by local socio-economic elites and central government civil servants' (Picard and Morgan 1985: 133). This is perhaps most evident in TLB memberships, often used by the ruling BDP to reward party faithfuls who have failed to make it to council or Parliament (Molebatsi 1994). Such a system creates rivalry and conflict between the tribal administration and the TLBs, and between the TLBs and District Councils.

Contrary to the above view, government publications and policy documents portray the planning system as decentralised and 'responsive to the needs, problems and priorities of local communities' (ROB 1979), while local government is 'designed to facilitate people's participation in development' with a 'long tradition of democratic consultation and devolved decision-making' (ROB 1991b: 445).

The centralisation-decentralisation debate notwithstanding, Botswana's planned economy has recorded impressive growth and is amongst Africa's fastest growing economies, a development partly attributed to the country's political stability. From independence in 1966, Botswana with its multi-party democracy and non-racial policies had a reputation as a 'shining star' of democracy in southern Africa, although the emergence of the new South Africa after multi-racial elections in 1994, and the rebirth of Namibia, have ushered in more inclusive democratic constitutions and more assertive civil societies in the region, exposing the limits of Botswana's democracy. Although the BDP has won all national elections since 1966, both local and national elections are hotly contested, providing a means for the electorate to bring pressure on politicians.

Prior to the 1999 elections, BDP support came mainly from rural areas, while the opposition drew support mainly from the urban areas. This pattern changed in the 1999 election, following a split in the BNF, and the parliamentary seats won back by the BDP included Mogoditshane. Multi-partyism and relatively free elections have resulted in the politicisation of several issues, particularly those perceived as unpopular by the electorate. Within the urban area, for example, the issue of service levy has often been used by the opposition to discredit the ruling party. Politicisation of issues on a partisan basis has often stalled possibilities for policy change, as any compromise by the government could be construed as capitulation to political rivals. The Mogoditshane land crisis has often been interpreted by those in power as lawlessness fuelled by opposition political parties.

The political and economic contexts within which land issues in Botswana unfold have some connection to what has been dubbed the neo-liberalism or the New Right. It can be argued that the de Soto thesis, the subject of this book, is anchored in neo-liberalism. 'Lifting the bell jar' can be construed as calling for the democratisation of capitalism. In the context of developing countries, this would include the State's willingness to embrace urbanisation activities organised outside the State apparatus by other city builders. Neo-liberalism advocates the freedom to build, with low-income groups presented as progressive builders and investors in housing. The advocacy recognises the multiplicity of players in city-building processes and calls for a streamlining and redefinition of roles, with the State confining itself to those things that people cannot do for themselves, facilitating and enabling rather than regulating and controlling (Cook and Kirke 1989). Instead of centralised housing delivery systems, this thinking emphasises the accommodation of the informal sector, through partnerships between stakeholders, and negotiations and mediations by actors inside and outside State organs. New Right thinking has, however failed to interrogate the socio-economic and political structures that generate uneven development and resource inequalities. Notwithstanding the above, the pluralism inherent in neo-liberal ideology offers opportunities that activists can exploit for the benefit of the under-privileged.

Neo-liberal thinking has found its way into Botswana's political economy through privatisation, cost-sharing and non-subsidisation of urban development, which are all topical in the country's development debates. The government has sometimes professed to adopt an enabling or facilitating role, with NGOs and CBOs as partners in development, exemplified by the community-based Rural Development Strategy.

## Land Tenure and the Administrative System

Land tenure and administration has always been a highly valued and sensitive issue in Botswana. The country's pre-independence history is scattered with warfare and skirmishes over land resulting in the current tribal territories, the boundaries of which coincide with those of the administrative districts. The colonial period saw further intensification of land pressure as huge chunks of prime land in the Gantsi Blocks and Eastern Botswana were ceded to white settler farmers. This picture has since changed, with prime land being transferred through the market to the country's political and economic elite. Some freehold farms, particularly on the outskirts of the capital Gaborone, have now been developed for housing or commercial use, as in the case of Phakalane Estate and portions of Mokolodi and Forest Hill farms. Freehold tenure has been discontinued since independence, and to date only 6% of the country's total land area remains freehold. The remaining 94% is distributed between State land (23%) and tribal or communal land (71%) (DTRP 1998).

A major development in the post-independence era was the introduction of a new land administrative system with the promulgation of the 1968 Tribal Land Act. The Act created the TLBs, which took over the chiefs' land responsibilities and were empowered to hold land 'in trust for the benefit of the tribesmen of that area', with the additional (and not necessarily consistent) aim 'of promoting the economic and social development of all the people of Botswana'. Twelve TLBs came into existence in 1970 (and over 30 subordinate TLBs created then and later), with powers over granting and cancelling land use rights, restrictions, and determining land use zones.

The TLB can issue three different types of land grant: customary grant, common law lease and Fixed Period State Grant (FPSG). Customary grant constitutes the overwhelming majority of titles issued in Botswana and has unlimited duration, but is not pledgable as collateral. The Tribal Land Act tried to overcome this perceived defect by introducing the so called common law lease (renewable, pledgable and surrenderable) under fixed terms, which were 50 years on commercial/industrial land and 99 years on residential plots. In tribal areas, ownership can be transferred to the State for national development purposes, for example, mining, which is how the towns of Orapa, Jwaneng and Sowa were established. Only citizens of Botswana are entitled to customary land rights (s 20 of the Tribal Land Act), while non-citizens and companies receive a common law allocation. The customary grant-holder has an exclusive right over his land, but only a right of usage, not of ownership. The Certificate of Customary Land Rights is perpetual, inheritable and transferable once the land has been developed. Information about the landholder is included in the certificate, with the identity card [*O Mang* = 'who are you?'] used to verify age, name and nationality. The certificate can be converted to a residential common law lease (99 years), which requires the expense of a full survey and payment of fees and can be 'hypothecated' for a mortgage.

The physical boundaries of residential plots are defined by fences or hedges, with corners identified by wooden pegs, iron bars or concrete posts. The plot-holder is expected to put in his own permanent pegs or posts within six weeks of allocation (although they are sometimes later moved or removed) and is supposed by law to develop his plot within a specified period (two years for common law grant, five for customary grant), after which the TLB has the right (rarely exercised) to cancel the grant on service of notice. Section 38 of the Tribal Land Act specifies development as 'to introduce or carry out works or improvements in accordance with the purpose for which the grant was made'; fencing, slabs and toilets are not considered development.

The statutory functions of the land board include monitoring of development, and a customary grant can be cancelled (under s 15 of the Tribal Land Act) if:

(a) the holder of the grant is no longer qualified to hold it;
(b) the holder of the grant fails to observe planning restrictions;
(c) the land has been used for a purpose not authorised by customary law;
(d) the plot has not been cultivated, used or developed to the satisfaction of the TLB.

Non-payment of lease fees is not a ground for cancellation, and in practice cancellation takes time and money.

The tenure patterns that exist on State land differ significantly from that discussed above. The most common form of basic tenure for low income groups is the Certificate of Rights (COR), introduced in 1975. Self-Help Housing Agency (SHHA) areas allow use of the land for an unfixed period, while the State retains ownership, but this does not confer access to credit from formal financial institutions. The COR can be upgraded to an FPSG, a long renewable lease. The system offers many advantages:

(a) no need for expensive surveys and conveyancing;
(b) rates not payable (only a fixed service levy);
(c) administered locally by the local authority;
(d) supported by the SHHA scheme;
(e) title transferable and upgradable;
(f) free plot (now subsidised with staggered payment).

COR tenure has now become the dominant urban tenure, accounting for 75% of all plots in towns. The scheme seems to work because of government institutional support (free surveys, physical planning and land administration) and the availability of open sites under State land tenure. The SHHA scheme is being extended to customary tenure areas to benefit 80% of the population, and, to cater for those outside the SHHA bracket (middle and high income groups), the government introduced the Accelerated Land Servicing Programme (ALSP).

## 'Towns', 'Urban Villages' and Peri-Urban Development

The existence of different land administration systems in areas physically next to each other (State and tribal land) has proved a major challenge to policy-makers and has contributed greatly to the peri-urban problem in Botswana. Peri-urban areas suffer from numerous land conflicts because of the co-existence of indigenous tenure with the received system of freehold and leasehold. Indigenous tenure is under pressure, but respected, and (as shown later in the case of Mogoditshane) lacks written proof of ownership, particularly in the older parts of villages where initial allocations were made by the chiefs without documentation but are acknowledged through the shared knowledge of the community.

Figure 2: Peri-urban land from the air. Part of the modern planned layout of Gaborone is to the right, meandering footpaths and peri-urban development on tribal land to the left and bottom, separated by a road (courtesy: R Home 2002)

The peri-urban challenge should be understood within the context of the country's rapid urbanisation and the public sector's failure to meet the land requirements of the growing urban population. Viewed from another perspective, the co-existence of the two systems is partly a result of the 1955 Township Act, which classified settlements into 'villages' and 'towns'. Towns were defined as those settlements on

Crown land, while the rest were to be referred to as villages. The classification was viewed to have effectively reduced indigenous Tswana settlements to village status, towns being associated with Europeans and villages with Africans (Hardie 1980; Molebatsi 1994: 133–39). Townships on State land were declared at Gaborone, Francistown and elsewhere. After independence, British-style planning was introduced (following reports by visiting experts in 1968 and 1974) by the 1977 Town and Country Planning Act, which replaced a former 1961 proclamation drawing upon South African legislation. Comprehensive planning was not considered necessary and the gazetted 'planning areas' were confined initially to the official 'townships'. Indigenous settlements were not considered 'ripe for planning control' by the visiting expert Desmond Heap, who recommended a strongly centralised control until 'time passes and understanding of the art of town planning and of the essential need to have it in a developing country becomes more and more understood' (Heap 1974: 26–27; Molebatsi 1994: 173–80).

The nature of urbanisation in Botswana is not different from that in other developing countries. It has been rapid and conforms largely to the geographical theory of the primate city. The proportion of urban to total population has risen rapidly, from 4% at independence (1966) to a striking 45.7% in 1991. This growth exceeds what the urban economy can absorb, and accommodating the incoming population with employment, housing and services is a major challenge (Molebatsi 1994). Gaborone offers a classic case of a primate city, dominating the national urban hierarchy, and is one of the fastest growing cities in the world. Between 1991 and 2001, Gaborone experienced an average growth rate of 3.4% per annum. The capital city in the primate city theory concentrates population in its region; the 1981 national census showed 50% of the national population living within 200 km of Gaborone, while by 1991, 50% were within 100 km (Molebatsi 1996).

The rapid rise in urban population is largely due to rural-urban migration, driven by the non-productivity of subsistence agriculture and a lack of viable livelihood strategies. The rural poor seek to improve their situation by migration, but they cannot be absorbed into the formal sector and so enter informal and irregular employment. One area that perhaps clearly demonstrates the challenges of urbanisation in Botswana has been the provision of land housing for low income groups. Urban land markets in Botswana serve high income groups and exclude the poor, and so squatter settlements arise as attempts at self-help, forcing a change of thinking from demolition to upgrading. Upgraded squatter settlements are a common feature of Botswana's urban landscape (many have grown up outside Gaborone, Monarch and Somerset East in Francistown, Peleng in Lobatse, and Botshabelo in Selibe-Phikwe) but remain poorly served with infrastructure; planning contraventions are common.

## The Peri-Urban Challenge

The peri-urban problem in Botswana revolves around access to land and the land transaction, which is negotiated and brokered outside State apparatus and viewed by the State as illegal. Such transactions defy State regulations and procedures, perhaps because individuals believe they are entitled to dispose of their land as they see fit. The peri-urban areas in Botswana are the space where indigenous land tenure interfaces with 'received' capitalist land markets. The State's policies toward such transactions can best be described as 'zero tolerance'. In the case of Mogoditshane, the State has through the Kweneng TLB sanctioned the demolition of developments on what was perceived by the State as illegally acquired land. Unrestrained by the public outcry that followed the demolition of houses in Mogoditshane, the State in Botswana has threatened to continue with demolitions anywhere in the country where contravention is detected. In the Central District, for example, the Ngwato TLB has resolved to demolish Jamataka, a settlement largely inhabited by San communities. The zero tolerance stance adopted by the government, and its ability to carry out demolition threats, should be understood within the context of Botswana's political structure, an argument developed later in this chapter.

Notwithstanding State hostility towards land transactions in the peri-urban areas, evidence from the present study shows that peri-urban areas offer services which the formal urban sectors fail to provide for significant numbers of the urban population. They provide affordable rental housing and opportunities for plot acquisition through unofficial transactions. The most common way of making money from property is through informal letting or sub-letting, and the poor are usually tenants in backyard accommodation who have not managed to find land of their own.

## Methodology and General Findings

Case study material was obtained from two peri-urban settlements, Old Naledi and Mogoditshane. Old Naledi (the name means 'star', supposedly from the period when its first residents slept without shelter, 'under the stars') started as a squatter settlement next to an industrial area and was occupied by building and industrial workers when Gaborone was growing rapidly after independence. It remains the most densely populated residential area in Gaborone. Formal recognition by the government resulted in upgrading programmes in 1977, 1988 and 1995. The 1977 programme included plot rationalisation, relocation of displaced plot-holders and (relevant to the present study) tenure security for plot-holders. Infrastructure and service improvements were undertaken by the government, and on-plot improvements were made by plot-holders with government support.

The second case study area, Mogoditshane, lies some 5 km north-west of Gaborone city centre, and is separated from the Gaborone administrative district by a land reservation for overhead electric lines serving the mining town of Jwaneng. Originally a cattle post for the Bakwena tribe, Mogoditshane was intended also to curb the expansion of freehold farms into Bakwena territory. Its population, 1,075 in 1976, exploded to 38,819 by 2001, recording an annual growth rate of over 10% in the 1990s. Surrounded by open farmland (arable and livestock), its proximity to Gaborone converted Mogoditshane into a dormitory settlement because of the shortage of housing in the city, and it also serves as overspill for Gaborone's commerce and industry, with several shopping malls being developed. Institutional fragmentation is reflected in the co-existence of tribal institutions like the *kgotla* and chieftaincy alongside the TLB and District Councils and the application of both the Town and Country Planning Act and the Tribal Land Act. Mixed land uses abound, with opportunities for multiple sources of livelihoods through rental accommodation and informal commercial activities.

The research undertook semi-structured interviews with 30 plot-holders in Old Naledi and 63 in Mogoditshane. The research team was formally introduced to Mogoditshane residents at a public meeting, attended by the chief, headmen and members of the Village Development Committee. To identify low-income plot-holders, the older parts of Mogoditshane and their poorer physical structures were identified and marked upon an orthophoto-map. Other key informants were interviewed (professionals, community leaders and civic organisations active in Mogoditshane and Old Naledi), focus group discussions were conducted and documentary evidence was used to augment other data sources. The results, especially for Mogoditshane, highlight the extent of the peri-urban land crisis in Botswana.

## Access to loans

Most plot-holders in Mogoditshane lack certificates of customary grant, which encourages illegal land occupation. Delays in issuing certificates result partly from the administrative inefficiency of the TLB. Many of the plots had been allocated by the chief before the TLBs were created, and still lacked certificates of ownership: in Mogoditshane, 40% of respondents had been allocated land by the chief, 16% by the Land Board, and 43% had inherited land. The TLB had only recently encouraged plot-holders to apply for their certificates. In Old Naledi, all the 30 plots covered were initially self-allocated, and formalised under the 1976 upgrading with the issue of a COR. In Mogoditshane, 56% of respondents had customary land grant certificates, 30% were awaiting their issue, and 13% had not yet applied. The Tribal Land Act required plot-holders to register their plots to formalise previous allocation, but this was rare, partly due to TLB capacity problems.

Evidence from the research suggests that security of tenure has not spurred the poor to seek mortgages, but has allowed multiple sources of livelihoods to be pursued through rental accommodation, on-plot trading, and the subdivision and sale of land. Even where plot-holders have title documentation, a combination of inadequate information, biased land and housing markets and the cumbersome procedures of financial institutions have made them reluctant to seek loans. Even in Old Naledi, an area already upgraded with title, plot-holders do not seek mortgages (or hypothecation); not a single respondent indicated ever using his or her plot as security in accessing loans from commercial banks. This can be attributed to three factors:

- *Inadequate information on collateralisation.* Development issues are usually communicated through public or *kgotla* meetings addressed by politicians, but these are poorly attended. Other ways of information dissemination are through the State-owned radio station and daily newspapers. Planning procedures are little known, and, even when the process of converting from customary grant to common law lease was explained, few respondents showed interest.
- *Cumbersome conversion procedures.* Conversion from customary grant and a COR to the FPSG is a lengthy and costly process, and financial institutions do

not accept customary grant or a COR for hypothecation purposes, since they are not legally registered or transferable (Kalabamu 2001). Also, the lack of infrastructure, compounded by planning contraventions (housing next to dilapidated and unimproved plots, beer-parlours and tuck shops), has the effect of devaluing property.

- *Fear of losing property to financial institutions.* More common than bank borrowing was borrowing and lending from friends and relatives, usually at no interest. In the 1980s recession, much publicity was given to the Botswana Building Society repossessing houses from defaulting customers, and the National Development Bank acting against defaulting farmers. To most respondents, the dreaded court cases (commonly referred to as 'In the Matter Between') published in the local newspapers captured the fate of those who might want to use property as collateral. A selection of case histories shows this ongoing fear of repossession proceedings.

**Figure 3: Incremental plot improvements in Mogoditshane. Traditional round hut in centre, concrete-block rental housing to right and rear, services in foreground (courtesy: R Home 2002)**

## Case 1: 'This piece of land is my life'

A man (aged 46) from northern Botswana lives in Area 8 of Old Naledi with his wife, 10 children and a nephew (a total of 13 individuals). He arrived in 1975 for building construction work and also ran a 'tuck shop' and *shebeen*. Now self-employed in construction, the respondent takes home a monthly income of P2000–3500, and lets six rooms on his plot at P125 per month each, while his wife engages in small-scale tailoring and selling health products. Like most residents of Old Naledi, he 'self-allocated' the plot, and subsequently received a COR. He started on the plot with six mud shacks, which he let out, and used the accumulated rent and other income to build two three-room structures (cement bricks, iron roofs), then a tuck shop, and later a three-room house (with water standpipe). While clearly enterprising, he would not contemplate using his plot as collateral for a mortgage:

> This piece of land is my life. I am who I am because it supported me and my family, and I can't change its title because I cannot afford to have it taken by a bank or anyone because I failed to pay back a loan. I have children who should inherit this plot, not a bank!

**Figure 4: Building materials for plot improvements. Self-allocated plot in Mogoditshane, with self-built housing at rear, building sand and materials waiting to be used (courtesy: R Home 2002)**

### Case 2: 'What if I fail to pay?'

A woman who came to Gaborone with her husband in 1977, from Bobonong via Francistown and Ramotswa, first rented a shack in Area 4 of Old Naledi, and later bought a plot with a mud hut. When the couple heard that the SHHA was 'decongesting' Areas 4 and 8 and allocating new plots, they 'self-allocated' their current plot in Area 2, which was later formalised during upgrading. The respondent lives with two children and nine grandchildren (including two orphans, one of her daughters having died). She has never had waged employment and, after her husband's death, became a street vendor (which she stopped when her daughters started having children). At acquisition, they built a shack with plastics and sticks, then two mud huts, then a two-room house, later extended by three rooms, all funded by her husband's salary from piece jobs and building work. She now rents out three rooms (at P100 each per month) to supplement her old age pension. She would like to build a bigger house with piped water, but lacks funds, or (because the surrounding area is dirty and over-crowded) wants to move to a better-serviced area. On credit, she said: 'Over my dead body! I cannot use this plot to access a bank loan. What if I fail to pay and the bank takes my plot! My husband died here, and he left me on this piece of land and I will also die here, unless I am moved by council to another area.'

### Case 3: 'You end up in prison'

The respondent lives with seven children and a grandchild. She came to Old Naledi in 1980, to Area 5, with two mud structures and a hut on her plot, but was relocated under the upgrading programme, and used her compensation to develop her new plot with two rooms, to which her children added three two-room blocks, with one room currently being used as a kiosk. She also has a residential plot and a ploughing field in her home village. To supplement her pension, she works for a project building the national stadium, brews traditional beer and is a traditional healer. She knew little about plot hypothecation for credit, but said: 'I don't want to find myself in money-related problems because you end up imprisoned.'

### Case 4: 'I am not interested'

A man and woman moved from Lobatse to Gaborone in 1974 to look for better jobs. Initially on a plot in Area 8, they were regularised by the SHHA in 1979, and built a two-room structure, followed in 1986 by a six-roomed house. The man worked as a plumber for Gaborone City Council from 1974 to 1999, the woman as a house-maid until 1994. They complained:

> Our government has a system of taking people's land without giving them other plots and the compensation is too low. We should go to government with our goods and stay with them ... Government allocate us plots but we do not have powers when government wants to demolish our plots. We are being abandoned now that they have depleted our strength. The Bible advocates for our control over land, but this government has turned itself into little gods.

When asked about future improvements, they said: 'It is hard to think of any developments because the banks do not give us elders money, NDB give loans to young people only.' They knew about hypothecation, but said: 'My child, this is one way used by government to confiscate people's plots. I am not interested! If you are not careful with some of these things, you will end up in trouble.'

## Patriarchy, inheritance and land

Extended families are still important in Botswana, and plot-holders often retire to their villages, leaving children in charge of their peri-urban plots (particularly common in Old Naledi, with its older average age of residents). The circumstances of plot development and ownership may be problematic and contentious, particularly when the current resident of the plot is the daughter of the plot-holder. Of the respondents. 70% were women heading low income households: 40% were single, 24% widowed and 24% married (the remaining either divorced or cohabiting). 85% were unemployed, 40% were pensioners, while 29% relied on rented accommodation as income. Cases 5 and 6 clearly illustrate the prevalence of patriarchy in matters relating to land titling.

Figure 5: Rental housing. A plot-holder in Mogoditshane stands on foundations of original round hut (now demolished), with the base of another demolished structure to left, rental housing behind, and building materials to right (courtesy: R Home 2002)

## Case 5: 'Property that is more important belongs to sons not daughters'

A single woman, from Siviya in North Eastern Botswana, stays with her three sisters and a brother (none fully employed, but doing casual or piece jobs), her four children and one grandchild. She came to Gaborone in 1993 and the plot she currently lives on belongs to her father. Following the death of her mother, her father went back to the home village, handing over the plot to her to look after. Her living expenses are met mainly from a tuck-shop, and she forwards the rent from three shacks on the site to her father. Her father came to Gaborone in the 1960s for work, rented a shack in Area 8, then found an empty space and built his own shack. When, in the 1980s, Gaborone City Council through the SHHA was trying to reduce congestion, he was moved and allocated his current plot. At acquisition, the plot was undeveloped, and he built two shacks, subsequently replaced by more permanent mud structures. He later used his salary to build 'two-and-half' cement structures, later extended to 'three-and-half'. The respondent's partner (now deceased) then built a tuck shop for her. She never thought of further improving the plot because of inadequate resources. The certificate was with her father in their home village. She was well aware of the possibilities of plot hypothecation, but was not interested because the plot would pass to her brother:

> In our tradition land, livestock and other major property that are more important to life are inherited by sons not daughters. You know, we women we are really cursed, my father gave me authority to look after this plot because the only son he has (my brother) is still young. When he comes of age he will tell me to move out, no matter what development I could have carried out here. Land is not for us women, whether you are married or not. In your father's home you do not have inheritance, especially land, it is only accumulated for your brothers, and in your home with your husband the property is his and the inheritance goes to his son. When he dies, no matter whether you are still alive, you know that after his death you lose the ownership and control of property.

### Case 6: 'I don't know where they get this law'

A woman, aged 37, from Lerala, has lived in Gaborone since 1981, staying with her four children, sister, two daughters and son. She has never worked except for occasional piece jobs, and lets two rooms out at P75 per month each. Her sister works in a firm and helps with groceries. Her mother was given this plot by her uncle, who 'self-allocated' it in the mid-1970s and had since retired to his home village and passed the plot to her mother, who received a COR from the SHHA. At that time, the plot had two structures roofed with iron sheets, and the mother (a street vendor) built a 'two-and-half' with pit-latrine. The respondent maintains that she helped her mother develop the plot, contributing income from her casual jobs, but, when her mother died and she tried to change ownership to herself, the SHHA office determined that the plot should be inherited by the youngest son in the family. 'I do not know where they get that rule from. It means I cannot even develop the plot!' Her uncles and grandmother support the SHHA decision, and so she wants nothing more to do with this plot, only to find a husband and leave. Because of the patriarchal nature of Botswana society, women lose out in these complex encounters. Although they may have had an important part in the development of the two plots described above, that is not considered when it comes to inheritance, and the brothers take the plot.

### Multiple sources of livelihoods

Income can come from renting rooms and informal commercial activities, such as beer-selling and tuck shops, and, in Mogoditshane, the sale of land. Over 80% of the plot-holders surveyed let out accommodation, usually with at least one structure specifically for renting. These houses, variously called 'train-houses' and hostels, were usually arranged in a row, each room leading into a yard with communal facilities (pit-latrines and standpipes). Rentals range from P100–P300 per month. Like the tuck shops that sell goods in small quantities (for example, cigarettes sold singly), rented accommodation in Mogoditshane is available in the smallest possible unit, a room, and the terms 'two-and-half' or 'three-and-half' refer to a number of rooms, the half being the kitchen. Family members may build rental rooms on a plot held by one of them, a son or daughter on the parental plot, with family members supporting each other financially; the rent goes to the developer, not the plot-owner. In Mogoditshane, 59% of respondents' plots had been undeveloped at the time of acquisition, and a further 32% had just one mud structure. Social networks contribute to fund-raising for plot improvement, remittances from relatives in 38% of interviews, while in Old Naledi building is often funded by the plot-holder's children. Rental income is generally undeclared and untaxed. Small-scale commercial activities include beer-parlours (*shebeens*, also known as *spoto* = spot), tuck shops (popularly known as *semausu*), car-repairs and brick-moulding. In Old Naledi, 25 of the 30 respondents had such businesses, contravening planning and building controls but tolerated or overlooked in practice.

## Extralegal Land Subdivision and Sale in Mogoditshane

Extralegal land subdivision and sale is a major activity in Botswana's peri-urban areas that has caused conflict between government and land-owners, most markedly in Mogoditshane. In 1992, the government instituted a presidential commission of inquiry into the land problems in Mogoditshane and surrounding areas, starting from the premise that 'in Mogoditshane and other neighbouring villages people do as they like with the land. They subdivide *masimo*, change use to residential plots, sell and allocate plots without the involvement of any lawful authority' (Kgabo Commission 1991: v). The Commission showed a good appreciation of the circumstances of extralegal land transactions in Mogoditshane and recommended that:

> ... the form and severity of punishment must in the interest of justice, take cognisance of mitigating factors, if any ... all wrong doers had no alternative plots available on which to build houses. All the agencies had turned their backs on these poor houseless people who legitimately had secured jobs in towns and had an opportunity to build a descent future for themselves and their families.

The Commission toured the villages, held public meetings, interviewed some 400 individuals and found over 800 illegally created plots, along with a general collapse of the legal procedures for allocating land. Specific abuses included unauthorised subdivision, unauthorised change of use from *masimo* land to residential, unauthorised sales, and irregularities in TLB procedures. According to the commissioners, this 'eating up of agricultural land by towns and villages' means that 'the best arable soils do not grow crops for human consumption but they grow houses for human shelter' (Kgabo Commission 1991: 110–12).

According to the Commission, illegal occupation was a result of non-delivery on the part of the government. The BHC had a waiting list of over 20,000 applications, the Department of Surveys and Mapping and the Department of Town and Regional Planning had no plots to offer, the SHHA scheme was frozen and could not help, TLB activities were frozen, while the Ministry of Local Government, Lands and Housing was not giving proper guidance to its agencies. The Commission saw clearly the link between non-delivery by government and lawlessness by the community: 'it is internationally an acceptable principle that when a government ignores the aspirations of its people, it loses the right to rule' (Kgabo Commission 1991). Such brave pronouncements should be understood in terms of its composition. The Commission was chaired by an ex-Minister, while the vice chairperson was a highly influential, outspoken and widely respected former civil servant and businessman. Other members included a former MP, former civil

**Figure 6: House foundations cut across unmade road. Unauthorised foundations for a house on illegal subdivision at Mogoditshane, with completed house in background (courtesy: R Home 2001)**

servants and legal practitioners from the private and public sector. The secretariat was drawn from the public sector.

Those involved with extralegal land transactions in Mogoditshane included *masimo* owners who supplied land to individuals from different income groups, but were usually individuals with steady incomes who could afford the prices quoted. Evidence to the Kgabo Commission indicated that prices for a 1600 sq m plot ranged from P400–10,000 (Kgabo Commission 1991: 25). The Commission observed that those involved in the extralegal land transactions were well aware of the illegality of their activities, and were indeed uncontrite and defiant in their evidence. The holders of tribal land rights, often handed down over several generations, believed they owned their land in perpetuity and could sell, subdivide or convert it to other uses, while no effective sanctions were available to the TLBs (Habana 2000). Participants in the extralegal transactions felt justified in their action, both because government had failed to allocate enough affordable housing land and because leading Batswana, including senior politicians, were exploiting the situation. 'Why should they sit back when these responsible people accumulate large chunks of land and enrich themselves?' (Kgabo Commission 1991). Such views were sparked by an incident in which land compulsorily acquired for a commercial centre was transferred by the Minister to an MP, overruling the TLB decision.

While sales of peri-urban plots benefit both purchasers and buyers, the unco-ordinated manner of the transactions caused concern, as did, in particular, the involvement of two cabinet Ministers. The situation was seen to be exploited by those in power for reasons of personal aggrandisement. The Commission recommended a tough line: 'Tribal land is our land, it is not to be sold ... We have to be ruthless. If people have acquired land illegally they have to suffer the consequences' (Kgabo Commission 1991: vi and 72).

The Commission's findings were published, and Government White Paper No 1 of 1992 provided an analysis and possible remedies to the identified problems, which can be summarised as follows:

- *Lawlessness*

Residents of peri-urban areas subdivide their *masimo* (ploughing fields), offer them for sale and new owners start building houses, contrary to the provisions of the Tribal Land Act that require customary land to be conveyed only by the TLB through a lease. Field-owners either sell the whole land, or subdivide it into 40m x 40m plots (1,600 sq m) and sell at prices ranging from P2,500–5,000 per plot. According to the Commission, these illegal land transactions are motivated by factors such as delays in land allocation by the TLB, convenient location of the fields, high land demand, and the amount of and delay in compensation.

- *TLB compensation*

Field-owners/occupiers complained that compensation was inadequate, with subdivision and sale giving better returns on the open market. The government maintained that tribal land was not owned by individuals and so could not be sold, with compensation payable for improvements only when it was required for public purposes under the Tribal Land Act (such as housing development). Irrespective of the location of tribal land, uniform compensation guidelines operated countrywide, making TLBs powerless to negotiate in recognition of local market conditions. The government tripled the then compensation payable to P700 per hectare in 1992, further increased it to P800 in 1998 and to P1,950 in 2000, yet these increases still did not match up to the 1992 open market prices, under which one hectare subdivided into 6 plots could get P15,000–30,000 (over 40 times higher than the official compensation).

- *Influx of people to peri-urban villages*

The high and unaffordable prices of serviced land and the shortage of housing was driving people into the peri-urban areas, with the attraction of tribal land greatest to those who could not afford official plots. Those with houses in Gaborone were paying field-owners market prices way beyond TLB compensation guidelines.

- *Lack of enforcement*

Illegal development was uncontrolled, with both TLBs and District Councils powerless to apply the legal provisions of the Tribal Land and Town and Country Planning Acts to curb the deteriorating situation. The government established a Land Tribunal to improve dispute resolution over land matters.

- *Establish a subordinate land board*

The immediate establishment of a subordinate land board was recommended for the area with greatest conflict (Mogoditshane), to be managed by a senior government officer (deputy board secretary) and provided with a survey section of qualified land surveyors.

- *Illegally acquired land*

All illegally acquired but unused and undeveloped land was supposed to revert to the TLB. Usually, undeveloped land in peri-urban areas had been ploughing fields allocated long before the TLBs were instituted, and ownership was difficult to prove, since chiefs did not hand over any records and land boards did not pursue them either.

- *Mandatory P5000 fine*

Those who had acquired land illegally, as identified by the task force in 1992, were to pay a minimum penalty fee of P5,000 per 1,600 sq m plot. About 3,000 individuals had this mandatory fine imposed, but by April 1999 only 99 had fully paid, while a further 18 were paying by instalments, contributing a total of only P680,000. There was a trade-off for paying the fine in the form of an automatic customary lease from the TLB, but most plot occupiers felt that the field-owners should pay the fine, since they had already paid.

## After Kgabo

Two test cases went before the courts. The Court of Appeal in one gave field-owners the right to dispose of their fields to whomever they wished, legalising allocations by field-owners before 8 July 1994 and compelling the TLB to issue titles for such land. The second case involved an individual who bought land and built an expensive house. The TLB petitioned the High Court and got an eviction order, but on appeal the Minister waived the court order. Thus, both cases failed to uphold the tribal land system, favouring occupiers' rights.

To implement the White Paper, a task force was instituted to monitor illegal land developments, assisted by nine police officers. The task force found that the TLB had effectively no records, and large-scale up-to-date maps of the area were not available, and so brought in the Department of Surveys and Mapping to map all subdivisions and structures. Illegal land development still continued, with the task force powerless to do more than warn the people to stop.

Throughout the 1990s, the remedial measures proved ineffective. Mogoditshane remained the fastest growing 'urban village' in the country (increasing its population from 14,246 in 1991 to 38,816 in 2001, at a rate of over 10% per annum). The plot demand as estimated by the government rose from 20,000 to 30,000 between 1993 and 1997 (Habana 2000). The Department of Town and Regional Planning in 1992 prepared detailed layout plans for 24,000 residential plots, based upon the planning area that had been declared in 1986, but permissions for subdivision and change of use had not kept up with change, and detailed planning layouts were ignored on the ground. The biggest test of the official planning process came when surveyors went on the ground to start placing beacons, only to find physical structures (houses, fences, etc) and land occupiers denying them access. The surveyors had no authority to remove obstructing property, and the TLB was powerless to act. The government offered inadequate compensation to acquire land for planned development under the standard national guidelines, making no allowance for land pressures, and thus was trying (ineffectually) to deny people the betterment value from their land and a chance to participate in the development gain from urban expansion.

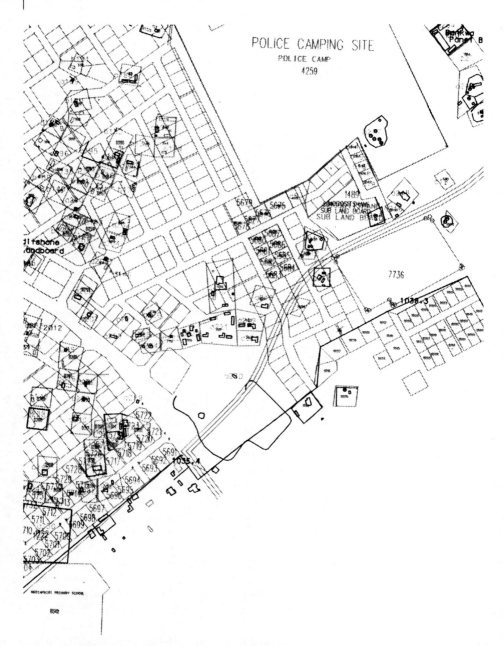

**Figure 7: Plan of illegal development in Mogoditshane. The official (unimplemented) layout is shown overlaid on the illegal subdivisions and developments, which follow different road alignments (courtesy: DSM, Botswana 2002)**

A tough stance against extralegal land subdivision and sale began in 2001. The period leading up to it was characterised by bitter confrontation between field-owners and government. The para-Statal corporations, such as the Botswana Power Corporation, had placed their infrastructure according to the approved plans, but high-voltage power lines could not be switched live without physically removing the structures that had been illegally erected beneath them. In some instances, plot-holders refused to make way for the planned layouts, and some of the more enterprising even prepared their own allocation lists and passed them over to the TLB as a basis for negotiation.

In 2001, residential developments viewed by the State as illegal began to be demolished, effected by the Kweneng TLB under the Tribal Land Act. Much consternation ensued, and protest reached a climax at a meeting in Mogoditshane addressed by the President of Botswana, who reaffirmed the government's view of the land crisis as simple lawlessness. In his address, a visibly angry President Mogae likened illegal land subdivision and sale to rape ('what you have done is like rape, it is not allowed', *Gazette*, 18 October 2000). The heated meeting was shown on the country's only television station, prompting a headline in the *Gazette* 'Sparks fly in Mogoditshane'. The meeting was largely interpreted as having been hijacked by political party politics, with those against the demolitions including the former MPs for Mogoditshane and Gaborone West and councillors from the opposition BNF. A later delegation, led by the MP for Mogoditshane, apologised to the President on behalf of the Mogoditshane people for the heated meeting. This conciliatory gesture was widely viewed as showing the good nature of Botswana and their concern for

**Figure 8: House marked for demolition. This modern house, illegally built, has been marked for demolition with a painted red cross (left of door) (courtesy: R Home 2001)**

the rule of law, but also showed the country's patron-clientilist politics at work and the tendency to appease those in power for future reward. This means that controversial issues are not openly debated, but reduced to partisan politics, making it more difficult to find alternative and perhaps innovative policy interventions in land issues. The ruling BDP sees land problems in Mogoditshane as manipulated by opposition parties seeking to discredit the ruling party and bring the electorate into their fold.

## Conclusions

Various conclusions can be drawn from the story of land titling and peri-urban development in Old Naledi and Mogoditshane. Perhaps the most obvious is the seemingly retrogressive and conservative position adopted by the State in Botswana towards extralegal land transaction, a position not found in the two other countries studied. While, in the late 1970s, the government had a policy of accommodation and tacit recognition of self-allocation of residential plots in what were then seen as squatter settlements, the same government has of late adopted a tough stance, best described as zero tolerance, towards extralegal land transactions, as evidenced by the 2001 demolition of developments viewed as illegal by the State. The present zero tolerance stance of the government runs contrary to other countries' approach and to neo-liberalist thinking that recognises the role and contribution of other actors involved in the city building process.

On the issue of land title and poverty alleviation, evidence from both Mogoditshane and Old Naledi suggests that conferment of land title to plot-holders did not encourage them into using their titles for hypothecation. Most plot-holders were engaged in informal sub-letting (erecting rentable space – the so called 'two-and-half' or 'three-and-half'), which may help alleviate poverty by bringing in extra income, often undertaken without recourse to bank loans. The thesis that land titling leads to poverty alleviation is thus not supported, because land title alone is not perceived as a sufficient condition for obtaining credit. Financial institutions tend to look at other aspects of creditworthiness before determining an applicant's eligibility.

## References

Colclough, C and McCarthy, S (1980) *The Political-Economy of Botswana: A Study of Growth and Distribution*, Oxford: OUP

Cook, D and Kirke, J (1989) 'Experiences and reassessment' in Meilke, S and Safier, M (eds), *Cities and People: Can We Plan the Future?*, London: DPU Working Paper 57

Dickson, W (1990) *Land Tenure and Management in a Developing Country: The Case of Botswana 1966–1985*, Gaborone: UB National Institute of Development Research and Documentation Working Paper 54

DTRP (Department of Town and Regional Planning) (1998) *Greater Gaborone Structure Plan*, Gaborone: Government Printer

Dunleavy, P and O'Leary, B (1987) *Theories of the State: The Politics of Liberal Democracy*, London: Macmillan

Good, K (1992) 'Interpreting the exceptionality of Botswana' *Journal of Modern African Studies* 30(1): 65–95

Good, K (1993) 'At the ends of the ladder: radical inequalities in Botswana' *Journal of Modern African Studies* 31(2): 203–30

Habana, G (2000), 'Field owners or squatters? Practical issues of land title and peri-urban settlement in Botswana', unpublished MSc thesis, School of Surveying, University of East London

Hardie, G (1980) 'Tswana design of house and settlement: continuity and change in expressive space', unpublished PhD thesis, University of Boston

Hardie, G (1982) 'The dynamics of the internal organization of the traditional capital, Mochudi' in Hitchcock, RR and Smith, MR (eds), *Settlement in Botswana: The Historical Development of a Human Landscape*, Gaborone: Heinemann and Botswana Society

Harvey, C and Lewis, S (1990) *Policy Choices and Development Performance in Botswana*, London: Macmillan

Heap, D (1974) *Review of Town and Country Legislation*, unpublished report to Minister of Local Government and Lands, Botswana

Holm, J (1985) 'The State, social class and rural development in Botswana' in Picard, L (ed), *The Evolution of Modern Botswana*, Lincoln: University of Nebraska

Holm, J (1988) 'Botswana: a paternalistic democracy' in Diamond, J (ed), *Democracy in Developing Countries* (vol 2), London: Boulder

Home, RK (2001) 'Eating farmland, growing houses: peri-urban settlements and customary land tenure in Botswana, Southern Africa' *Trialog* 69: 30–35

Kalabamu, F (2001) 'Effects of gendered land rights on urban housing by women in Botswana', paper to conference on land tenure issues, Cape Town, South Africa

Kgabo Commission (1991) *Report of Presidential Commission of Inquiry into Problems in Mogoditshane and other Peri-urban Villages*, Gaborone: Government Printer

Low, N (1991) *Planning, Politics and the State: Political Foundations of Planning Thought*, London: Unwin Hyman

Molebatsi, C (1994) 'Towards understanding policy practice disjunction in urban planning: a case study of Kanye, Botswana', unpublished PhD thesis, University of Newcastle-upon-Tyne

Molebatsi, C (1996) 'Towards a sustainable city: Gaborone, Botswana' *Ambio* 25(2): 126–33

Molomo, M (1989) 'The bureaucracy and democracy in Botswana' in Holm, J and Molutsi, P (eds), *Democracy in Botswana*, Gaborone: Macmillan

Molutsi, P (1989) 'The ruling class and democracy in Botswana' in Holm, J and Molutsi, P (eds), *Democracy in Botswana*, Gaborone: Macmillan

Molutsi, P and Holm, J (1990) 'Developing democracy when civil society is weak: the case of Botswana' *African Affairs* 89(356): 323–40

Murray, A and Parsons, N (1990) 'The modern economic history of Botswana' in Konczacki, Z et al (eds), *Studies in the Economic History of Southern Africa (Vol 1: Frontline States)*, London: Frank Cass

Noppen, D (1982) *Consultation and Non-Commitment: Planning with the People in Botswana*, Leiden: African Study Centre

Parsons, J (1983) 'The trajectory of class and State in dependent development: the consequence of new wealth for Botswana' *Journal of Commonwealth and Comparative Politics* 21(3): 38–60

Parsons, J (1984) *Botswana: Liberal Democracy and Labour Reserve in Southern Africa*, Boulder, Colorado: Westview Press

Parsons, J (1985) 'The labour reserve in historical perspective: toward a political economy of the Bechuanaland Protectorate' in Picard, L (ed), *The Evolution of Modern Botswana*, Lincoln: University of Nebraska

Parsons, J (1990) 'Succession, legitimacy, and political change in Botswana 1956–1987' in Parson, J (ed), *Succession to High Office in Botswana: Three Case Studies*, Ohio: Ohio UP

Picard, L (1979) 'District councils in Botswana: a remnant of local authority' *Journal of Modern African Studies* 17(2): 285–308

Picard, L (1980) 'Bureaucrats, cattle and public policy: land tenure changes in Botswana' *Comparative Political Studies* 13(3): 313–56

Picard, L (1987) *The Politics of Development in Botswana: A Model of Success?*, Boulder: Lynne Reiner

Picard, L and Morgan, P (1985) 'Policy, implementation and local institutions in Botswana' in Picard, L (ed), *The Evolution of Modern Botswana*, Lincoln: University of Nebraska

Reilly, W (1983) 'Decentralisation in Botswana: myth or reality?' in Mawhood, P (ed), *Local Government in the Third World: The Experience of Tropical Africa*, Chichester: John Wiley

ROB (Republic of Botswana) (1979) *District Planning Hand Book*, Gaborone: Government Printer

ROB (1984) *Francistown Development Plan*, Gaborone: Government Printer

ROB (1985a) *National Development Plan 1985–1991*, Gaborone: Government Printer

ROB (1985b) *Report of Workshop on Extended Gaborone Planning Area*, Gaborone: Government Printer

ROB (1986) *Kanye Development Plan 1986–1996*, Gaborone: Government Printer

ROB (1987) *Report of the Working Group to Facilitate the Provision of Serviced Land: Part 1 Urban Areas*, Gaborone: Ministry of Local Government and Lands

ROB (1989a) *Southern District Development Plan IV*, Gaborone: Government Printer

ROB (1989b) *Report of the Review of the Tribal Land Act and other Land Related Issues*, Gaborone: Government Printer

ROB (1989c) *Report on the First Physical Planners Workshop*, Gaborone: Government Printer

ROB (1990a) *Introduction of Town and Country Planning Act 1977 to Major Villages in Botswana: Consultation Report*, Gaborone: Government Printer

ROB (1990b) *Report on the Proceedings of the Third Physical Planners Seminar*, Gaborone: Government Printer

ROB (1991a) *Report on the Proceedings of the Physical Planners Seminar on Plan Implementation*, Gaborone: Government Printer

ROB (1991b) *National Development Plan 1991–1997*, Gaborone: Government Printer

ROB (1991c) *Population Census Preliminary Results*, Gaborone: CSO

ROB (2000) *Botswana Multiple Indicator Survey: End of Decade Review for the World Summit for Children*, Gaborone: CSO

Segodi, R (1990) 'Financing district planning in Botswana' in Helmsing, AHJ and Wekwete, KH (eds), *Subnational Planning in Southern and Eastern Africa: Approaches, Finance and Education*, Aldershot: Avebury

Serati, E (1990), 'Urbanization, urban development planning and management in Botswana: an overview', paper to Workshop for Rural and Urban Planners in Southern and Eastern Africa, Harare, Zimbabwe

Silitshena, R (1979) 'Chiefly authority and the organization of space in Botswana: towards an exploration of nucleated settlements among the Tswana' *Botswana Notes and Records* 11: 55–67

Silitshena, R (1984) 'Urbanisation in Botswana' *Norsk Geogr Tidssk* 38: 109–28

Silitshena, R (1990) 'Tswana agro-town and rural economy in Botswana' in Baker, J (ed), *Small Town Africa: Studies in Rural-Urban Interaction*, Uppsala: Institute of African Studies

Southern Africa Regional Poverty Network (SARPN) (2001) *Botswana Poverty Reduction Tender*, Newsletter No 4, November

Wiseman, J (1978) 'Conflict and conflict alliances in the Kgatleng district of Botswana' *Journal of Modern African Studies* 16(3): 487–94

# Chapter 6
# Trinidad: 'We Are Not Squatters, We Are Settlers'[1]

*Charisse Griffith-Charles*

## Introduction

The southernmost of the Caribbean States, the nation of Trinidad and Tobago, comprises two islands: Trinidad (4,828 sq km) and Tobago (300 sq km, not included in this study). Colonised successively by the Spanish, French and British, the two islands became one colony in 1889, achieved national independence in 1962, and declared a republic in 1976. The colonial plantation system exposed the country to commodity price fluctuations, but its current reliance upon petrochemicals rather than sugar has made it one of the richest Caribbean countries. Its population (primarily of African and Indian origin) of 1.3 million makes it the second most populous English-speaking Caribbean country (after Jamaica). In spite of its relative prosperity, there is significant poverty, linked to issues of access to land and its colonial history. Private land-ownership was concentrated in large-scale commercial estates, often with absentee proprietors, cultivated first by slaves imported from Africa, then by indentured labourers from East India (Blouet 1977). In the 19th century, both plantation-owners and government were concerned about labour shortages, and land prices were kept high, both on State and private land, to discourage the former slaves and indentured labourers from becoming independent land-owners. Since land, however, was freely available on abandoned estates and unused State land, those not able to buy (including immigrants from elsewhere in the Caribbean) resorted to squatting. Under the threat of eviction, they had little incentive to build more permanent structures, and so developed the building form known as the 'chattel-house', made of temporary materials for easy transportation if required (Wylie 1986; Watson and Potter 1993). Private owners now have 47% of the land, and the State owns the rest, much of it being forest reserve (Smart 1988; Stanfield and Singer 1993). Inequalities in land-ownership invite claims of ethnic and political discrimination, which are difficult to extricate from the historical and cultural idiosyncrasies of the country. The legal and institutional structure and inefficiencies and under-resourcing of State land administration have contributed to such inequalities, while archaic and irrelevant English land law, mixed with other colonial influences, and poor maintenance of the title registers have encouraged informal dealings in property.

The State has periodically attempted to allocate land to those in need of it, although the term 'squatter' with its negative connotations has survived longer in the English-speaking Caribbean than elsewhere in the Third World. The colonial administration from the 19th century would periodically attempt land settlement schemes (Blouet 1977). During the recession of the 1930s, for instance, a government committee was created which in 1944 recommended leasing 15,000 acres to resettle the poor (CO 295/643/2, 1945). After independence, the government built some

---

1 All quotations are from recorded interviews undertaken in the course of the field research, unless otherwise indicated.

**Figure 9: Peri-urban housing on hilly land in Trinidad (courtesy: R Home 2002)**

low-income housing, but the economic decline of the mid-1980s led to increased extralegal occupation and development of land (Gelb 1988; Pamuk 1998), a problem exacerbated by the cost and complexity of formal development and titling, which the Sou-Sou Lands initiative attempted to address (see below). An accelerated land distribution programme attempted to issue new statutory leases for agricultural small-holdings, but was handicapped by bureaucratic procedures.

Thus, government land administration was characterised by various problems: lax management of State lands, inadequate or inappropriate laws, lack of an institutional structure for formalisation and lack of recognition of *de facto* property rights. From the 1980s, various land law reforms were attempted but met with limited success mainly because of lack of implementation capacity. Legislation enacted in 1981 alone included the Landlord and Tenant Act, the Land Law and Conveyancing Act, the Trustee Act, the Limitation Act, the Condominiums Act, the Land Registration Act and the Succession Act.

In the 1990s, the government, with funding assistance from the Inter-American Development Bank, developed a major initiative to improve land management, and within it the Land Use and Policy Administration Project (LUPAP) was aimed to achieve a more open, accessible land market, and address the institutional causes of tenure problems. Research and consultancy support was provided by the Land Tenure Center (LTC) of the University of Wisconsin, and new legislation followed with the State Land (Regularisation of Tenure) Act 1998, the Land Adjudication Act 2000, the Land Tribunal Act 2000 and the Registration of Titles to Land Act 2000, all supporting the systematic titling and registration of land, with mechanisms for clarifying questionable title (Wisconsin LTC 1999).

The Wisconsin LTC researchers attempted to estimate the extent of tenure insecurity in 1991 from a small sample of 219 households (on both private and State land), extrapolating the results against the 1990 census figures of 300,592 households in the country (Stanfield and Singer 1993). The finding was that some 40% of households on private land had inadequate or no documentation; on State land, 48% had no document, and a further 39% had no formal deed or lease. The Land Settlement Agency (2001) estimated the number of squatter households in 1998 at 25,000, which broadly corresponded with LTC estimates, comprising about 8% of the country's population.

Executive capacity and complex procedures delay the process of regularisation, with the Lands and Surveys Division struggling to meet the demand for land from a growing population. State cadastral survey records are often incomplete and inaccurate (Barnes 1995; Opadeyi and McLaughlin 1996). Revised legislation included the Land Surveyors Act 1996 and associated regulations, with draft revisions in 2000 (Griffith-Charles 2002). The topographical map database has been digitised from 1994 aerial photography, and some of the existing paper-based cadastral sheets have been scanned.

Thus, the postcolonial State struggles with the colonial legacy: difficulty in gaining land title, combined with official disapproval of squatting, and poor basic services in some areas. Official attitudes and policy are changing, and there is a growing recognition that the informal structures need to be formalised and that some basic services, even in an unsatisfactory and inadequately planned environment, are better than none. The research interviews for this book revealed widespread scepticism about government, one respondent having waited 26 years for regularisation of his tenure:

> The NHA not giving you no okay, then, to say you could build, you know? People building, some waiting for NHA. I ain't waiting on them.

> The government tell us we can't develop anything as far as I know. Everybody you see here developing is because they take their own risk.

> They [officials] always keep telling us, don't build in concrete, so I am always suspicious of that ... they [the settlers] put up a house in the back there, and they [officials] come and they break down the concrete structure. Yes, they break it down.

> Long time they [NHA] used to push down your fence you know? ... You ain't entitled to put no fence, you already illegal here on the land.

## Pumpkin Vine: the Tenacity of the Family Land Institution

'Family land' as a Caribbean cultural institution symbolises a social response to oppressive colonial land regimes. Defined as co-ownership of land in undivided shares by the descendants of the original purchaser, family land provides a social link between the many members of the 'punkin (or pumpkin) vine family'. Pumpkin vine in the Caribbean describes the tenuous but valued links to distant relatives by analogy with the pumpkin plant, which spreads along the ground over large distances, the main plant linked to the other fruiting plants by branching stems. Even where family land is legally transferred to heirs, it is not uncommon to find a person retaining an interest in a 1/300th undivided share of a parcel. Family land is also variously called

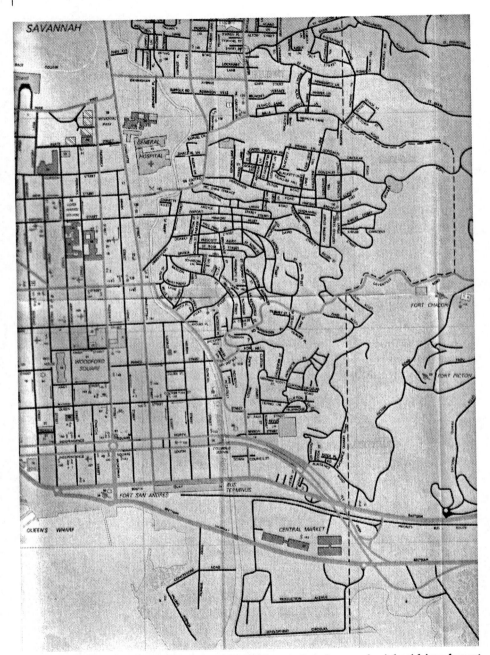

**Figure 10:** Urban and peri-urban Port of Spain. Street plan shows colonial grid-iron layout to the left (with the Savanna park at top and port at bottom), and the unplanned, self-built peri-urban area of East Port of Spain to the right, across the Dry River. Clearance of the unplanned development by compulsory purchase was refused after a judicial inquiry in the 1970s (courtesy: R Home 1992)

generation (or generational) land, children's property, succession ground and (by lawyers) owner-like possession (Crichlow 1994; Maurer 1997). Family land arises typically when the original purchaser dies intestate, and the heirs do not obtain letters of administration (perhaps because of the cost and complex procedures), instead preferring to let the land pass down the generations in undivided shares.

The extent of family land is, by its nature, difficult to quantify. Estimates for different Caribbean islands range from 15% to 35% of land parcels, while Stanfield and Singer (1993) found 12.9% in their Trinidad sample. Official disapproval has condemned family land as preventing agricultural modernisation and withholding land from the market, yet it has deep historical roots, retaining functions of tribal or customary land transferred in memory across the Atlantic (and perhaps also a survival of pre-colonial Caribbean communal land rights). By acquiring title, usually at some cost and difficulty from a hostile land regime, a former slave could re-establish autonomy, kinship and community by consolidating what he might see as customary rights to land, representing a kind of cultural defence against the penetrative effects of global capitalism. The coloniser's law of primogeniture was not followed, nor was African customary land descent (through either paternal or maternal lines), for family land descended in both lines, becoming a positive cultural creation rather than a merely passive retention of African practice. This Creole descent system validated 'illegitimate' kinship lines and bestowed scarce land rights upon the chattel slaves from the pre-emancipation period. Similar tenancy forms had existed in the so called provision grounds, which allowed slaves to grow their own food (in substitution for expensive imported food) and sell the surplus at markets. In the towns, the tenure form of barrack or house-yards provided rooms for rent with a similar pattern of extended family sharing.

The social status of an undivided share of family land exceeds its economic value and symbolises for the individuals such concepts as personhood, prestige, security, status, continuity, solidarity, sovereignty and freedom. The land has a long-term symbolic role, reflected in voluntary non-use of the land while retaining the interest. Residents on family land are often regarded as caretakers, stewards or trustees for the kin group. Plots may be left empty because family members have migrated to the towns or abroad, and absentees in need may return for temporary residence. The land may fragment into multiple house 'spots' with both intensive and symbolic cultivation, based on multi-cropping (which is officially regarded as commercially uneconomic), and the rights of dispersed kin may be symbolised by gifts of food or picking from the fruit trees. Thus family land is an unofficial transformation of freehold into communal tenure, applying different methods of validating and transmitting land tenure (Wilson 1973; Besson 2002).

There are pressures in the opposite direction, from communal toward individual tenure. Those holding the deed documents may be unwilling to part with them. Residents sometimes seek possessory title (thereby excluding absent relatives) so as to access credit, and population growth is increasing competition for land and land values. Nevertheless, official attempts to abolish family land tenure have hitherto failed, and proposed legislation in Jamaica will reinforce its legal status, in recognition of its strong cultural roots, while such land may be recognised through registration as a family trust or tenancy-in-common.

## Certificates of Comfort and the Land Settlement Agency

After the failure of an earlier (1986) Act, the State Land (Regularization of Tenure) Act 1998 was passed, establishing for Trinidad a Land Settlement Agency (LSA) to deliver secure tenure and some settlement planning for the informal occupants of State lands (in Tobago the Act is administered by the House of Assembly). The LSA's statutory responsibilities include the investigation of legal title, the conducting of surveys (sociological, physical and cadastral), the undertaking of planning and research, the establishment of settlement councils for fostering local governance and social cohesiveness, the processing of Certificates of Comfort (COC) and deeds of lease, the creation and maintenance of a database on the process, the fostering of small-scale enterprise, and the adjudication of land disputes. The Act applied to some 250 settlements, which were separately listed in an accompanying schedule but were not identified by reference to a map. Settlements can be added to or removed from the schedule, but not where they are already allocated for non-residential uses, considered environmentally sensitive or required for public purposes.

The COC was a key new feature in the step-by-step procedure under the Act. Certificate of comfort in normal legal practice refers to a letter written by a parent company or a government giving comfort to the lender about a loan made by a subsidiary or public company, which may or may not have legal or contractual effect. In Trinidad, tenure regularisation, the COC is a letter that confirms 'protection from ejectment' to qualifying occupants of State land. It does not create a registrable interest in the land, but gives the holder a personal right that he or she will not be removed from the house plot, unless it is deemed necessary for him or her to relocate and an alternative plot is identified and offered. It is thus an assurance of somewhere to live, either on the 'spot' occupied or an alternative. All squatters living on State land before 1 January 1998 were eligible and, by late 2001, 22,573 applications had been received, with none failing (although some were delayed pending production of supporting documentation). The COC was intended to facilitate connection to services and give those eligible some tenure security while the more thorough legal processes were being addressed. Although not recorded in the Land Registry, it arguably creates an unwritten interest in equity and recognises the permissive possession of the land, but is not accepted by banks. Another unstated implication is that the applicant acknowledges the authority of the State over the land, and thus severs any claim to possessory title that may have been entertained.

The holder of a COC (being a citizen or resident, a legal adult, and not possessing or owning other land in the country) can progress to a non-transferable statutory lease for a fixed 30-year period (upgradable to 199 years) on payment of rent, infrastructure development charges, survey and legal fees and stamp duty (which collectively comprise a not inconsiderable financial cost). To control speculation, within the first five years of the deed of lease period, the government has first option to purchase the land, while subsequent assignment requires official consent.

While intended to be simple, the COC requires considerable resources. A preliminary cadastral survey has to be undertaken to define the legal limits of the settlement, a planning layout formulated and accepted by the planning authority, followed by a subdivision survey, infrastructure construction and the drafting and issue of deeds-of-lease. Individual applications have to be checked against the survey, title investigated and advertised in local newspapers. Since private surveying fees can be $US400 per parcel, the LSA has experimented with GPS technology to reduce costs and prevent multiple claims on the same parcel but has encountered resistance from the vested interests of professional surveyors, who claim their professional fees are being squeezed enough by competitive forces. The plot-holders interviewed were interested in obtaining title, but wary of the cost:

> I would be willing to pay, under my terms ... I have a wife and a little son, my salary is not big, cost of living is very high, so when they come if they come to an understanding like that, which I will really appreciate.

In 2001, the UNC government summarised its tenure regularisation achievements to the Istanbul+5 Habitat conference (LSA 2001), as follows:

(a) acceptance of applications from 85% of the estimated 25,000 squatter households on State lands;

(b) conferral of 448 letters of comfort;

(c) regularisation of expired tenancies on State land with 88 30-year statutory leases and nine 199-year leases;

(d) training of 500 low income households in the construction of low cost starter homes (based upon research and development by its Shelter Support Centre);

(e) infrastructure for 600 serviced plots, reserved for low income households, large households and persons with disabilities.

A new PNM government succeeded the UNC government and is, at the time of writing, redirecting the work of the LSA.

## Case Study Methodology and General Findings

The DFID research project in Trinidad visited four case study areas for survey interviews, chosen to represent a variety of peri-urban, low income settlements without formal titles. Peri-urban areas were defined as being along or adjacent to the urbanised routes, with densities of at least 16 households per hectare. Numbers of households were estimated from 1998 aerial photographs (although settlements have grown since), and 97 households were interviewed during the first half of 2002 (some being tape-recorded). Three of the settlements were on State land, listed for regularisation in the 1998 Act as follows:

(1) Race Course (Arouca South): 28 interviews conducted (of about 200 households).

(2) Bois Bande (near the town of Sangre Grande): 20 interviews (of about 150 households).

(3) Bon Air (in the Northern Range): 24 interviews (of about 160 households).

The fourth case study, Carlsen Field in central Trinidad, was private land, unofficially subdivided by the Sou-Sou Lands Company, but, unlike other Sou-Sou Lands projects, the occupants remained in tenure insecurity. Twenty-five households were interviewed there (of about 200). In addition, interviews were conducted with government officials and banks.

Female-headed households represented a quarter of those interviewed (fairly evenly distributed between the case study areas). There are no restrictions in Trinidad law on women's access to land, and the LSA encourages women (of whatever marital status) to apply for title. Some inappropriate attitudes, however, remain, such as the LSA progress report statement that settlement design should reflect tasks 'traditionally performed by women'. Most respondents felt that women had the same opportunities as men (or better) to acquire land, often helped by the children's absent father or a new male figure in a 'visiting' relationship. Financial status was seen as more important than gender ('the rich go get it faster'). As respondents said:

> It would be equal. For example when I was working in the Cayman Islands it was I who came home and bought the land with my money. I went straight to them and bought my land, it wasn't a problem. I don't think we have that problem here about buying land at all (from a woman).

> I think it fair enough. Everybody would like to have their own. Even though somebody and their husband should break up there is equal rights for the woman.

> Equal! Even a little better. Whereas people will help women you think anybody would come and help me? (from a man).

> If a woman come inside this area and want a tree cut down ... unless she have a man alongside her, she can't pull a cutlass, pull a rake.

Asked about sources of income, 52% of the households interviewed had regular income (although often small), the highest proportion being in Carlsen Field (84%) and the lowest in Race Course (10%). Average monthly income per household of three or four was about US$320 in Race Course, US$376 in Bon Air and US$212 in Bois Bande; incomes were significantly higher in Carlsen Field. Salaried income came variously from pensions, public assistance, nursing and construction jobs. Other sources of income covered a wide range: taxi driving or conducting, small shops, remittances from abroad, car painting, domestic work, salvaging, food sales, help from a parent, carpentry and construction work, horse grooming, baking, fishing, barbering and bartending. 'You get a little something to do and you make it do.' 'Sometimes months pass (to tell you the truth) and I don't work for a dollar.' Few relied on agriculture for a living (even when squatting on agricultural land), but gardening on plots supplemented income: 'Like half of the year you could plant garden and live and half of the year you have to be looking for little hustle, is only rainy season you could plant.'

Plot sizes varied around the generally recognised plot size of 5,000 sq ft (50 ft x 100 ft). The word 'averaging' was used to describe how the informal settlers, without benefit of a formal survey, laid out their plots by pacing out. They felt the official plot size was sufficient for most needs: enough space to distance the latrine suitably from the living area and for an allotment (provision ground):

> If you don't have a lot, you can't put latrine and shower-bath and these type of things, you understand? Or plant a little pepper or something. Look I have a portugal here; I have a peas there. If you have land you could plant about ten tree of tomatoes and see about them, or an acre, you could get about five hundred dollar.

> I have a piece which I feel is a lot ... It is not quite a lot because everybody just average a piece. I halfway measure it then, it smaller than a lot. But I say when the real people come they will give me it. But if it 40 x 80 or however I measure it, I have it right now. I satisfied.

If I have to get less (ie surrender some land) to make another person comfortable, I happy with it.

With the exception of Carlsen Field, the homes visited were mostly constructed of galvanised iron roofing sheets (cheap and often salvaged second-hand), which enables the house to be moved easily if necessary (a legacy of the uncertainties of the colonial chattel-house). 'I did build a little galvanise house on the land, they could have come and break down that any minute.' The occupiers had little choice but to use cheap, discarded wood: 'I had old wood from an old house ... what I couldn't use, they had weevil and so on, I throw them out and I burn them.'

**Figure 11: Galvanised iron house. Self-built house of second-hand roofing materials at Race Course, Trinidad (courtesy: M Ndengu 2001)**

Incremental development occurs as the occupants consolidate their money over a period of time and also become more secure in their tenure. Brick building materials signified security and a willingness to invest and were used in a quarter of the case study areas on State land. In Carlsen Field, all the homes visited were constructed of brick, since, despite the lack of formal deeds of ownership, the occupants felt secure, and household income was higher than on the other settlements.

The settlements generally had one main, well-paved roadway, with access to houses via footpaths. In Bon Air, the government began constructing a new road up the hill to the squatter settlement during 2001, but the project was discontinued with the change of government, leaving a dusty, gravel track (much to the annoyance of the settlement). Sewage disposal was normally to individually built pit-latrines (sometimes inside the house, with modern sanitary fittings and plumbing connected to water tanks). Water was usually provided by communal standpipes installed and paid for by the residents, often at some distance from their homes, supplemented by occasional water lorries and by plastic drums or tanks for rainwater run-off from roofs. Transportation was usually by taxis, and garbage was sometimes collected by official trucks, sometimes buried or burned locally. Electricity is usually supplied (although not in Bon Air, which was seen as a serious failing), but not all households are connected. Telephone lines are rare, and mobile phones are generally used.

On the issue of mortgages, 26% of those interviewed had attempted to access credit, and those succeeding had regular income. Most of the others were averse to official credit:

> When you go to the bank you have to have something before you get something, but I don't even think that that is wise to do because the few things that my friends give to me the bank going to take away all of it. And then that is one thing I don't believe in, credit.

> I never really put it in thought borrowing money. I always have it in myself that it is better I work. I wouldn't have to study about paying back the bank.

> If you don't have you can't get. You take a loan and the next thing you know they come to take what little you have so where you going?

Financial institutions (one credit union, one mortgage bank) were reluctant to give mortgages without formal tenure and did not accept the COC. They wanted more properties brought into the formal property registration system to increase numbers of potential borrowers, reduce lending risks and enlarge their portfolios, but borrowers' ability to repay (regular income, value of other assets and credit track record) was more important than title deeds.

## The Case Studies: 'Poor People Catching They Tail, Government Jumping in the Mud': Sou-Sou Land in Carlsen Field

In 1987, the International Year of Shelter for the Homeless identified 10 demonstration projects worldwide, one of them being Trinidad's Sou-Sou Land Company, which was described as 'an experiment through private initiative of distribution of home sites to the homeless' and 'an attempt by a former colonial people to discover a novel method of providing land for the landless by drawing on the wisdom of indigenous approaches to self-reliance and the ability to economise in a situation of limited resources' (Habitat 1986).

The concept behind Sou-Sou Land derived from an informal savings institution, traditionally practised in Trinidad and Tobago (the term 'sou-sou' in French patois meaning penny-by-penny). Participants put small sums of money periodically into a communal fund managed by one of the group, and each person in turn would 'draw a hand' or receive all the contents of the communal fund, available for a major deferred purchase. The practice may have been introduced from West Africa through the slave trade and is used at all levels of society (Pamuk 1998). Its advantages are small group sanctions over default, simple administration and a flexible participatory nature. No interest is charged, and a round usually covers one year.

The Sou-Sou Land Company started in 1983 as a private initiative developed by an opposition politician (supported by officials in State housing and settlement agencies), applying the sou-sou principle to self-help housing for the poor. Participants paid in small sums until they reached the cost of a plot and then received an agreement that documented the monies paid, while the fund was used to buy old, abandoned rural estates at low cost, and provide minimal infrastructure and services. Stuesse and Ward (2001) discuss similar schemes for Mexican immigrants to the United States. The first project in Trinidad, with 19 families buying an abandoned estate of 117 acres, ended in eviction by the government, but the company continued over its first three years to buy 2,000 acres, with 12,000 participants and TT$18 million. By 1997, the Sou-Sou Land Company owned 11 projects on a total of some 2,300 acres, with some 400 resident households; the plots sold for US$2,500–5,000 per plot, compared to an estimated open market value for comparable plots of US$8,000–10,000.

The land was not approved for residential use, being usually abandoned estates of the former plantocracy next to existing estate villages, and the company operated in contravention of planning regulations, motivated by a frustration at the shortage of affordable housing land. Success depended on high-level political support guaranteeing acceptance by the State, and the experimental programme of land redistribution was intended to revitalise rural areas, mobilise grass-roots support and strengthen local government through community initiative.

The on-site development began with the 'walk-over': the participants visiting the site, walking over it and planning the development and community organisation, which was based upon small-scale farming organised around family units. Basic infrastructure was to be installed (paved roads, earthen drains, water) by community self-help and local government assistance. Mixed residential and business use was allowed under one roof, with settlers deciding on commercial or industrial activity, livestock rearing, tree-crop or food-crop agriculture so as to inform the settlement design. Parcels could not be resold for a fixed period (to prevent land speculation), and the settlers organised mixed use, environmental sanitation, fragmentation and land speculation themselves through area committees, with technical teams for planning, land surveying, engineering and project management (Sankersingh 2002; Laughlin 1986). It was thus a precursor to the 1998 tenure regularisation programme.

Some of the Sou-Sou Land settlements were successfully regularised, with infrastructure and title deeds provided, but this did not occur in Carlsen Field, where the soil conditions on the hilly site were held to be unsuitable for soak-away foul drainage, and so planning permission for housing subdivision was withheld pending the installation of an expensive sewerage treatment plant (although householders claim that their individual soak-aways are adequate). Roads were poorly maintained by the residents, and the government refused to improve or adopt them. Investing in the settlement risked dooming the home-owner to an unsaleable asset, with no access to credit and no infrastructure upgrade.

Fifty-six per cent of the households interviewed had lived there since inception of the project in the late 1980s, but others, frustrated by the lack of improvements, had sold up within the last five years. Some homes had been abandoned, probably for financial reasons or lack of potential purchasers:

> We have a committee. Well, just who living here does really pay those who have land and not living here, so what we does you are supposed to pay $10 an acre or part thereof, we does pay $20 a head ...

One householder expressed his frustrations about the scheme, the community's inability to resolve the tenure problems and the inadequacy of government programmes:

> Somebody come to find out what going on here, because I find it's stupidness. And poor people catching they tail. Don't mind you see what going on here, is my pension money ... They sell us here with the intention that we would get lights, water, and everything ... After paying off that money, when we come – no lights, no water. We had to end up now paying for the lights. To get pole run and all of that, all of our money have to chum up ... they take names, all the houses and so on. And they say all right we'll get our connection. The next thing bills coming in and nobody get pipe ... Yeah, they fool us man ... The smartness with them is they don't want to give the deed, because why? They want to make a profit still on the land, because if they leave they have no claim here again. We have to pay your land tax straight in to the government warden office ... I showing you it is a whole scheme in it and they don't want to give us the deed. A lot of them just talking and they not coming out to say anything.

Another interviewee said: 'We purchase the land already. Is just that we don't have the final deed ... They will have to kill me if is anything ... I build the house, but the most important thing is to get the deed. When you get the deed you more secure. They will have to buy the land, they will have to buy the house.' Another was using his pension for incremental development on his parcel, secure that:

> This is mine here. This is mine! They can't tell me to go nowhere else again! This is mine! This is bought lands. Is scheme they want to come with and mess up people inside of here ... I didn't bother to go to government because it look like all of them is like going from pillar to post and jumping in the mud.

The interviewee supported the aims of the 1998 Act:

> At the beginning I lose friend and all when I say give UNC a chance. Some say oh Indian, Indian. I say I not racial ... I glad that they raise the old people pension and so on. But ... it's no sense you giving me a hundred dollar and you taking a thousands, millions for yourself. I start to talk about that. And all the road paving they say they pave, what done smooth already. They pave again just for a show? That don't make sense ... Water? ... Look is a big main so 12 or 16 inch main running straight across, and you want to say you can't run water for people in here? All you do is put standpipe and telling people that you taxing them? If is one thing the government is supposed to do is the standpipe rate, they supposed to change that. A lot of people, WASA billing them and they ain't have no water ... If you put water in my yard I will pay water rate (you understand?), but don't tell me you sending bills for me and I don't have water in my yard. Everybody get their own form to fill out whether they want tap in the house, the size of the house and all that.

The interviewee would like credit to develop the plot: 'I would like to do that ... They may send a letter to me, well, look you qualify, or what ... If I can't pay back I not borrowing.' He has built incrementally, placing great emphasis on boundaries of the site: 'That went up first, before I started to build anything. Then I put up a board house, a small board house, and from there I sacrifice, sacrifice. I buy blocks and did that ... I bought the material piece, piece, piece, piece, so if I get a little loan I don't mind.'

## *'Have Mercy on the Ground Dove': Race Course*

Race Course, which takes its name from the adjoining Arima Race Club, lies on State land, leased in 1960 for 99 years. Part of the area was intended for the training, exercising and pasturing of horses, but this was squatted, initially by the grooms, jockeys and other staff of the club, and then expanded onto both the leased State land and neighbouring private land (the boundary between the two being unclear). Those on State land were protected by the 1998 Act, while those on private lands are confident that they will not now be evicted. At the time of the interviews, the LSA had undertaken social (but not cadastral) surveys and allocated numbers to existing dwellings; while the occupants had applied for certificates of comfort, none had been issued. Some dwellings added after the LSA initial surveys were removed, while the fate of others (constructed later by individuals) was undetermined. The oldest household claimed to have been there for 26 years, the average being about 10 years. The stated policy of removal of new households (those added after 1 January 1998) was not rigidly enforced, and there was a general sense that occupation of State land was a right to be enjoyed as a citizen of the country, it being not politically expedient to remove such households. As expressed by the President of the Evergreen Community Group:

> I feel secure because I am a citizen of Trinidad and Tobago. Where I was squatting before I was asked to locate somewhere else and I did so at that time ... I feel more secure as the time goes by because my motivation goes a lot of way in this country ... as citizens of Trinidad and Tobago we have rights. We are not squatters; we are settlers. And this is something they have to change in the Act; don't call us squatters.

**Figure 12: Self-built housing in scattered development, Trinidad (courtesy: R Home 2003)**

Race Course had the most organised community group of the four case study areas, with elected executives, regular meetings and a meeting-house (galvanised iron roofing on iron posts, with seating reclaimed from the race course). A pioneering spirit motivates the occupants to improve both the area and their individual plots. As various respondents stated:

> Whatever you have is that what you develop. Whatever you develop it is that you entitled for.

> We just full up the place, here was swamp, here was water and we full it up. Nobody would even dream to come there. So what we do now, truckloads by the truckloads come, and we had to pay for it. So whatever money we had we prefer use to fill up the land so we could build something to live.

> I had friends. There were people that I worked with, now that I am old they pass by and I ask them for a couple of blocks or a load of sand. Just now a man promised me he would send a load of gravel for me. I was very kind in my young days so in my old days it is paying off.

> We the villagers tend to stick together. We get together and try to speed it up.

Provision of services by the utility companies increased the sense of security on the land: 'that is why we feel secure or they wouldn't have put down all this.' Because of their investment in the settlement, few would willingly relocate if required. Most respondents (71% of 28) claimed to be secure or very secure on the land they occupied ('I still have confidence that I wouldn't be moved'), but would not be absolutely secure unless they held a deed of ownership. 'Of course I would like to have one. Only when you have that you have the real security.' Some felt that the COC would add nothing or remove nothing: 'I did not go for a letter of comfort because I already read about the conditions that if where you live they have to pass a road or they have to build something there.' When asked if the COC would make him feel any more secure, one replied bluntly, 'at all [not at all]'.

The lack of title documents deterred a few from investing in permanent structures: 'I want to go into [concrete] blocks but I don't want to do it unless I surely getting the deed of comfort. I see people done start going block-wise already. I have materials put down but I can't do nothing unless (I get) the deed of comfort.' They saw structures that had been allowed to be constructed by others and gained confidence that they could do the same without fear of demolition: 'So I reach this point now where I am going to start my house. This is not a place for my family. I waiting too long.' Many were only deterred from building more substantial structures by the lack of funding: 'I have no money to walk in a bank ... I want to start to save some for my foundation.'

They had little confidence in State initiatives:

> You are going to feel secure ... if the fellah up there say have mercy on the ground dove down there and throw some feed on the ground for him. Them chicken-hawks and all them feeders in the air that is Manning and Panday (current and former Prime Ministers). Ground dove like me, I feed on the ground, so if you don't throw some feed for me I can't fly high up there to get it.

One of the householders was interviewed in depth. She was 71 years old, had been on her parcel for 26 years, and was raising grandchildren there, living off her State pension, with help from her children and their families close by. She can think of living in no other area:

> Yes I like it. From the time we came here they tell us to cut about 5 acres. So we average it, and we plant grapefruit, orange, all them mango trees that is what we plant. People (counter-claimants) start setting fire, they burn half and I start to get frightened now. And they (the responsible State agency) say you can't build house.

Her definition of security of tenure is simple:

> I want to know that if I can't live here till I dead. To move now in my old age ... That is all I does study ... I will be glad to get one [title deed], very glad to get one, that is what I want. It was me and my husband and them same set of children, one of the daughters over there [on another plot]. They [officials] come and they tell us you can't do that [build without permission of the State]. We had everything down in the back there. We had to let it grow back in bush, but we does clean it. When they come they must have somewhere to throw we.

> Look I plant some young trees there, so that when they (government land agents) come they could see what you plant. We plant all those things: roucou trees, lime trees everything, everything, everything we plant, because it is pure woodland we cut down.

Another respondent, who was 58 years old, was born in St Vincent and came to Trinidad when young to seek a better life. He had come to Race Course seven years before his interview. He saw his role in the settlement as a teacher to the youths of the area: 'I ain't like it, I love it. I ain't satisfied with it, but I love it. And these youths for instance. I try to see if I could sit down and talk to them and try to see if I could find out what in their head ... They get a lot of teaching from me because I old.' He does not want to access credit to develop the parcel: 'If you get the Certificate of Comfort then they might lend you some. If I even take something ... you make a down payment, you leave it in the store and pay for it until you finish. I think it is a little better than taking credit from the store. When you done you done pay for it.' He relies on small carpentry jobs and help from old friends (some of them abroad): 'I buy and then sometimes they pass by and I get something ... I have a friend sometimes send a few cents for me.'

At Race Course, the settlers felt secure on the land, although the government regularisation programme was handicapped by inadequate information on the plots, its own inability to manage its land, and leases which allowed squatting to become entrenched. Feeling secure encouraged occupiers to invest in both their own and communal facilities, but they were mistrustful of credit institutions. There was a strong community spirit, and the acquiescence of the State allowed the improvement of the services by self-help. Regularisation through COC was incomplete, and it seemed that it would make little difference to obtaining credit.

## 'I Rake and I Scrape to Put Up': Bois Bande

Bois Bande, a State-owned forest reserve, was gradually invaded by squatters over the past 15 years and listed for regularisation in the 1998 Act. At Bois Bande, the occupants have acquired a feeling of security from the time elapsed since occupation, and this feeling has increased with the recent provision of some services. An informal land market barely operates now that the LSA has started survey and tenure regularisation under the 1998 Act. Some occupiers felt that the

**Figure 13: Government tenure regularisation and settlement upgrading in progress in hilly area of central Trinidad (courtesy: M Ndengu 2001)**

promise of a COC would improve their security of tenure: 'I feel secure since the LSA, they gave us the deed of comfort. We sure that in the area nobody can't put us out without giving us somewhere else to go.' Others felt secure from having been allowed to live there for the length of time that they had: 'I feel more secure, you have to make yourself secure. Because what make me feel more secure, they [the government] putting lights in the village, they bringing water in the village, they bringing telephone in the village. It make you feel more secure that we could own we place.'

One informant (73 years old) had lived in the settlement for seven years and was patiently awaiting the provision of services: 'Yes, we expecting, but it very slow. If they come reasonable, and we have to, we have to. Things doesn't run free, the government have people working too.' He found the government tolerant towards squatters: 'this is about seven years now, in a different country they done throw you out already. In Trinidad and Tobago, we in a paradise here, man, because I lived a few places, Canada and in the States.'

He feels that he should be compensated if the regularisation process required him to move, 'because me ain't young again to work again, you know. I rake and I scrape, and I rake and I scrape to put up ... if I didn't do this I would be in the ground already outside'. The land he considered unsuitable for farming: 'They say they have a portion for agriculture, but nothing ain't coming. You could watch there and see, you see cashew? Cashew coming, lime coming, if you plant one or two peas yes but any other thing, it acid, acid ... When it is dry season, it hard like concrete, and when rain falling it come sappy.'

**Figure 14: Laying out roads and plots in upgrading programme, central Trinidad (courtesy: M Ndengu 2001)**

Another householder was unlucky in not meeting the regularisation criteria. Allowed by the original occupier to build a small hut on an existing parcel, he had only finished his own house after January 1998:

> I had moved in here before '98 but I didn't have this house. This house started to build and finish in '98. What happen, we had a little galvanise thing. It was really I alone living here. And this block of land was really my father-in-law own. I get a little place to stay right here... In '98 I had to demolish there, it was a little thing I had. The number was on it, but the whole thing just gone through ... They (the LSA) didn't know anything they just demolish everything.

Another informant lived with her three children (aged from one to 18 years) and claimed to be the first person to move into the area, six years earlier:

> I was the first person to come and live inside here, it didn't have nobody. And when my husband was alive (he died now), he make road and thing for material to fix the house ... And then people start coming and coming. So that was years aback. The only house it had here was that one over there and this one. Well, my husband died (I shouldn't say husband because we ain't married), he died. He was working on the house ... and he died.

She now survives on public assistance and help from a male companion:

> I have a mister does visit me you know ... I is a sickly person so I does get public assistance for me and the children, it's TT$480 a month ... So then this father of this one, I picked him up, he helping me. I come and get a child for him, he helping me. I ain't moving to go nowhere, because I have nowhere to go. I don't want to go by my mother.

> I does be frighten here in the night, but thank God the mister come and he wire the house for me and I have a little light to see, because sometimes is only me and my daughter alone here. Maybe as how they find that I am alone living here they would take advantage. But I doesn't study them. I does just pray ... The mister, he put up this wall. He tell me that he would leave some money. I don't want to go, I want to stay here. I mean I here so long, so much years, I had to struggle for what I want. If the mister come and die, everything end up in a hole. God bless me, I picked up another old mister. I getting something (you know), thank God. And then the little public assistance helping me to buy little food, and when I want something, I does put aside a little change. I want something from the store, I go and buy it. I want the next thing from the store, I go and buy it. I take it on terms and finish pay off for it and it coming.

Another respondent moved to Bois Bande two years before, after separating from her husband. She purchased her plot through the informal market but was having difficulty funding the project:

> I bought from that gentleman and he showed me a lot ... I built the house. When I came here it was a little galvanise structure. How I was able to get materials? I have an arrangement with a hardware. The last set of materials I took came to TT$2800. Every month I pay towards the materials I took ... They didn't tell me to put concrete, I put concrete at my own risk – that's my funeral, I'm watching the situation ... I don't have electricity as yet because I don't have the cash. Right now I have three-day work domestic like cleaning, cooking and things. The three days a week for the month I get TT$600 ... I am a bookbinder by trade, I also make fudge and tooloom [a sweet made of molasses and grated coconut] and things, but I started having trouble with my hand.

The financial support that her sister used to provide ended after the respondent began visiting her partner against the sister's advice: 'My sister ... every three months she would send something but now she stopped since I went back home.'

## 'You See from Small You Have to Dream, This Come Like a Dream Too': Bon Air

Bon Air was State land which had been leased to individuals for commercial agriculture in the fertile foothills of the Northern Range, but which had been occupied residentially because of its accessibility to Port of Spain and Arima. High on a hill with a scenic view of the surrounding plains, yet near the urbanised East-West Corridor, the aptly named Bon Air was loved by its inhabitants:

> You see this breeze you getting, I have to enjoy it now because in my old age I might not be able to, it might have so much of concrete structures ... Windy Hill! And we have a river. Talk about river, the water does rush down. It divided, it have a shallow pool, it have a deep pool. You could jump from a height, all kind of thing. Up here nice you know, up here nice. And then we have a spring, it have a place where the water does be filtered, the water cleaner ... we get water all year. You see, if I want to wash tomorrow, I going up there.

About a third of households interviewed had lived there for over 10 years, and two-thirds (63%) felt secure on their land. 'You see from small you have to dream. This come like a dream too.' 'I feel secure. You are not sure to stay where you are, because I don't know this government what they will do.'

One informant moved to Bon Air nine years ago after a relationship ended:

It was very hard for me because my children was smaller and I didn't have the job ... When I came up here everybody wash their hands of me. I shamed the family. ... You trying to do something for yourself but you don't want to depend on them. I came up here I didn't have to ask them for anything. Everything I took it one day at a time ... Like my bigger daughter, she gone away, she just used to sit down and cry and say Mammy, I can't take this. ... If I could have done better ... I trying to see if I could leave something for all you, so I trying to see if I could get the land. She [elder daughter] want to go, I sent her away [abroad]. I have my mother away, like it is a relief, you know, because she [daughter] gone, I know she happy.

She worried about her next in line, a girl of 19 years of age, currently working as a clerk in an office: 'This one want to study, she want to study medicine. Where I getting the money?'

She had little confidence in government programmes and criticised the lack of firm information on tenure upgrading:

It had a big bacchanal here. I wasn't here at the time, I went to work, but they say that these cars come up the road, people looking for the land that they already started to pay for, and we on the land and we ain't start to pay for nothing yet? Big bacchanal, yes, because they already start to make some kind of payment. ... So who could I trust? ... Look, my daughter pick up a drop [took a lift] a time, and the same mister who give her a drop say he paying for land up here, but he say he didn't know the place have no water and no lights. So he come up and say he going back and ask for his money back, and the man talking proper English! You wouldn't have come up here five years ago, you know.

Another informant explained her reasons for squatting:

I from a home with plenty children, my mother had 13 children ... I couldn't stay there. He [partner] from south, he from a home with only boys. And you know when we get together and married and thing ... you have to go on your own. You can't stay by parents no time, so we start renting ... We take chances, like every year we put a room. Is only 2 rooms the house have, you know, a drawing room and a kitchen, to be honest what you seeing there ... That is old thing we use that we got cheap, we buy and we put it, all them ply and thing. It looking good from the outside, but it not good, is very thin ply because that is the box board and thing what come with the vehicles ... This is wood that come from them cars that they assembling in Trinidad, in the factory there ... it is not anything that classic. And the galvanise now is people who change from they roof, they sell me over it for a price, TT$10 a sheet. Them is used already, that must be make about 30 years before they change it. But the important thing that I don't do is to borrow or beg ... I never have an account nowhere. As I say, I never borrow and I never credit goods or foodstuff or anything. It is according to the amount I earn, I live by that.

## Conclusions

All the informants felt relatively secure in their tenure, because of the tolerant State policy, which had evolved over the years from enforcement against squatting (by demolishing at least the most substantial structures), through a politically expedient toleration, to the current initiatives for regularisation and upgrading. The numbers, growth and tenacity of the squatters have forced upon the government a need for more proactive, complex and developed solutions. There are certain key findings from this research that may be used to develop best practice guidelines for land-based poverty alleviation solutions for low income, peri-urban households. These include the following:

- *Solutions for different income groups*

The average income of the Sou-Sou Land settlers in Carlsen Field was higher than those on State land in the other settlements, and solutions that would satisfy the Sou-Sou land settlers would be less applicable to others. Poverty can run the gamut from temporary periodic poverty to chronic poverty. The land allocation solutions provided to alleviate poverty must therefore be tailored to suit the intensity of the problem, and general solutions such as suggested by de Soto (2000) would not be applicable in all cases. Financial institutions are reluctant to honour land, titled or untitled, as collateral for loans if the borrower has no established and stable income. The size and established nature of the informal settlements, together with the histories of those interviewed, show a need for multi-layered, low cost solutions to the problem.

- *Perceptions of security of tenure*

The perceived security of tenure is high and is linked with visible service provision rather than intermediate tenure mechanisms, such as the COC. This suggests that the millions of donor agency dollars being invested in land administration projects, focusing upon land individualisation, land titling, land registration and cadastral development projects, with accompanying legislative change, may not always be cost-effective in meeting development goals.

- *Access to credit*

It is argued that security of tenure, provided through pro-poor titling programmes, allows the new land-owners to access credit, which can be invested in business enterprise and productivity-enhancing ventures. In Trinidad, however, the evidence does not suggest a dramatic increase in land market and economic activity on completion of the land privatisation and land titling programmes. A level of security of tenure already exists without the completion of the programme, and the occupiers of the informal settlements were reluctant to pledge their hard-won plots to obtain credit for improvements. The Trinidad case suggests that the importance of secure tenure, achieved by land privatisation, titling and registration, may lie less in its use as capital to generate market activity and economic development than in the well-being it generates in the individual beneficiaries. The land titling process, together with complementary social and service provision programmes to improve pro-poor opportunities, can help to foster and maintain feelings of well-being, which are far more important than economic development. In the words of the respondent from Bon Air who expressed her appreciation for the intangible benefits of her simple, meagre surroundings: 'Up here nice, you know, up here nice.'

# References

Barnes, G (1995), 'An assessment of the cadastral surveying and land registration system in Trinidad and Tobago', report submitted to the Inter-American Development Bank

Besson, J (2002) *Martha Brae's Two Histories: European Expansion and Caribbean Culture-Building in Jamaica*, Chapel Hill and London: UNC Press

Blouet, BW (1977) 'Land policies in Trinidad 1838–50' *Journal of Caribbean History* 9: 43–59

CO 295/643/2 (1945) *Trinidad Land Allocation Policy*, London: PRO

Crichlow, MA (1994) 'An alternative approach to family land tenure in the Anglophone Caribbean: the case of St Lucia' *New West Indian Guide* 68(1 and 2): 77–99 de Soto, H (2000) *The Mystery of Capital: Why Capitalism Triumphs in the West and Fails Everywhere Else*, London: Black Swan

Dujon, V (1997) 'Communal property and land markets: agricultural development policy in St Lucia' *World Development* 25(9): 1529–40

Gelb, A (1988) 'Trinidad and Tobago: windfalls in a small parliamentary democracy' in Gelb, A and associates (eds), *Oil Windfall: Blessing or Curse?*, New York: OUP

Griffith-Charles, C (2002) 'Developing land survey legislation to support the establishment of geographic and land information systems in Trinidad and Tobago' *Surveying and Land Information Systems* 62(2): 109–14

Habitat (1986) *Report on Settlements*, Nairobi: UNCHS

Home, RK (1993) 'Transferring British planning law to the colonies: the case of the 1938 Trinidad Town and Regional Planning Ordinance' *Third World Planning Review* 15(4): 397–410

Laughlin, I (1986) 'The Sou Sou Land story: a non-governmental, non-profit land reform initiative in Trinidad and Tobago', Port of Spain, Trinidad: UNCHS/Sou-Sou Land Ltd

Lemel, H (1993) 'Data analysis and findings on tenure, documentation and land use' in Stanfield, D (ed), *Land Tenure and the Management of Land Resources in Trinidad and Tobago Part 1: Land Tenure*, Madison, Wisconsin: LTC

LSA (2001) *Trinidad and Tobago Country Report Habitat Agenda Istanbul+5, June 2001*, Port of Spain: Land Settlement Agency

Maurer, B (1997) *Recharting the Caribbean: Land, Law and Citizenship in the British Virgin Islands*, Ann Arbor: Michigan UP

Opadeyi, JAS and McLaughlin, J (1996) 'Cadastral records in Trinidad and Tobago' *Surveying and Land Information Systems* 56(1): 37–42

Pamuk, A (1998) 'The price of land for housing in Trinidad: the role of regulatory constraints and implications for affordability' *Urban Studies* 35(2): 285–300

Sankersingh, L (2002) Personal communication, 13 February

Smart, M (1988) 'A new policy for land distribution and agricultural development' in Robertson, M (ed), *Land Information Management: Problems and Perceptions*, St Augustine: UWI

Stanfield, D and Singer, N (1993) *Land Tenure and the Management of Land Resources in Trinidad and Tobago*, Madison, Wisconsin: LTC

Stuesse, A and Ward, PM (eds) (2001) *Irregular Settlement and Self-Help Housing in the United States*, Cambridge, Mass: Lincoln Institute of Land Policy

Trinidad and Tobago Ministry of Agriculture, Land and Marine Resources (1994) 'Programme of institutional strengthening of the Lands and Surveys Division', Cabinet Minute 2193 of 1994

Watson, IB and Potter, RB (1993) 'Housing and housing policy in Barbados: the relevance of the chattel house' *Third World Planning Review* 15(4): 373–95

Wilson, PJ (1973) *Crab Antics: A Caribbean Case Study of the Conflict of Reputation and Respectability* Prospect Heights, Illinois: Waveland Press

Wisconsin LTC (1999) *Project Profile – Land Use and Policy Administration Project*, University of Madison, Wisconsin: LTC

Wylie, JCW (1986) *The Land Laws of Trinidad and Tobago*, Port of Spain: Government of Trinidad and Tobago

# 'Having a Place of Your Own' in Kitwe

*John Kangwa*

## Introduction

Land tenure has been defined as consisting of the social relations and institutions governing access to, and ownership of, land and natural resources, and sometimes as a 'bundle of rights' associated with land and property (Simpson 1976; Maxwell and Wiebe 1998). Land titling or land registration is a procedure that serves both public and private functions. Public functions relate to the need for States to maintain records of their land resources for fiscal or other purposes, while private functions are concerned with individual needs to create and transfer rights in land. Security of tenure is simply the state of being safe or secure in the holding of land; it can exist whether or not there is documentary proof of its existence. Under customary tenure in many parts of Africa, for example, the occupant of a piece of land enjoys security of tenure without necessarily having any documentary evidence to prove the fact. For de Soto (2000: 53), formal property also has the effect of creating individuals from masses, by transforming people with property interests into individuals who can be called to account. For de Soto, individualised property systems bring people with interests in property into complex webs of connections that involve both the State and the private sector. The property system, it is said, 'draws out the abstract potential from buildings and fixes it in representations that allow us to go beyond passively using the buildings only as shelters' (de Soto 2000: 60). Moreover, formal property systems protect and enforce property transactions, making land easily transferable.

The peri-urban areas of many cities in Africa (like Kitwe, the focus for this chapter) reflect their citizens' desire to own property and be independent. In this, they are no different to their counterparts in other more developed areas, both in the same cities and around the globe. The term 'peri-urban' has come to be associated with unregulated development, and their residents frequently characterised as social misfits. Existing formal systems of property ownership tend to cater for those better off. Okpala (1987) has argued that the theories employed in African urban studies have been borrowed from European conceptual frameworks, leading to largely ineffective prescriptions and recommendations, which compound and exacerbate urban problems. His view is that African society is inadequately documented, and the absence of documentary evidence or official permits and approvals simply reflects weak administration and institutions. The concept of legal title has little meaning to house-owners in the so called 'unauthorised areas', even though the implications of this have governed official policies on land management for some time (Okpala 1987: 140–41).

The analysis presented here supports a middle ground between Okpala and de Soto, the latter arguing that the wholesale application of formal land titling systems is the way forward. Squatters are, by and large, 'ordinary folk making a claim for better opportunities and standards of living, and a brighter future for their children while making the best of a bad situation in anticipation of better things to come' (Mulwanda 1994: 118). They deserve a place they can call 'home' without the danger of eviction or displacement.

Zambia is a large country (covering 753,000 sq km), and is also heavily urbanised, with 40% of its inhabitants living in towns and cities. The movement to the towns, and towards permanent urbanisation, developed over several decades. The discovery of copper ore deposits in the north of the country was the principal driver of urban development from the 1920s (Simons 1979). The history of low cost housing in Zambia is tied to this economic and industrial expansion driven by colonial capitalism, which required labour to run the mines, and the farms that provisioned them. To mobilise the abundant labour in the rural areas, a 'hut tax' was imposed, compelling villagers to seek jobs in the fledgling towns. Squatter settlements developed after independence, when strict regulations dating from the colonial period were relaxed. Population growth across the Copperbelt then slowed from the 1980s, with a decline in industrial activity following the controversial privatisation of the mines. The proportion of Zambia's population living in the Copperbelt Province has recently fallen, but it remains relatively densely populated, and peri-urban communities continue to grow.

Zambia is now classified as one of the poorest nations in the world, with estimates that 80% of the population live on the equivalent of US$1 per day. By contrast, at independence in 1964, the country had a strong mining-based economy, but it suffered a sharp decline in copper prices from the mid-1970s, compounded by oil price rises. The Structural Adjustment Programme (SAP) imposed by the International Monetary Fund and World Bank from the early 1980s failed to significantly address the poverty challenges, and Zambia was one of only four countries in the world to experience a reversal in human development in that decade. That deterioration continued during the 1990s, when many other countries in the region also saw a similar decline, so that, for most of Zambia's city residents, many of the benefits of urban living have either failed to materialise or have dissipated (UNDP 2003: 40).

Privatisation of the mines in the Copperbelt has resulted in the loss of thousands of jobs and the removal of important economic safety nets, creating impoverishment and economic uncertainty. Privatisation was a policy of the Movement for Multi-Party Democracy (MMD), which defeated the United National Independence Party (UNIP) government of Kenneth Kaunda in 1991. The mines on the Copperbelt, which include one of the largest open-pit operations in the world, were disposed of finally in April 2000. Privatisation has been criticised for disregarding the interests and wellbeing of the people, with no regulatory framework to protect employees during the sell-off or monitor conditions afterwards (Kenny 2000). The legally constituted agency for privatisation was bypassed, and a separate body created to deal only with the mines, raising issues of accountability and transparency. With the loss of mining jobs, many families also lost access to medical, educational and recreational facilities that had been provided as employee benefits by the State-owned Zambia Consolidated Copper Mines (ZCCM) (Kangwa 2001). It is now widely accepted that Zambia needs to diversify away from copper mining into tourism and agriculture, while the hardships of Zambians have become worse for the majority of the population estimated to live below the poverty datum line. Life expectancy has fallen in the period 1996–2001 from 46 to 37 years for men, and from 45 to 37 years for women (CSO 2001).

## Problems of Land Administration Post-Privatisation

Job losses in the mines have had secondary impacts on land in and around the Copperbelt towns, such as the pressure to 'degazette' forest reserves for subsistence farming, and increased squatting on private, State and mines land. Available evidence indicates that there has been considerable encroachment onto forest land, because Forest Department staff had licensed charcoal burning activities in parts of the gazetted forests as a measure to clear land for pine plantations. When the land was cleared, the charcoal burners were supposed to leave but did not, instead turning to farming (Palmer 2001). In most cases, these same squatters have organised themselves into branches of the ruling party in order to gain legitimacy for their settlement and put the political system on their side. They have then elected their own leaders, who in turn have begun to allocate land to newcomers. Such political manoeuvering continues to play a large part in the management of land issues on the Copperbelt since mines privatisation. While such informal settlements may be illegal, politicians on their part often exploit this illegality to seek votes from the communities, dangling the carrot of legalisation and service provision if the community vote in their favour. This is particularly true for the party in power. The Forest Department has, on its part, been concerned with the level of degradation of the forest reserves, which has had an impact on the catchment area for the Kafue River running through most of the Copperbelt. At a workshop organised by Oxfam to discuss land problems on the Copperbelt, officials from the Department indicated that the issuing of charcoal-burning permits was intended to discourage the indiscriminate destruction of forests, but the Department was insufficiently resourced to enforce the permit system (Kangwa 2002).

Such land problems have come to the surface in many Copperbelt towns since the mines were privatised. For instance, a scheme started over 20 years ago by ZCCM to resettle retired miners on part of its surface rights area in Mufulira backfired when the mine was sold, because no titles had been formally issued to the resettled former miners. The new mine owners insisted on removing everyone until civil society action compelled the company to negotiate. In another example, a community of more than 100 families had been faced with eviction from State land where they had been squatting for more than 20 years, because the local authority concerned had started allocating small-holder plots assuming that the land concerned was vacant State land. At the time of writing, little had been done to formalise security of tenure for the community. In a similar case, another community of about 500 households had squatted on private land, apparently unaware that the land was privately owned. When informed of the illegal nature of their settlement, they negotiated successfully, with the help of an advocacy group, for the excision of the land into community control. In this case, the owner set aside a block of 150 hectares for exclusive use as agriculture to benefit widows and orphans in the community.

In order to mitigate the problem of informal settlement on mine land, Mopani Copper Mines plc, one of the new mining companies on the Copperbelt, has also created a system of permits whereby land is made available in its surface rights areas to subsistence farmers every rainy season from November to March. These seasonal farming permits have strict conditions attached to them, allowing only use for agriculture and forbidding permanent structures. Once a grant is made, it cannot be extended beyond the agreed boundaries, is only effective for the agreed period, and must be renewed annually. The mining company employs its own land rangers to ensure that the system is enforced.

NGOs and CBOs are thus playing a positive role in addressing issues of land tenure and access to land and housing for the urban poor. Oxfam runs a programme aimed at livelihoods improvement and supports advocacy for land access for retrenched miners and the urban poor, while World Vision has been involved in providing low-cost housing solutions for orphaned children and child-headed households, responding to the impact of HIV/AIDS. As a direct result of these and other land problems on the Copperbelt, the NGO sector has recognised the need to set up a land rights centre, which can advocate for the land rights of poor peasant farmers and other land holders and serve as an advice centre and 'one-stop-shop' for information dissemination on all land matters on the Copperbelt. This centre will press for pro-poor land policies and ensure that the poor have protection from exploitation and forced eviction from the land. It is envisaged that such a centre will also provide education programmes and awareness-raising campaigns on the provisions of the current land law in Zambia, provide networking facilities with other programmes around the region and globe with similar objectives, and provide communities with a voice and a platform to encourage women's access to land.

Access to land for the urban poor on the Copperbelt is crucial to the maintenance of food security for many residents, particularly in the post-privatisation period. The loss of mining employment for many has meant that, without secure access to land, they are deprived of the one ingredient essential for a viable livelihood and food security. A review of land policy in the country has begun, but unless it includes all stakeholders, and particularly the poor, the final product is unlikely to reflect the real needs of the people who are most at risk from lack of secure access to land. A major complaint targeted at the land delivery and management system in Zambia is that the titling process is too cumbersome, favouring the rich rather than the poor, while there are not enough licensed land surveyors to carry out the surveys, and the licensing process is itself too restrictive.

The sale of houses to sitting tenants has affected a significant proportion of Copperbelt residents. Some former miners bought their homes as part of their redundancy packages, only to find that they cannot maintain their former lifestyle after retrenchment and have to sell or rent their homes, transferring into the informal peri-urban areas. This 'downshifting' has affected large numbers of former miners, increasing pressure on the already heavily populated informal areas. The Zambian Copperbelt is thus a suitable study for the mechanisms by which the poor gain access to land and housing, and for whether giving title to home-owners in peri-urban areas improves their circumstances.

# Land Tenure in Zambia

Zambia's land tenure system is embedded in the country's colonial history. English statutes as at 1911 were given force of law in Zambia, making English land law Zambian land law, although a strong and intact tribal land holding system did survive. Before 1911, Northern Rhodesia was administered as two units: North-Eastern Rhodesia and Barotseland North-Western Rhodesia. In 1889, Lewanika had signed a concession giving absolute and perpetual control to the British South Africa Company (BSA) of an area vaguely described as 'North Bechuanaland and the Transvaal and East of Portuguese Angola', under which the BSA claimed mineral and land rights in North-Eastern and North-Western Rhodesia (except Barotseland) (Hansungule 1994). The company administered the territory until 1924, when the British Crown assumed a protectorate (Mvunga 1980: 4).

The British Colonial Office took steps to protect existing land interests by way of promulgating the Northern Rhodesia (Crown Land and Native Reserves) Order 1928, creating different categories of land for purposes of administration (Chulu and Beele 2001). Crown land could be alienated to European settlers under English law, but native reserves were set aside 'for the sole and exclusive use of the natives of Northern Rhodesia'. In 1947, a new category of trust land was introduced, said to be 'for the sole use and benefit, direct or indirect, of the natives of Northern Rhodesia', but within which non-natives could acquire interests up to 99 years. Following independence, all land in Zambia was vested in the President, and Crown land (some 6% of the total) became State land.

In 1975, there was major reform through the Land (Conversion of Titles) Act (GRZ 1975), which replaced freehold titles with statutory leases for 100 years, and was particularly driven by concern about property speculation. In what became known as 'The Watershed Speech', President Kaunda argued that the ruling UNIP regarded land as a gift from God, which should not become the subject of speculation. According to African tradition, he said, 'land was never bought. It came to belong to individuals through usage and the passing of time ... land cannot be made and does not grow ... it is the source of man's life and its sacredness can only continue to be if all of it is held by the State for the good of all' (Kaunda 1975). Kaunda had consolidated political power behind his party and nationalised industrial and commercial interests, but, despite the party's long-standing hostility to colonial land laws, it was a decade after independence before the system inherited was reformed to confront entrenched land interests (Chulu and Beele 2001). The President banned the operation of real estate agents (held responsible for inflated prices of land and housing) and prohibited housing loans to expatriates. Landlords had five years to phase out their businesses and sell their properties to the State, and building loans were no longer available for constructing rental accommodation. Local authorities were ordered to enforce against unauthorised buildings, and anti-corruption measures were applied to the allocation of council housing.

The 1975 Act did not apply to customary land, but effectively extinguished the land market and introduced the notion that 'land has no value', particularly through banning the sale of vacant, unused land. In fixing a maximum sale price, the value of the land was to be disregarded and only the 'unexhausted improvements' upon the land could be valued and sold. The Act required State consent for all dealings in land, with government valuers fixing the value of unexhausted improvements, but the valuers could not cope with the work volumes created, so that consent was often delayed for months. Hansungule (1994) argues that the 1975 reforms gave only psychological comfort to Zambians, reducing land speculation but not opening up access to land. Some of the current difficulties in access to land can be traced to these reforms, which pushed the poor into invasions of land perceived as vacant, or illegal allocations by local party officials. In 1985, following repeated complaints from the general public about their difficulties in securing land, Land Circular No 1 set out general policy guidelines for land administration, but remained little-known or applied, so that the reforms failed and indeed hampered development. Mortgages could not be created on unused land, and long delays and fixed sale prices frustrated both vendors and buyers, creating a black market in land transactions. Controls on the housing rental sector, such as limits on sub-letting, also created a thriving illegal market (Mulenga 1995; Schlyter 2002).

The MMD promised a reform of land law when it came to power in 1991, after defeating Kaunda, and stated in its manifesto that:

> [We] shall institutionalise a modern, coherent, simplified and relevant land law code intended to ensure the fundamental right to private ownership of land as well as to be an integrated part of a more efficient land delivery system ... [In] order to bring about a more efficient and equitable system of tenure conversion and land allocation in customary lands; land adjudication legislation will be enacted and coordinated in such a way that confidence shall be restored in land investors ... The MMD shall attach economic value to undeveloped land and promote the regular issuance of title deeds to productive land-owners in both rural and urban areas.

It was argued that land administration lacked capacity to deliver either serviced land in urban areas or agricultural land elsewhere, while customary tenure needed reinforcing and discriminatory laws corrected. The Land Act 1995 (GRZ 1995) was the outcome, which:

(a) provided for the continued vesting of land in the President and the alienation of land by the President;

(b) provided for the continuation of leasehold tenure;

(c) established a Land Development Fund and Lands Tribunal (for efficient and cheap land dispute resolution); and

(d) repealed the Land (Conversion of Titles) Act 1975, and various related Orders.

These changes ended the legal fiction that 'land has no value' and restored a land market, although it also abolished the distinction between State and tribal land, both falling under the same regulatory framework. The President cannot alienate customary land without taking into account local customary law and consulting the local chief and district authority, thus embedding a hierarchy of laws which makes customary law inferior to modern or statutory tenure (Machina 2002). Land cannot be alienated for more than 99 years unless in the national interest and approved by a two-thirds majority of the National Assembly.

The Land Act 1995 provided for the control of settlements and land husbandry practices in the interests of environmental conservation. Section 9(1)(2) of the Act empowered eviction for any unauthorised occupation of vacant land. Squatting occurred mostly on land long vacant, or with no identifiable owner, and tribal land tenure was recognised by the community, with the consent of the headman for settlement, so the new Act provided little help to those who may have occupied the land for many generations (Machina 2002). Customary tenure could be converted to 99-year lease, with the approval of the chief and an approved land survey, under the same procedure as for State land. The new Lands Tribunal was criticised as too expensive, over-technical and dominated by lawyers (Kangwa 2002; Machina 2002), and proposals were made for local, more accessible tribunals.

The Act, aiming to return the Zambian economy to free market conditions, was accompanied by privatisation of the mines and housing. From 1996, through presidential decree, all council houses, most government houses and most mine houses were offered to sitting tenants at a discount, often as part of redundancy (or 'retrenchment') packages (Schlyter 2002).

## Security of Tenure and the Peri-Urban Poor

Statutory leaseholds have since 1995 applied to both State land and customary land and offer the most secure form of tenure, but the 1995 Land Act 'is a law of the rich who can afford to use it to their advantage' and does not cater for the needs of the poor (Machina 2002: 5). The need for housing by the majority of Zambia's population on limited incomes has been addressed in a variety of housing policies over a long period, including the building of low-cost housing, aided self-help schemes and squatter upgrading. In the colonial period, barrack or bachelor accommodation was succeeded by single-family dwellings under a policy of 'stabilisation of labour' (Home 2000). From 1966, sites-and-services schemes were introduced, catering for the middle classes, with plots sold fully serviced with access to water, street lighting, road frontage and drains. More basic sites-and-services schemes followed, although the poor found even such plots unaffordable. Zambia thus has a long history of projects, initiated by government, local authorities and NGOs, designed to improve or upgrade informal, unplanned settlements, and recognising that such unauthorised areas represent an investment of social and economic capital that cannot be ignored (Kasongo and Tipple 1990; Rakodi 1989). The Housing (Statutory and Improvement Areas) Act 1974, with its provisions for improvement areas and statutory housing areas, prepared the way for the implementation of a squatter upgrading programme with World Bank support.

For a squatter settlement declared an improvement area, the local authority prepares a layout plan and, once approved by the Surveyor General, acquires a head lease for the area, installs roads, water and other services, and regularises plot sizes through a land readjustment procedure. In such areas, 30-year occupancy licences can be awarded to plot-owners during upgrading, and certificates of title can follow once permanent structures have been built with planning approval, as if the land-owner were obtaining a direct lease from the government (GRZ 1974). The Act thus marked a government commitment to basic infrastructure for informal areas, but, while successful in Lusaka, it had little practical effect on the peri-urban areas because of insufficient investment (Knauder 1982; Mulwanda and Mutale

**Figure 15: A place of our own. Family on sites-and-services plot at Luangwa, Kitwe (courtesy: J Kangwa 2002)**

1994; Rakodi 1989). Between 1976 and 1989, the proportion of upgraded units in total housing stock actually fell, from 20.4% to 10.3%, while the numbers of squatter dwellings rose.

In 1996, the Minister for Local Government and Housing launched a new National Housing Policy (GRZ 1996) after nationwide consultation. With only a third of total housing stock being formal and approved, the policy set various goals confirming previously undocumented reforms. Its support for home-ownership as the means of providing security, stability and economic power to households was reflected in the sale of council, mine and government houses to sitting tenants. This action was referred to as a 'Housing Empowerment Scheme'. The transfer of mine, civil service and local authority housing to the private sector created a large demand for survey services and placed great constraints upon the Survey and Lands Departments of the Ministry of Lands, who needed extra resources to cope with the increased workload. The downside of this action was that local authorities, especially on the Copperbelt, found overnight that they could not collect rates from the former mine townships as they had done under the previously State-owned ZCCM. Prior to privatisation, ZCCM had paid block rates for all the mining townships on the Copperbelt to the local authorities. The 1974 Act provides that a township must be declared a statutory housing area in which the owners are eligible for individual titles from the local authority before rates can be levied in that area. Local authorities are also required to carry out five-yearly valuations of properties in their jurisdictions for this purpose. The sale of houses to sitting tenants created a cadre of home-owners who were not recorded on the local authority valuation rolls. They could not therefore have rates levied against them until their properties were registered and their rates were fixed.

This was meant to be a 'rates for rents' policy shift, in which councils would move from collecting rents and begin collecting rates from affected home-owners. It was intended that this move away from rentals would improve revenue collection, as local authorities would enforce the collection of rates more effectively than rents. However, rates are only payable on properties that are registered in the lands and deeds registry, and for registration to be effected, a property must be surveyed and title issued and registered in the lands and deeds registry. In the Copperbelt mining townships where this process has not been completed, uncertainty has been created among the home-owners who have benefited from the Housing Empowerment Scheme. Since then, Kitwe City Council, for instance, has processed more than 10,000 title deeds in those townships where it already had jurisdiction. With land alienation and registration procedures seen as too centralised and cumbersome, and the rating system inequitable, administrative reform has included decentralisation of the lands and deeds registry, a new office being opened in the Copperbelt at Ndola.

## The Nkana-Kitwe Case Study

Nkana-Kitwe is a mining town whose official population was recorded at 388,646 in the 2000 Census, but is unofficially estimated at 1.5 million, largely because many peripheral settlements have gone unrecorded. The name Nkana-Kitwe reflects its history as one of the 'twin townships' of the Copperbelt. Nkana was established in 1928 by the Rhokana Corporation as a mining township to exploit the area's rich copper ore deposits, while the colonial protectorate administration set up a duplicate public township at Kitwe because of its opposition to the principle of company towns (Gardiner 1970; Mutale 2004). A management board ran the public township from 1936, and later there was a local council (granted city status in 1966), but the mines area remained outside the local government structure under mine company policing and control.

Colonial urban policy saw towns as European creations, primarily for European occupation, with race and class structure rigidly maintained. While Africans provided most of the mine labour for the mines and for industrial and agricultural infrastructure, the South African experience was that these migrant workers would live in temporary barracks of single-room mud huts until they eventually returned to their villages. Some employees were accommodated in self-built huts in peri-urban areas, overcrowded and with limited services (Rothman 1972). The council built housing estates from the 1950s and, after independence, 'aided self-help' housing schemes and new rental housing. Squatting was largely prevented through rigid controls during the colonial period, but this changed after 1969, when an easing of regulations allowed many settlements to develop near employment opportunities. In Kitwe, for example, the Turf Club and Chambishi Mine gave rise to Racecourse and Chambishi, while other areas were located near charcoal-burning areas and near high-cost residential areas, where domestic work was available (KCC 1973). At present, there are about 21 informal settlements around Kitwe, seven of them at various stages of upgrading. For this field research, one upgraded area (Luangwa) and one informal peri-urban settlement (Racecourse) were selected.

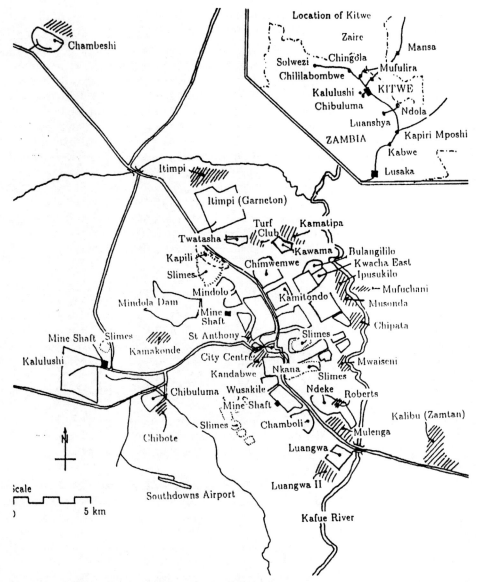

**Figure 16: Map of Nkana-Kitwe. Racecourse at top (next to Turf Club and Twatasha), Luangwa to south (courtesy: Kasongo and Tipple 1990)**

## Luangwa Township

Luangwa Township began as a sites-and-services scheme in 1970, on land belonging to KCC, in response to government Circular 29 of 1968, which encouraged councils to resettle squatters. In order to reduce costs, councils were to provide basic schemes, with plot-holders encouraged to provide their own pit-latrines (Kasongo and Tipple 1990). KCC created two schemes: Twatasha in the north and Luangwa in the south, while the Nkana mine authorities pressed for squatter settlements at Chibili and Kapili to be moved because they were in mining operational areas subject to subsidence. The government circular brooked no resistance to relocation, and field interviews undertaken for this research, with two elderly residents of Luangwa, confirmed that the schemes were resolutely implemented, those relocated being provided with transport to move their belongings to the new site once they had built their initial pole-and-*dagga* houses on their allocated plots (Kasongo and Tipple 1990). Luangwa Township now covers an area of about 90 ha, divided into some 1,700 residential plots, each 12 m x 25 m, with an estimated population of 8,500 (assuming an average household size of five persons). The area is represented on the city council by a ward councillor, has two schools, a trading area, churches and community facilities. The main access roads to the nearby Ndola-Kitwe highway were originally tarmac surfaced, but are now in poor condition. There is no piped water (most plots have a well), no street lighting, and few electricity connections, although lines are available throughout the township.

## Racecourse

The Racecourse area has a population of about 14,500 (Kleemeier and Malama 2001) and covers an area of about 85 ha. The land was re-zoned as a residential area in 1995, bringing it under the jurisdiction of the KCC. Originally, part of the area was council-owned, while the rest formerly belonged to the now defunct Kitwe Turf Club (this part is still known as the 'Farm House', referring to the former stables and clubhouse). When the Club was constructed in 1961, a number of Africans were employed as stable hands. Aerial photographs taken in 1969 show a small group of huts near the racecourse, but after independence, the numbers grew as settlement rules were relaxed and relatives of workers at the Turf Club and migrants from rural areas moved in. A KCC survey of squatter settlements (1973) found 119 houses there, built mainly of pole-and-*dagga* with corrugated iron roofing. At that time, the settlement had unmade roads and few other facilities; water came from the Turf Club tank (borehole) or, when that was empty, residents had to walk to the nearby bus company depot or Chimwemwe compound (KCC 1973). The settlement has now grown to over 2,300 houses, with access by a poorly maintained tarred road off the main Kitwe-Chingola road. Its proximity to Itimpi (Garneton) allows opportunities for domestic and gardening employment, mining jobs at Chambishi and Mindolo mines, and work at some commercial farms, forestry reserves and explosives factories along the Kitwe-Chingola and Kitwe-Mufulira highways. Within the settlement, the residents themselves, working with a facilitating NGO (Project Urban Self-Help – PUSH), have improved roads to gravel standards. A ward councillor living in the township represents the area and is also a trustee of the Residents Development Committee (RDC), which is responsible for all developmental issues; the councillor interacts with outside bodies such as NGOs on behalf of the residents. Racecourse has a community school, a privately-run community health centre charging minimal fees and a trading site with market and grocery shops selling basic foodstuffs. The community is promoting the construction of a health centre with support from the Microproject Unit (funded by the European Union Development Fund). In 1995, the KCC re-zoned the Racecourse area from industrial to residential in anticipation of its declaration as an improvement area, but such a declaration has not yet come.

**Figure 17: Community health centre foundations. The foundation trenches were dug with voluntary effort; plans for a substantial building exist, but no funds as yet (courtesy: J Kangwa 2002)**

## Survey results

For the field research, 75 households were selected by random sampling, using maps and house numbers supplied by the KCC Town Planning Section. Male respondents formed 61% of the sample (a relatively high proportion, attributed to increased unemployment levels following privatisation of the mines). In 1998, male unemployment was 25% on the Copperbelt, but 61% of those surveyed. There was a more equal division, however, between males and females in the Luangwa survey, probably because Luangwa is closer to sources of employment, including the Nkana mine, farms bordering the Kafue River and a sawmill.

The proportion of elderly respondents in the survey sample was high, with 55% aged above 50, and 45% in the range 14–49 years. Racecourse had more elderly residents, while Luangwa was more evenly divided among the age groups. As both settlements dated from the 1970s, older heads of households were to be expected, having lived there for at least two decades with apparently little turnover in plot occupation and ownership. National statistics (1998) show a younger population for the country (69% younger than 25, 45% under 15, and only 2% aged 65 years or above, according to CSO 1998).

Most of the respondents (71%) were married and living with their spouses at the time of the survey, with similar figures for the two areas. Only 6% had never been married, 23% were widows or widowers and none in the sample were either divorced or separated. National statistics for 1998 are comparable, with high proportions of married persons (88% of men aged 30–49, 87% over 50, although only 45% of women in this age range were currently married). Nationally, widows comprised some 41% of over-50 women, divorced 11%, and separated 2% (CSO 1998). Of the 23% of the sample who were widowed, more than two-thirds were women. This can be attributed to the loss of healthcare services after the privatisation of the mines having a negative impact on many former miners, leading to many early deaths and highlighting a need to improve security of tenure for women, particularly widows (Owen 1996; Machina 2002).

Most (58%) of the sample had received some primary education, although a substantial minority (16%) had received no schooling at all; 26% had attended secondary school (more common amongst Luangwa residents). Thus, a somewhat better educated and younger population inhabits Luangwa, compared with Racecourse, explained partly because Racecourse is an older settlement and has been illegal for much of its existence.

Unemployment rates were high (61%), with only 10% in formal employment and 29% self-employed (in various activities including trading, farming, tin-smithing, building materials supply, tailoring, and shop-keeping). The national urban unemployment rate was astonishingly high at 67% in 1998 (CSO 1998). There was little difference in employment status between the two settlements, or between men and women. Asked how they survived day-to-day, one respondent said, 'We survive by the grace of God'. Lack of employment and steady income excluded most of these peri-urban residents from institutional credit; the Zambia National Building Society (with a branch in Kitwe City centre) has a policy of lending only to those in regular employment. Farming only provides a livelihood in the rainy season, unless there is access to wetland areas (*dambo*, where vegetables can be grown throughout the year).

**Figure 18: Children at Racecourse. On a public space outside a club, with anthill in background (courtesy: J Kangwa 2002)**

A quarter of Luangwa respondents had access to a farm plot (equally divided between men and women), but only 6% of the Racecourse sample, a disparity due to their relative location and land tenure arrangements on the surrounding land. Racecourse is bordered to the north by well-established small-holdings at Itimpi (Garneton) and a forest reserve. Itimpi (Garneton) was established as a suburban township, predominantly for expatriates, and many of its former residents engaged in market gardening, supplying the city and its mining communities with fresh fruit, vegetables, flowers, poultry, pork, etc. It was originally named Garneton but was renamed Itimpi after independence with the two names used side-by-side since. To the west of Racecourse, the land is predominantly under mine licence, with no legal access for farming activity; to the east is a former State ranch, subdivided and sold to individual small-scale subsistence farmers. Luangwa, by contrast, is next to an area of customary land (the Lamba-Lima Reserve), and also to forest reserve land at Misaka, Kakolo and Maposa (off the Ndola-Kitwe highway) which has been degazetted to provide small-scale farming opportunities to those who had lost their jobs at the mines. Thus, residents from Luangwa have greater access to farm plots.

Of respondents, 61% reported a family size of four to six persons, which conforms closely to national census figures (an average of five). Family size in Luangwa was larger, with three generations living on some plots. There were a number of cases where grandparents were looking after orphaned or destitute grandchildren (whose parents could not support them due to illness or lack of resources).

Respondents were asked to state in whose name their plots were registered to assist in understanding issues of women's security of tenure, where women may be dispossessed by their husbands' relatives when they die. Such 'property-grabbing' has been increasing with the prevalence of HIV/AIDS (Owen 1996; Nampanya-Serpell 2000). Of the respondents, 26% of men and 4% of women indicated that the plot was registered in their name alone, 16% reported that the plot was registered in the name of a deceased husband, and 10% of men reported that the plot was registered in the name of a wife. This finding departs from what is generally understood, that men do not register property exclusively in their spouse's names. CBOs often hold meetings, awareness seminars and drama sketches attacking the practice of 'property-grabbing', particularly when husbands die, and it seems that some of this awareness raising is beginning to have an impact.

A substantial proportion (19%) of plots were registered in the name of a relative, usually someone older than the respondent, such as a father, uncle or grandfather, who either lived there or had retired to a home village. Another 6% indicated that the plot was registered in the name of a landlord, or that change of ownership had not yet been effected. The remaining respondents did not know in whose name the plot was registered. There were no cases of joint registration (Machina (2002: 12) also found joint titling of plots by married couples rare), and this may reflect an institutional bias (the plot application forms not allowing joint applications). At a workshop organised by Oxfam to discuss land problems on the Copperbelt, it was suggested that the city council rejects applications from women if the husband has been allocated a plot. Schlyter (2002) found that married couples in a range of housing situations in Lusaka rarely discussed joint ownership, and the concept was widely rejected, at least by husbands.

Thirty-nine per cent of respondents said that they had a 30-year occupancy licence from the Council. (In Luangwa, even after the settlement had been declared an improvement area, 45% remained unsure what documentation existed for the plot.) For instance, a widow aged 56 and living with five children stated: 'I don't know very much about title deeds, all I know is that we have a paper from the council for the house.' Sixteen per cent claimed to have no documents of ownership, and one 84-year-old man, who had lived on his plot in Luangwa since 1972, said: 'The council did not give us any help with anything ... we just had to do it all ourselves. I have not been given any papers by the council to show that I own this plot.' Many respondents could not produce documentation, either because they did not know where it was, or said that a close relative was holding it.

Regarding length of residence, 22% of respondents had lived in their settlement for more than 30 years, a further 29% for more than 20 years, 10% 10–20 years, and 39% less than 10 years. With so many having invested much of their lives in these communities, a need for improvement is suggested. In Mulwanda's words:

> ... squatters ... have allocated themselves land where the formal authorities have failed to assemble and service enough land to allocate to them ... they have provided themselves with shelter where formal housing agencies have fallen short ... [but] they are called squatters because they live on land which is not their own and to which they have no title deeds (1994: 118).

Access to credit would help plot-holders make improvements, and under adverse possession rules most could claim possessory title. Asked how they funded their

Figure 19: Waiting to develop. In Luangwa, the plot-owner stands on the base for a modern house structure, which would require an upgrading of his tenure. Existing mud-brick house in background, and matured boundary hedges (courtesy: J Kangwa 2002)

**Figure 20: Preparing for plot improvements. Sun-dried mud bricks for further building on plot at Luangwa. Euphorbia hedge in background (courtesy: J Kangwa 2002)**

house building, most (58%) indicated personal savings or money from their employment (for example, Christmas or productivity bonus or salary arrears) and said that they put aside small amounts of money for building materials. (Saving for births, deaths and weddings, or for family obligations, such as support of orphaned children or aged relatives, was unknown.) Only 10% of respondents had used redundancy or pension benefits to construct their dwellings, and 6% had used other means, such as loans from employers. A 32-year-old woman in Luangwa (whose husband was a self-employed joiner) explained:

> When we came to Luangwa we rented a house ... but the owner of our present dwelling decided to move to the village, so my husband got a loan from his employers to buy the house, but it is quite dilapidated ... The money we have used has been saved from my husband's earnings ... we enlarged it to make three rooms and added an outside kitchen.

A quarter of respondents (26%), mainly those renting from a landlord or living on relatives' property, did not know how building was funded.

A relevant study of informal settlements at Mulenga (Kitwe) and Kapisha (Chingola), partly to investigate access to income and basic services (Oxfam 1998), found money being raised for micro-enterprises by borrowing from friends, relatives and moneylenders, without formal loans. Women in particular operated *chilimba* (micro-credit) schemes, where up to five women pool agreed amounts of money each month and take turns to borrow from the purse (Oxfam 1998). Such money-raising appears to be a generally accepted way of financing shelter in developing countries. Mutizwa-Mangiza (1991: 53–54) states that 77% of resources invested in housing in India comes from such informal sources, the proportion in

Sri Lanka and Tanzania being even higher. A 73-year-old respondent in Luangwa said: 'We would rather build using our own resources because getting a loan means you have to pay back and if you fail then you can create problems for yourself.' Micro-finance institutions may fill the gap for business enterprises, but not for house construction. One respondent in Racecourse (living with a wife, four children and three grandchildren) said: 'At the moment I want to increase the height of the walls and put new roofing sheets. I think I can apply for a micro loan for my carpentry business and then I can use some profit to improve my house.'

Only four respondents were paying rent (two men, two women), which was attributed to the 'action orientation' of these peri-urban communities, traditional societies being accustomed to villagers building their own huts with community help, and renting being an alien concept.

## Physical Structures and Improvements

Respondents' houses were either built of mud brick or concrete blocks. Most housing structures (64%) comprised between one and three rooms, 25% had four or five rooms, and 10% had six or more. The majority (74%) lived in mud-brick houses (these more common in Racecourse than Luangwa), and those with concrete block construction were mostly found in Luangwa where there was greater shelter consolidation. The respondents often used salvaged sheet metal, asbestos, corrugated iron sheets and flattened oil drums for roofing (a mixture of these materials was used by 45% of respondents). Those living in Luangwa used consistently better materials than their counterparts in Racecourse, although tile roofs were unknown. These differences between the two communities can be explained in part by the different legal stati of the two settlements, and because the poorer population in Racecourse had fewer job opportunities than in Luangwa, limiting their chances in improving their shelters even with greater tenure security.

The use of local materials can be regarded as one indicator of poverty within peri-urban communities. Building regulations require house construction with permanent materials in formal layouts. One retired man in Racecourse (living with his wife on a plot with an occupancy certificate from the council, which he had not collected) commented: 'Here in Racecourse we have been allowed to build mud brick houses because people here are poor. Those who go to build in Twatasha [an adjacent sites-and-services area] have to build with concrete blocks. I am not doing anything about this house because it might be demolished.'

Asked about their level of satisfaction with their house and its condition, 26% of respondents were 'totally dissatisfied' and a further 45% 'rather dissatisfied'. Some indicated that, in their opinion, either the house needed to be replaced or needed considerable rehabilitation. Fifty-five per cent of respondents wanted improvements to walls and roofing, 10% better quality doors and window frames, and 29% more rooms. One respondent said: 'When visitors come from the village there is no space for them to sleep. If we had a bigger house (more rooms), we would be able to accommodate more visitors more comfortably.' The 16% satisfied with their housing invariably lived in houses built to conventional standards with permanent materials. The 13% of respondents who declined to rate their accommodation included the small group paying rent, who probably did not want to give an opinion where the property did not belong to them, indicating perhaps their

**Figure 21: Making bricks. Sun drying mud bricks on outskirts of Luangwa (courtesy: J Kangwa 2002)**

vulnerability and need to accept sub-standard housing. One respondent expressed eloquently that renting is a poor substitute for a place of one's own: 'When you are renting, you are at the mercy of the owner. They change the rentals anytime they feel like or they put in their relatives to stay with you. I have found it difficult because we have had to move several times and it's very hard for the children. That is why I am looking for a plot where I can build my own house.' Another tenant said: 'I am not happy with the condition that the house is in, but it's such an inconvenience moving all the time from place to place that I just stay.'

Most respondents (84%), including all those living in Luangwa, used well water. A piped water supply was installed in Racecourse with the help of a World Bank loan, and 31% of respondents there had access to this supply. A network of 35 water-vending kiosks (26 of them operational at the time of survey) existed within the settlement, opening between 0600 and 1800 hours daily, run by residents, and charging K50 for 20 litres of water. Those not using the kiosks said: 'We only pay for drinking water (because it's treated).' 'Considering our disposable incomes, the kiosk water is expensive, so we prefer to use well water because it's free.' 'The kiosks are far from this area; they were not brought this far because the land here still belongs to the Farm House.' 'We cannot use water purchased from the kiosk to make bricks, it would be too expensive.' 'I have no money to spend on kiosk water, I depend upon our neighbour's well.' Luangwa Township had a piped water supply installed as part of the original sites-and-services programme, but pipes had been removed because residents were unwilling to pay for the water. As a result, in the dry season it suffers serious water shortages as the water table recedes, and water has to come from shallow wells and holes scooped from the sandy banks of the nearby Kafue River.

While a study of Lusaka found 23.9% of residents in similar housing areas went more than 200 m in search of water (Kangwa 2000), 97% of respondents in this survey had a water source within a radius of 100 m. In the Lusaka study area, formal water supplies had been installed but vandalised, with sections of piping missing. In the Kitwe case, untreated well water was available, with a risk of water-borne diseases (especially cholera and dysentery). Thirty-nine per cent had well water on their own plot, and a further 45% access to water within 50 m (usually the well of a neighbour), demonstrating the communal way of life in the settlements and mutual dependence. Traditionally in African society, a well is communal property and cannot be denied to a neighbour or stranger.

Poor sanitation represents a significant health hazard. In 1991, a cholera outbreak killed over 1,000 people in Kitwe District, and the District Health Management Board linked cases of diarrhoea with potentially contaminated water sources in peri-urban communities. The Board has instituted health promotion and community education through extensive radio, television, drama, leaflets and posters, with emphasis on the treatment of drinking water with chlorine and the washing of hands with soap. Most respondents in the survey had access to a pit latrine, either their own (84%) or shared with neighbours (13%), but 3% had no access to a toilet. The plots are small, and most residents position wells at the front and latrines at the back. As one respondent said: 'Do you think I am happy to build a pit-latrine where I know it will contaminate my neighbours well?'

With only 13% of respondents connected to electricity, the most used sources of light were candles and paraffin. Official statistics for all Zambian provinces (except Lusaka) show that most households use kerosene/paraffin for lighting: 51% of the

Figure 22: Privy in back yard. Pit latrines such as this (at the back of a plot in Luangwa) can contaminate well water supplies (courtesy: J Kangwa 2002)

**Figure 23: Drawing from the well. Many plots in Luangwa depend upon their own wells (courtesy: J Kangwa 2002)**

urban population and 78% of rural residents. Only 3% of rural residents nationally have access to electricity. In low-cost urban areas, those using candles and paraffin is 62%, indicating a level of deprivation inconsistent with urban living. The respondents in this survey used charcoal for cooking, which was generally on sale. Luangwa is near the charcoal-burning areas of Maposa and Kakolo, where land has been cleared for small-scale farming, while Racecourse is near a similar charcoal-burning area. A bag of charcoal weighing about 15–20 kilos sells for about K10,000–12,000.

Only 7% of respondents had no direct road access to their plot, all of them in Racecourse. According to the KCC, when a decision is made to upgrade a settlement, the area is surveyed for road layout, with the aim of giving each property a road frontage, but dirt rather than tarred roads are the norm (3% of respondents, all in Luangwa, had access to tarred roads but the roads had mostly deteriorated to a strip of tar in the middle). Drains are important in the rains to prevent storm water entering the plots, particularly where houses are built of mud, and such homes have collapsed during heavy storms, particularly near the Kafue River. Nearly half of the road frontage of respondents had drains.

## Conclusions

The research undertaken in Kitwe found impoverished communities, with households averaging five or six persons living in two-room homes, with limited access to services. Most relied upon well rather than piped water (unreliable in the dry season), pit-latrines, charcoal for cooking fuel, and candles or kerosene for lighting. The communities in the study were marginalised, not only in access to basic services, but also in their lack of voice in governance and institutional structures. Definitions of housing adequacy, however, are relative to economic and cultural milieus (Koebel and Edwards 1998), and Okpala (1987) argues that concepts of 'slums' and 'squatter settlements' can embody the transfer of Western cultural values, with insufficient attention to indigenous socio-cultural value systems. More than 80% of urban households in African cities have originated from rural areas, bringing rural habits and customs with them which are still undergoing adjustment, and may explain in part the current relatively low quality of urban systems and environments (Okpala 1987: 146).

The field research found that many families do not equate the absence of title papers with a lack of tenure security and show little awareness of the normal documentation that proves ownership, although the concept of title deeds is understood. Thus, property rights in these settlements do not currently provide the opportunity or protection for residents that could transform their prospects in the way that de Soto envisages. The system for delivering title deeds is slow and usually linked to upgrading, the implementation of which lies beyond the resources of the peri-urban poor. Given the limited institutional capacity, existing titling arrangements appear to work adequately, and the provision of intermediate forms of title, such as land record cards or occupancy permits, makes little difference in improving access to credit. In the Zambian case, an intermediate form of title seems merely to create the feeling of tenure insecurity and falls short of the collateral security necessary to access credit. Transactions that involve buying and selling property take place without legal documents regarding ownership, and both buyer and seller depend upon the social mechanisms of goodwill and traditional custom/trust to make the transaction binding. Martin (1975) has argued that informal settlements exhibit the organisational characteristics of a village lifestyle, and this represents a rational response by individuals trying to achieve their aspirations under circumstances where the official system, whose rules they do not fully understand, has failed to meet their needs.

The Zambian case found formal institutional credit effectively non-existent, with high levels of unemployment preventing residents from qualifying for loans from established financial institutions. Economic decline and government policies have led to massive job losses and rendered many incapable of achieving decent housing. While institutional capacity in managing pro-poor urban development is weak, even if residents in peri-urban areas could qualify for such loans, few respondents in this study would put themselves at risk of dispossession. They have built and/or bought their homes with informal funds, from savings, redundancy pay, pension benefits or money raised through small-scale enterprise. Building improvements take place incrementally as each household's situation permits. Linking micro-finance to the production of building materials, and locating these activities at community level, would allow more effective home improvements, drawing upon these communities' pools of skilled labour.

Mulwanda (1994) makes the plea that, if the poor are to benefit from initiatives aimed at raising them from their poverty, the only valid approach is to involve them directly in improving their environment, as well as to mobilise support from other sectors of society. The rigid application of existing systems of urban planning will not assist because of the informal nature of peri-urban settlements, which should be raised to the level of conventional settlements before applying the rules to them, as is the case with the policy of upgrading. Governance structures need to evolve to address the needs of the poor without necessarily viewing those needs through the same lenses applied to the more fortunate. Existing regulatory frameworks are rooted in colonialism and were not devised to deal with either illegality or informality. If anything, they were designed to thwart such development. Such frameworks cannot be used to uphold what they were designed to suppress.

# References

Chulu, M and Beele, EM (2001) 'Land law and policy in Zambia after Kaunda' in Lungu, J and Akombelwa, M (eds), *Land Policy and Reform: The Moses Kaunda Memorial Lectures*, ICARES Workshop Proceedings, No 2, Kitwe

CSO (1998) *Living Conditions in Zambia – 1998*, Lusaka: CSO

CSO (2001) *Selected Socio-Economic Indicators 2000*, Lusaka: CSO

de Soto, H (2000) *The Mystery of Capital: Why Capitalism Triumphs in the West and Fails Everywhere Else*, London: Black Swan

Gardiner, J (1970) *Some Aspects of the Establishment of Towns in Zambia During the 1920s and 30s*, Lusaka: University of Zambia Institute for African Studies

GRZ (1974) *Housing (Statutory and Improvement Areas) Act 1974*, Lusaka: Government Printer

GRZ (1975) *The Land (Conversion of Titles) Act 1975*, Lusaka: Government Printer

GRZ (1995) *Land Act 1995*, Lusaka: Government Printer

GRZ (1996) *National Housing Policy*, Lusaka: Ministry of Local Government and Housing

Hansungule, KM (1994), 'The land tenure system in Zambia and prospects for investment', unpublished paper for Land Bill Workshop, Lusaka

Home, RK (2000) 'From barrack compounds to the single-family house: planning worker housing in colonial Natal and Northern Rhodesia' *Planning Perspectives* 15: 327–47

Kangwa, J (2000) 'The impacts of fragmented settlement patterns on provision of infrastructure and services in Lusaka', unpublished Masters dissertation, University of Zambia, Lusaka

Kangwa, J (2001) 'Privatization and social management', unpublished paper for Mining, Minerals and Sustainable Development Project, African Institute of Corporate Citizenship, Johannesburg

Kangwa, J (ed) (2002) 'Report of Proceedings: Copperbelt Land Workshop', Mindolo Ecumenical Foundation/OxfamGB Zambia Copperbelt Livelihoods Improvement Programme, Kitwe

Kasongo, BA and Tipple, AG (1990) 'An analysis of policy towards squatters in Kitwe, Zambia' *Third World Planning Review* 12(2): 147–65

Kaunda, KD (1975) *The 'Watershed' Speech*, Lusaka: Zambia Information Services

KCC (1973) *Squatter Settlements and Contractors Compounds in the Kitwe Area*, Kitwe City Council

KCC (1976) *Low Cost Housing in Kitwe: Its Characteristics and Implications on Housing Policy*, City Engineers Department, Kitwe City Council

Kenny, T (2000) *Zambia, Deregulation and the Denial of Human Rights*, Oxford: Refugee Studies Centre, Queen Elizabeth House, Oxford University

Kleemeier, E and Malama, A (2001) 'Assessment of the Community Management Approach', Peri-urban Pilot Water Supply Project, Zambia

Knauder, S (1982) *Shacks and Mansions: An Analysis of the Integrated Housing Policy in Zambia*, Lusaka: Multimedia Publications

Koebel, CT and Edwards, PK (1998) 'Housing and marginalized populations: introduction' *Habitat International* 23(1): 1–3

Machina, H (2002) *Women's Land Rights in Zambia: Policy Provisions, Legal Framework and Constraints*, Lusaka: Zambia National Land Alliance

Martin, R (1975) 'The evolution of a traditional morphology in an urban setting: Greater Lusaka' *Zambia Geographical Journal* 29/30: 1–19

Maxwell, D and Wiebe, K (1998) *Land Tenure and Food Security: A Review of Concepts, Evidence and Methods*, Madison: LTC Research Paper 129, University of Wisconsin-Madison

Mulenga, SP (1995) 'Zambia urban land policy dilemma', unpublished paper presented at CBU, Kitwe

Mulwanda, M (1994) 'Minding their own communities' *Habitat International* 18(3): 117–25

Mulwanda, M and Mutale, E (1994) 'Never mind the people, the shanties must go: the politics of urban land in Zambia' *Cities* 11(5): 303–11

Mutale, E (2004) *The Management of Urban Development in Zambia*, Aldershot: Ashgate

Mutizwa-Mangiza, ND (1991) 'Financing urban shelter development in Zimbabwe – a review of existing institutions, problems and prospects' *Habitat International* 15(1 and 2): 51–68

Mvunga, MP (1980) *The Colonial Foundations of Zambia's Land Tenure System*, Lusaka: Historical Association of Zambia

Nampanya-Serpell, N (2000) 'Social and economic risk factors for HIV/AIDS-affected families in Zambia', unpublished paper to Aids and Economics Symposium, Durban

Okpala, DCI (1987) 'Received concepts and theories in African urbanisation studies and urban management strategies: a critique' *Urban Studies* 4: 137–50

Owen, M (1996) *A World of Widows*, London and New Jersey: Zed Books

Oxfam (1998) *Kapisha/Mulenga Livelihoods Analysis*, Draft Report, Kitwe

Palmer, R (2001) *Land Tenure Insecurity on the Zambian Copperbelt, 1998: Anyone Going Back to the Land?*, Oxford: Oxfam GB

Rakodi, C (1989) 'Self-help housing: the debate and examples; upgrading in Lusaka, Zambia and Hyderabad, India' *Habitat International* 13(4): 5–18

Rothman, NC (1972) 'African urban development in the colonial period: a study of Lusaka, 1905–1964', unpublished PhD thesis, NorthWestern University, Evanston, Illinois

Schlyter, A (2002) 'Privatisation of public housing and exclusion of women. A case study in Lusaka, Zambia', submitted for publication to Institute of Southern African Studies, University of Lesotho

Simpson, JR (1976) *Land Law and Registration*, Cambridge: CUP

Simons, HJ (1979) 'Zambia's urban situation' in Turok, B (ed), *Development in Zambia: A Reader*, London: Zed Books

UNDP (2003) *Human Development Report 2003*, New York and Oxford: OUP

According to development policy-makers, accessible and transparent property rights are a key to linking the poor and marginalised in society with market opportunities and democratic governance, an argument recently sharpened by Hernando de Soto's *The Mystery of Capital* and the Habitat Global Campaign for Secure Tenure. This book has been testing these linkages through interviews in peri-urban settlements of three countries of Africa and the Caribbean, examining whether legal and institutional reforms can help the poor to 'leverage their property into improved, sustainable livelihoods' (USAID 2002).

Our research was in countries with British colonial backgrounds, reporting the voice of the poor themselves and their experience of tenure reform in peri-urban informal settlements. Our research team brought together the two main professions directly involved in land titling (land surveyors and lawyers) and others with experience in planning and social anthropology. The team was experienced in both academic research and professional practice. We chose peri-urban areas as intermediate zones between urban and rural conditions, where poverty, ambiguous tenure and 'cloudy' title might be found. The Botswana research visited two such areas around the capital city of Gaborone, one where tenure and conditions had been upgraded (Old Naledi), the other where tribal land was being converted into extralegal housing (Mogoditshane). The Trinidad research visited four settlements, three where loose land-owner control had allowed piecemeal occupation (Race Course, Bon Air and Bois Bande) and one (Carlsen Field) where the informal settlers had acquired their own land. The Zambian research visited two areas, one where the city council had prepared a sites-and-services housing area (Luangwa), the other where voluntary relocation or 'down-shifting' had taken place by those dislocated due to the collapse of the mining economy (Racecourse). Compared with the claims of other studies, we found little evidence of 'market eviction' (the poor forced off their land as market prices increase) or of violence, corruption and ethnic politics (although African-Indian political rivalries figured in the Trinidad case).

In these conclusions we summarise our findings. First, the voice of the poor themselves: what they think about the land titling process, based upon their everyday life experiences. Secondly, the law, institutions and processes of land titling: the historical construction of illegality from the colonial period, how (or whether) an integrated system could be achieved, the capacity constraints upon government, and the potential for local initiatives. Thirdly, the situation on the ground: the physical occupation and plotting out of land, dispute resolution procedures, the structures and improvements on the plots, and the infrastructure provision of roads, water, electricity and drains.

## Everyday Life and the Voices of the Poor

De Soto tends to call the potential beneficiaries of his ideas 'the poor', as if they are a homogeneous and undifferentiated mass. He likens them to 'a still lake', with policy-makers as engineers looking to 'transform the placid lake's potential energy into kinetic energy of tumbling water that can rotate turbines, and generate electricity' (*New York Review of Books*, 31 May 2001). Such an image hardly acknowledges the complexity and diversity of 'the poor', and his talk of 'listening to the barking dogs' devalues the contribution of humans in these matters. Formal systems interact with informal cultures and structures through the lives and strategies of individuals. The State may see itself as conferring property rights from above, but these rights operate within basic kinship relations, between partners, generations and siblings. Our interviews with plot-holders reveal individuals embedded in nets of strong, reciprocal commitments, and put family bonds and obligations closer to the centre of the picture.

Finding the voices of 'the poor' is now officially sanctioned, even mandated, by policy-makers. A focus upon individual histories and identity can help to interweave human and socio-political development, opening up different dimensions of lived totality. Oral historians, for example, have adopted life-history methods as tools of emancipation and empowerment, reaching those sections of society, both past and present, whose experience could not be adequately reached through documentary or formal survey sources. We found talking directly to our respondents a refreshing and liberating experience, revealing the divide between the languages of official and academic discourse and the often vivid, clear, courteous and direct language with which poor people talk about their everyday lives and concerns. They revealed a healthy caution and realism about government and used expressions that related official language to everyday life, like 'averaging' boundaries and 'self-allocating' plots.

We found that people were strongly attached to their plots, which they viewed as both shelter and security for the future, rather than a marketable asset. Some were willing to adjust plot boundaries, or even move for upgrading, but a repeated theme was their identification with the land and reluctance to sell. 'This piece of land is my life. I am who I am because it supported me and my family.' 'This is mine here. This is mine! They can't tell me to go nowhere else again! This is mine! This is bought lands.' 'I want to know that if I can live here till I dead. To move now in my old age, ... that is all I does study.'

Land thus was a basic security and welfare support. The Caribbean institution of family land, officially disapproved of, expressed the social importance of land for extended families. In Africa, tribal land was seen as an important common property resource, indeed a defence against the forces of globalisation, and in Botswana, its conversion to individual ownership through unauthorised subdivision and sale had become a major political issue. There was resistance to market pressures (although rental housing thrived in Botswana and Zambia), irrespective of legally recognised title. We found limited evidence of a market in peri-urban plots, with plot-holders more likely to pass their land to relatives (perhaps on retiring to their villages) than sell. One young man who wanted to regularise title to the family plot in Gaborone was accused by his father: 'You are a crook, you could sell us with this yard, and leave us not knowing what is happening.' In Trinidad, the market was regarded with suspicion: 'a big bacchanal here ... these cars come up the road, people looking for the land that they already started to pay for, and we on the land and we ain't start to pay for nothing yet.'

Government was remote from, and insensitive to, the day-to-day concerns of our respondents. 'A lot of them just talking, and they not coming out to say anything ... poor people catching they tail.' 'I didn't bother to go to government ... all of them is like going from pillar to post and jumping in the mud.' 'Botswana Government allocate us plots, but we do not have powers when government wants to demolish our plots. We are being abandoned now that they have depleted our strength. The Bible advocates for our control over land, but this government has turned itself into little gods.' Government prepared layouts without checking the facts on the ground, so that land surveyors arriving to peg out the plots found the land already occupied. Even under threat of eviction, the plot-holders were convinced of their rights. In Botswana, 'self-allocation' was a recognised term for the poor acquiring land. In Trinidad, recent legislation provided protection from 'summary ejectment', and a community leader said: 'I feel more secure as the time goes ... as citizens of Trinidad and Tobago we have rights. We are not squatters; we are settlers.'

De Soto emphasises the importance of 'paperising' property rights, and all three countries we researched offered some form of intermediate land title linked to incremental improvements. Some plot-holders valued a documented title. 'When you get the deed you more secure.' 'Of course I would like to have one. Only when you have that, you have the real security.' 'I'll try, I will be glad to get one, very glad to get one. That is what I want.' 'I would be willing to pay, but ... under my terms ... my salary is not big.' But more were indifferent or unwilling, usually because of the costs and procedures involved, or vague about where their papers were, if they had any. 'I don't know very much about title deeds, all I know is that we have a paper from the council for the house.' 'We have no documents for the plot, because we have to pay to effect the change of ownership; at the time when we bought the house, the previous owner did not give us any papers at all.' In Trinidad, asked if intermediate title would make him feel more secure, a plot-holder replied, 'at all [not at all]'. 'I did not go for a letter of comfort because I already read about the conditions that if where you live they have to pass a road or they have to build something there.' Some improved their plots without waiting for title; others did not. 'I have materials put down but I can't do nothing unless the deed of comfort.' 'When the council began to sell houses, that is when this issue of title deeds became important ... the council allocated plots freely without giving title deeds. After a person built a house, that is when he got a card to show that he was the owner of the house.'

Land tenure regularisation is supposed to facilitate access to finance, but we found poor plot-holders in all three countries understandably risk averse, reluctant to pledge title deeds in case they lost their land. A striking feature of our research was the similar and forceful language used to express the fear of debt: 'this is one way used by government to confiscate people's plots. I am not interested! If you are not careful with some of these things, you will end up in trouble.' 'Over my dead body! I cannot use this plot to access a bank loan. What if I fail to pay and the bank takes my plot! My husband died here, and he left me on this piece of land and I will also die here, unless I am moved by the council to another area.' 'If you don't have, you can't get ... the little you have now, you try to make it do. You take a loan and the next thing you know they come to take what little you have, so where you going?' 'I can't change its title because I can't afford to have it taken by a bank or anyone because I failed to pay back a loan. I have children who should inherit this plot, not a bank.' 'If I can't pay back I not borrowing.' Funding institutions interviewed were reluctant to lend to the poor in informal settlements, even with legal title, because repossession would be difficult and politically risky, they lacked confidence in repayment and made little profit from such small-scale lending. Poor families improved their housing conditions with personal savings and informal borrowing, for which formal legal title was not needed. 'I never borrowed money to build ... it is better I work. I wouldn't have to study about paying back the bank.' 'I don't get help from nobody, the only people I get help from is like somebody have a drain to dig or somebody to cutlass.' Micro-credit facilities were more likely to fund business enterprise than housing improvement. 'The micro finance people only give loans to marketeers but this is not fair. We also need assistance to improve our house conditions, and anyway not everyone can go and sit at the market.'

Land titling reform envisages a stronger role for NGOs acting from below in a kind of local re-establishment of land rights for the poor. We found community-based associations well-organised in some cases (Old Naledi in Botswana, Carlsen Field and Race Course in Trinidad, Racecourse in Zambia). At Race Course (Trinidad), the community had organised the building of roads and a meeting-house (where we were received to discuss our work). In Zambia, international agencies had become involved (notably Oxfam through the Zambia National Land Alliance), and the Racecourse residents had excavated foundations for a community health centre that they hoped would attract funding. Generally, however, the peri-urban poor were understandably preoccupied with day-to-day existence, rather than engaged with time-consuming solidarity activity.

Gender discrimination and denial of children's rights were particularly found in property inheritance matters in Africa, where constitutional guarantees meant little at the local level. 'We are in the middle of the court cases. They want me to leave, they claim I was not married to him.' One woman in Botswana expressed it eloquently:

> ... we women are really cursed, my father gave me authority to look after this plot because the only son he has (my brother) is still young. When he comes of age he will tell me to move out, no matter what development I could have carried out here. Land is not for us women, whether you are married or not. In your father's home you do not have inheritance, especially land, it is only accumulated for your brothers, and in your home with your husband the property is his and the inheritance goes to his son. When he dies, no matter whether you are still alive, you know that after his death you lose the ownership and control of property.

In Trinidad, however, women were seen as having equal rights or even better.

In both the African cases, property transfer and inheritance were increasingly problematic with the impact of HIV/AIDS upon family and social structure. We found many peri-urban plots where the most economically active age groups were missing (although respondents were reluctant to acknowledge the cause). Land-grabbing by relatives is common, either on death or when the sick return to their home village, leaving partners and children vulnerable and often unsupported by social institutions.

# Property and Legal Process: Paperising or Pauperising?

For de Soto, if the poor's property assets are not 'paperised' through the formal legal structures common in the West, these assets cannot function productively as capital. In his earlier work, *The Other Path*, de Soto claimed that, 'The real remedy for violence and poverty is to recognize the property and labour of those whom formality today excludes' (de Soto 1989: 258). Property rights systems, he asserts, are the hidden infrastructure that can help achieve sustainable development goals. 'Integrating dispersed information into one system' is the second of his six 'property effects', which can build 'a bridge, if you will, so well anchored in people's own extralegal arrangements that they will gladly walk across it to enter this new, all-encompassing social contract' (de Soto 2000: 182). Such a reform raises complex issues of law, policy, institutional capacity and process, which our research explored.

De Soto sees legal systems functioning as a 'bell jar', excluding the poor, and our research confirmed the role of colonial and postcolonial governments in constructing exclusion and illegality. The three country case studies were all former British colonies or protectorates, with legal systems constructed in their different periods of colonisation: Trinidad brought under British law in the 1790s, Botswana a protectorate from the 1880s, Zambia initially a mining concession, then a protectorate from the 1920s. The peri-urban poor fell under different jurisdictions (land in Botswana, State land in Trinidad, and local authority or mine township land in Zambia) but in all cases were in situations where land was loosely managed and ownership rights were 'cloudy'.

In the British colonies, all vacant or unused land was claimed by the State, so that those occupying land without approval could be designated as squatters, even in the land of their birth, and subject to eviction (or 'summary ejectment', as termed in jurisdictions under the common law tradition). Eviction is now increasingly seen as an inappropriate option, which does not resolve the problem and carries a high cost, both locally and internationally. In Botswana, the rapid growth of 'self-allocated' plots on tribal land met a 'zero tolerance' reaction by the government, but was successfully challenged in the courts for its inhumanity and lack of due process. Continuing illegality and official disapproval limit plot-holders' opportunity to improve their living conditions, and the enforcement regime may tolerate temporary, but not more permanent, structures. 'They always keep telling us, don't build in concrete ... they come and they break down the concrete structure, yes they break it down.' 'They come and they tell us, you can't do that [build without official approval]. We had everything down in the back there, we had to let it grow back in bush, but we does clean it. When they come [to eject] they must have somewhere to throw we.' 'Everybody you see here developing is because they take their own risk.' 'I didn't take the risk to fence ... You ain't entitled to put no fence, you already illegal here on the land.' 'We have been allowed to build mud-brick houses because people here are poor ... I am not doing anything about this house because it might be demolished.'

Often, the inefficiency of the colonial State in managing the land over which it claimed ownership might allow occupiers a possessory title through lapse of time, but the procedures were discouragingly slow and expensive. By contrast with South

America, where the civil law practice of *usucapio* was followed, adverse possession ('squatters' rights') under British land law has long suffered judicial disapproval, seen as conflicting with the 'fundamental concept of indefeasibility of title' in registered land. With de Soto's advocacy of pre-emptive rights, citing the example of homesteaders on the American frontier who squatted on the 'public lands', adverse possession is increasingly, if reluctantly, seen as an option, creating private property from the bottom rather than the top. The Trinidad 'certificate of comfort' gave the holder a personal right not to be removed from his plot, while possessory rights were more often used to claim ownership against absentee family members.

All three country case studies had a sophisticated Torrens system of State-guaranteed land registration, and had frequently reformed their land laws in recent years (in the Caribbean, hardly a year goes by without States passing some new land law). Incremental tenure upgrading has been linked to upgrading programmes, which include registering all plots and occupiers, providing basic services, resolving land disputes and allocating property rights to recognised claimants. If the occupiers felt secure, tenure was not a priority or a subject of concern, and services could be received without title, provided they could be paid for. A major finding of our research was the mismatch between intention and reality in State land administration, which had limited capacity and resources for such complex and costly procedures. All three countries had incremental tenure regularisation procedures, but the costs of land survey and record-keeping were high, even with the supposedly simpler intermediate surveys. Government suffered from capacity constraints, not necessarily a shortage of trained surveyors, but a difficulty in building and running good record systems. The Botswana Tribal Land Boards and Zambian local authorities were starved of resources for accurate surveys and records, resulting in thousands of unplanned 'self-allocated' plots. In Botswana, central government had the resources to place trained surveyors and administrators in the Land Boards, tasked with improving the quality of service. In Zambia, the councils had planned layouts, with procedures for upgrading tenure linked to phased building of modern structures, but, with the collapse of the local mines economy, few households upgraded, preferring to build cheaper structures for rent and 'downshift' by relocating into informal peri-urban areas. In Trinidad, new legislation in 1998 introduced tenure regularisation on State lands, but progress towards full title was slow because of bureaucratic processes and costs. The effects of regularisation can be short-lived if the titles granted have restraints on alienation which are ignored in practice, or if only registered titles are accepted as valid yet the occupiers do not register their rights. Laws intended to redistribute ownership may have opposite effects because of the costs of regularisation, institutionalising certain acquired rights, sharpening status divisions between owners and renters, landlords and tenants, and reproducing the same dependencies that tenure security was supposed to remove. Those who suffer most are women. As the postcolonial State disengages from direct provision of development housing land, formal registration and mass titling becomes difficult to achieve. Thus, the failing State finds itself unable to reduce the poverty and human suffering of its citizens, even in an age of technology and plenty, or to resolve land disputes. Tenure policy needs to operate within a wider context of land-related State activity: managing State land portfolios, providing services, regulating land use, environmental protection, etc.

If the 'modern' land titling system struggles to maintain itself, even when pursuing intermediate or incremental tenure regularisation, then a more localised land tenure arrangement may fill the gap. In the Caribbean, family land survives, against official disapproval, outside the official system and the commodified land market, and survives tenaciously because of the support it offers the 'pumpkin vine' family. In Africa, an equivalent role on a larger scale is fulfilled by tribal land tenure, which in Botswana and Zambia covers three-quarters or more of the land (if not the best land, which was captured by the colonial State). So called customary, communal or tribal land tenure was deliberately maintained within the British colonial dual mandate system and now offers potential for a more flexible system, as some advocate. The local community (itself a sometimes slippery concept) may protect its interests by keeping control of land use and allocation, without recourse to the integrated property system offered by the State. For a long time, the modernising State devalued customary law and even sought to destroy it (what Santos calls 'epistemicide', the killing of alternative sources of knowledge or social agencies). Once seen as a vestige of the past bound for evolutionary extinction, customary or communal law is now 'an underground resource to be rediscovered and exploited', even in the West (Guadagni 2002).

Constructing appropriate institutions for managing and regulating land, that most basic of resources, is a major commitment for government, requiring good, fair and open administration. British colonialism attempted to build democratically elected local authorities, separating technical functions from the politicians' role, and also to maintain a modernised form of traditional authority in Africa. Trained specialists are needed to run a modern land registry, especially legal executives and land surveyors, following the Weberian model of the impartial professional or official who applies a defined body of professional knowledge under an ethical code of public service. In the British bureaucratic tradition, officials should be 'on tap, but not on top', but a modernising State needs to promote equal and effective relationships between poor people and the State, assessing the poverty impact of public policies, strengthening poor people's assets and capabilities, through pro-poor policies, correcting gender inequity and children's vulnerability and protecting poor people's rights. The land surveyor has traditionally boasted attributes of objectivity, accuracy and integrity, respecting and following the rules, but now is also a mediator, combining technical expertise with process management, dispute resolution and communicative skills, which have not been part of his or her traditional training. The professional training of planners and surveyors thus needs to embrace the techniques of what has been called 'deliberative and discursive democracy', incorporating a consensual element into professional planning and surveying work (Larsson and Elander 2001).

The scope of partnerships in achieving social aims includes developing local community-based organisations and coalitions, with new styles of advocacy and dispute resolution. A community can keep its own registers of rights, and indeed maintain its boundaries against outside forces by such practices (undertaken in the pre-enclosure open parishes of England) as beating the bounds, the whole community turning out to reassert boundaries and break down any unsanctioned land enclosure. In peri-urban areas, such confident, homogeneous and self-defined communities may not exist, allowing outside elites to manipulate processes for their own advantage. Attempts to create modern institutions following such conventions as membership lists, minutes of meetings, audited reports and land records may fail, with the oral record distorted when codified in writing, and the very complexity of land laws can create difficulties in communicating them to the poor who are supposed to benefit from them. The institutional capacity to demarcate and transfer land parcels and deal with disputes can be embedded in customary structures which operate adaptable and articulated rules and practices, but their adaptability creates room for multiple interpretations and manipulation.

Local recording of land rights can emerge through some form of local court or tribunal, applying hybrid law. Informal property rules in squatter settlements may correspond in large measure to formal legal institutions, providing squatters with practical recourse to protect their possessory interests and to make title-related claims. To interpret such institutions within the wider framework of neo-liberal globalisation, they can be seen as a form of globalisation from below, subaltern forms of legality which use traditional indigenous law as a 'contact zone' between the global and the local, resisting pressure to include them within de Soto's integrated property system. Thus, local law may be used to bring about a counter-hegemonic transformation, a reterritorialisation at local level (de Sousa Santos 2002).

## Meanwhile, on the Ground ...

Whether or not land titling can transform the poor into enterprising capitalists, land tenure regularisation may help to integrate informal peri-urban settlements into the formal and legal housing and land economy, and also should be able to assist physical, everyday improvements in local conditions: better housing structures, access to services and properly planned layouts. Without some form of local regulation, as the Botswana example of Mogoditshane shows, informal subdivision results in haphazard development which lacks form and structure, either that of the traditional village or the modern planned road layout.

We found the initial occupation of the peri-urban areas studied had typically been piecemeal, sometimes initiated under government programmes. There tended not to be organised land invasions, planned in advance with political support (except for the Sou-Sou Land project in Trinidad). The informal settlements of Old Naledi and Mogoditshane in Botswana, Race Course, Bon Air and Bois Bande in Trinidad, and Racecourse in Zambia all grew opportunistically and sporadically in response to work opportunities or by expanding an existing development. Even where roads existed, the informal subdivisions followed the irregular web of footpaths, and in Mogoditshane structures were built disregarding existing paths and roads.

When it came to marking out their plots, the squatters or homesteaders were usually aware of official planning norms and sought to follow standard plot sizes, although usually demarcated without benefit of a costly professional survey. In Trinidad, the squatters 'averaged' (as the expression went) the standard residential plot of 50 ft x 100 ft, or the five-acre smallholding. In Botswana, the customary grant through the Land Board allocated a residential plot of 30 m x 30 m, which illegal developers followed in demarcating their plots, even if they were irregularly formed.

Even when the Mogoditshane TLB was allocating land, the plots were often paced out on the ground without the benefit of a technical land survey, and the records identified the plot with a simple sketch rather than an accurate plan.

The physical means of marking plot boundaries varied. Sometimes, there was little to show where a plot ended, but more usually exclusive ownership was marked by a variety of fence or vegetation, with the euphorbia bush preferred as an effective boundary hedge in Zambia and Botswana. The more expensive fencing materials (such as post-and-panel or concrete block) were rarely affordable, but we found an imaginative use of half-buried tyres, saw-mill timber off-cuts and other recycled materials. Neighbour dispute resolution procedures seemed generally to be kept within the local community, which would sometimes marshal its resources to improve roads or build a meeting-place (at Race Course, Trinidad, the seating was recycled from the racecourse itself after refurbishment).

Structures on plots were simple and often of temporary construction, reflecting limited funds, availability of second-hand building materials and the risk of official enforcement and demolition. In Botswana and Zambia, mud-brick construction was the norm, whether in the traditional round hut (rondavel) or modern rectangular form, while in Trinidad, a variety of reclaimed materials were used. In Botswana, plots initially acquired through 'self-allocation' were progressively developed, rondavels being replaced with more permanent concrete-block buildings, especially if they were intended as rental rooms (called locally the 'one-and-half', 'two-and-half' or 'three-and-half'). Piles of building materials (blocks, sand, pipes, cement bags) often lay around, with concrete bases awaiting the owner's time and money to improve the plot further. 'We take chances, like every year we put a room.' In Zambia, colonial housing policy had from the 1940s sought to replace bachelor accommodation in barracks or hostels with single-family housing ('one family, one plot') and set the physical planning norms for self-build housing thereafter (Home 2000). Toilet arrangements were usually pit-latrines in separate structures, and water came from standpipes or kiosks (or from wells on the plots), but diseases from untreated water appeared to be relatively rare because of the low densities of occupation. Private taxis were usually available, but the time and energy needed for getting about and transacting day-to-day life was considerable, with long journeys to work (and that work often casual and unreliable). Small shops ('tuck shops' in Botswana, 'parlour shops' in Trinidad), usually on house plots, served the basic needs of the community.

Planning policies may exclude the poor, either by denying their existence or setting physical standards unrealistically high, and so official regulations and titling could hold back on-plot improvements. At Luangwa (Zambia), plot-holders were discouraged from building better structures because that would result in a requirement to extend their leases. The plot-holders wanted better services and infrastructure, not paper title documents. 'What make me feel more secure, they [the government] putting lights in the village, they bringing water in the village, they bringing telephone in the village. It make you feel more secure that we could own we place.' The potential of the land readjustment method for achieving better layouts, little recognised in countries from the British planning tradition (Home 2002), but promoted in Fourie's chapter, has yet to be explored in any of the countries studied, although the Mogoditshane case in Botswana is a salutary example of how the informal market can bypass slow and miserly land acquisition and compensation by the State.

## The Way Forward

What of the way forward? We found that British colonialism through the Torrens system had installed a State-managed land registration system that protected private property rights, but that it was expensive, procedurally complex and insensitive to pro-poor strategies. All three countries studied had attempted incremental land tenure regularisation, linked to physical *in situ* upgrading, but we found that that was often not significantly cheaper, simpler or more flexible than the full titling system it was supposed to feed, and that it was being phased out in both Botswana (certificates of right and the SHHA programme) and Trinidad (certificates of comfort). Structural adjustment, neo-liberal economic policy, the impact of HIV/AIDS in Africa and other factors had weakened the implementation capacity of both central and local government, contributing to the phenomenon of the 'failing State'. State land management efforts were seen as remote and irrelevant to the everyday lives of the peri-urban poor, who rarely saw a government official, avoided going to the offices of government or banks, and had little interest in 'paperising' their land tenure (even when the bureaucracy could deliver the documents). Thus far we confirmed the de Soto thesis about the burdens and irrelevance of State bureaucracy for the poor, and the failure of government to go down into the streets and talk to the people.

One achievement of the new thinking about tenure security has been, however, to soften official hostility to 'squatter' settlements, changing attitudes towards an acknowledgment of the rights of the poor to secure tenure on land. An unfortunate exception was the 'zero tolerance' policy adopted by the government of Botswana to the high-profile abuse of the customary land process in Mogoditshane. Other governments have come to recognise the political costs of squatter eviction and have responded to pressure exerted by the poor, who regard themselves less as squatters than settlers, or even homesteaders in the American tradition of frontier settlement. So de Soto's message is reaching both governments and 'the poor' themselves. The potential of adverse possession law (or grant of possessory title), which has been realised in countries in the Roman law tradition under the term *usucapio*, has hardly been applied in our country case studies with their British colonial and common law heritages.

In the African country studies (and in Trinidad through the family land tradition), customary or communal land tenure, long seen as in inevitable evolutionary decline, is now viewed more favourably and seems to offer a local, accessible and accepted institutional framework for land management and dispute resolution. It is, however, under pressure to bureaucratise and 'paperise' its processes and collective memory. In the hybrid and transitional conditions of peri-urban areas, its flexibility renders it vulnerable to manipulation by outside forces, and it is an insufficient guarantor of the rights of women and children (as the Botswana case particularly showed). For most of the peri-urban poor, local institutions have some meaning, but de Soto's world of paperised property rights, official upgrading and mortgages remains remote from their everyday concerns, at least until translated into tangible benefits on the ground.

The way forward would seem to be through capacity-building and empowerment of local community-based associations or organisations, while recognising the limitations of the concept of community (Torstensen and others 2000). Narayan and Petesch (2002: 487–93) have suggested that the State could become more effective agents of poverty reduction through five actions: promoting pro-poor economic policies, investing in poor people's assets and capabilities, supporting partnerships, addressing gender inequity and children's vulnerability, and protecting poor people's rights. These potential actions all converge upon the land resource. CBOs could set the limits and content of their territorial remit, perhaps through a variant of the 'beating the bounds' carried out by English pre-enclosure parishes, or of the 'walk-over' practiced by the Sou-Sou Land pioneers in Trinidad. CBOs can act as advocates for their communities and mediate the rights of absentee paper owners with the actual occupiers of the land. Supported by better record-keeping which exploits the vast potential of modern technology, CBOs could mediate links to micro-credit systems for both business and property development and use the energies of collective community action for materials and services procurement and infrastructure upgrading. Government, for its part, should recognise that reform of land law and procedure operates under severe capacity constraints, and that the traditional professional skills of surveyors and lawyers need to be supplemented by the more political skills of mediation, alternative dispute resolution and local coalition-building. Without more participatory local strategies, the management of land, that most basic resource of the modern territorial nation-State, will not meet the needs of 'the poor' and will contribute to the dangerous drift towards the failing State, with the risk of increased violence and civil disorder. To revisit the English slang expression cited in Home's chapter (p 13), it would be undesirable and dangerous if poor people can only become land-owners when they are in their graves.

# References

de Soto, H (1989) *The Other Path: The Invisible Revolution in the Third World*, New York: Harper and Row

de Soto, H (2000) *The Mystery of Capital: Why Capitalism Triumphs in the West and Fails Everywhere Else*, London: Black Swan

de Sousa Santos, B (2002) *Towards a New Legal Common Sense*, London: Butterworths

Guadagni, M (2002) 'Trends in customary land property' in Sanchez Jordan, ME and Gambaro, M (eds), *Land Law in Comparative Perspective*, London: Kluwer

Home, RK (2000) 'From barrack compounds to the single-family house: planning worker housing in colonial Natal and Northern Rhodesia' *Planning Perspectives* 15: 327–47

Home, RK (2002) 'Why was land readjustment adopted in British India but not in Britain? A historical exploration', unpublished paper to Workshop on Land Readjustment, Boston: Lincoln Institute of Land Policy

Labourn-Peart, C (1998) 'Planning practice in South Africa: the image and substance of participation' *Planning Practice and Research* 13(2): 171–82

Larsson, J and Elander, I (2001) 'Consensus, democracy and the land surveyor in the Swedish cadastral executive procedure' *Planning Theory and Practice* 2(3): 325–42

Narayan, D and Petesch, P (2002) *Voices of the Poor: From Many Lands*, New York: OUP, for the World Bank

Smit, W and Mbona, D (1996) *Low-Income Housing Consolidation Processes in Metropolitan Durban*, Durban: University of Natal, Built Environment Support Group Paper 1

Torstensen, A and others (eds) (2000) *Associational Life in African Cities: Popular Response to the Urban Crisis*, Uppsala: Nordic Africa Institute

USAID (2002) *Promoting Effective Property Rights Systems for Sustainable Development*, Washington DC